HEREDITARY
WITCHCRAFT

I think about the words of my teachers. I think about the old beliefs that without the Strega, the sun and moon will no longer rise. I remember the teaching that unless the old rites are performed, season to season, Nature will withdraw from humankind. In all of this I embrace the metaphor, and I know that there must always be one who will tell the Strega's story. There must always be one who will tend the ancient campfire. For it is the Witch and the kindred fairy who gives the life essence to the mundane world of men and women. We are the possibilities and the unshattered dream, we are what gives life magick. So, I will recount the old tales here and try to preserve them for yet another generation. It is my hope that after I am gone, another will come and blow upon the embers, and tend the old campfire for yet another who may someday come. Let us turn then and hear of things once whispered only in the night, before the glowing hearths of family Witches.

About the Author

Raven Grimassi was trained in the Family Tradition of Italian Witchcraft. He has also been an initiate of several other traditions including Brittic Wicca and the Pictish-Gaelic Tradition. Raven has been a teacher and practitioner of the Craft for over twenty-five years. His former students include authors Scott Cunningham and Donald Kraig. Raven is the author of several books on Wicca and Witchcraft including *The Wiccan Mysteries* which was awarded Book of the Year 1998 and First Place — Spirituality Book by the Coalition of Visionary Retailers. It is his life's work to ensure the survival of ancient Witch lore and legend along with traditional ancestral teachings on the Old Religion.

The author has been both a writer and editor for several magazines, including *The Shadow's Edge* and *Raven's Call* magazine, a journal of pre-Christian religion. Raven has appeared on both television and radio talk-shows in the San Diego area, in his efforts to educate the public about the positive practices and natures of Wicca and Witchcraft. He lectures on a variety of topics such as folklore, magick, and ritual structure. Raven is active in lecturing, holding workshops, and teaching formal classes.

To Write to the Author

If you wish to contact the author or would like more information about this book, please write to the author in care of Llewellyn Worldwide, and we will forward your request. Both the author and publisher appreciate hearing from you and learning of your enjoyment of this book and how it has helped you. Llewellyn Worldwide cannot guarantee that every letter written to the author can be answered, but all will be forwarded. Please write to:

Raven Grimassi
℅ Llewellyn Worldwide, Ltd.
P.O. Box 64383, Dept. K256–9
St. Paul, MN 55164-0383, U.S.A.

Please enclose a self-addressed, stamped envelope for reply or $1.00 to cover costs.
If outside the U.S.A., enclose international postal reply coupon.

HEREDITARY WITCHCRAFT

*Secrets
of the
Old Religion*

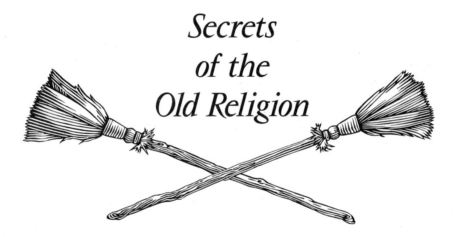

RAVEN GRIMASSI

2001
Llewellyn Publications
St. Paul, Minnesota, U.S.A., 55164—0383

FIRST EDITION
Third printing, 2001

Cover design by Anne Marie Garrison
Cover art by Tom Clifton
Interior illustrations by Anne Marie Garrison (pp. 60, 61,110, 115, 142,161);
    Hollie Kilroy (pp. 141, 143, 146, 148, 150, 151, 156);
    Tom Clifton (pp. 1, 3, 65, 105, 157)
Photographs by Stephanie Zarrabi (pp. 7, 31, 33, 72, 96, 109, 122, 172, 177, 189);
    Raven Grimassi (p. 27)
Interior design and editing by Connie Hill

Library of Congress Cataloging-in-Publication Data
Grimassi, Raven. 1951-
    Hereditary witchcraft : secrets of the old religion : drawn from old family texts and oral teachings / Raven Grimassi.
        p.   cm.
    Includes bibliographical references and index.
    ISBN 1-56718-256-9 (trade pbk.)
    1. Witchcraft.—Italy—History.   I. Title.
BF1584.I8G745   1999
133.4'3'0945—dc21   99-29164
                                                                        CIP

Llewellyn Publications
A Division of Llewellyn Worldwide, Ltd.
St. Paul, Minnesota, 55164-0383, Dept. 1–56718–256–9, U.S.A.

Visit our web site at http://www.llewellyn.com

 Printed in the U.S.A. on recycled paper.

Dedication

In memory of
Charles Godfrey Leland
(1824–1903)
the father of modern Witchcraft,
who, like all geniuses, suffered the fate
of being misunderstood.

The critics of your era are gone now
and forgotten in time, but your work lives on.
Perhaps there can be no greater justice than that.

Other Books by the Author

The Book of the Holy Strega
    (Nemi Enterprises, 1981)

The Book of Ways, Vols. I & II
    (Nemi Enterprises, 1982)

Whispers, the Teachers of Old Italy
    (Moon Dragon Publishing, 1991)

Teachings of the Holy Strega
    (Moon Dragon Publishing, 1991)

Italian Witchcraft (formerly *Ways of the Strega*)
    (Llewellyn Publications, 1995, 1999)

Wiccan Mysteries: Ancient Origins & Teachings
    (Llewellyn Publications, 1997)

Wiccan Magick: Inner Teachings of the Craft
    (Llewellyn Publications, 1998)

Encyclopedia of Wicca & Witchcraft
    (Llewellyn Publications, 2000)

Contents

Part Two: Myths and Lore

Part Three: The Rituals

Illustrations

Acknowledgments

I wish to express my appreciation and thanks to my dear friend Maggie Macary for sharing her research on fourteenth-century Italy, particularly relating to the cult of Guglielma.

Thanks also to Jenny Gibbons for keeping an eye out for material related to my research themes. She has pointed out the "needle in the haystack" on more than one occasion.

Also a note of appreciation to Sabina Magliocco who always adds balance to my research by pointing out alternative interpretations related to my discoveries.

Last, but certainly not least, my special thanks to Stephanie Zarrabi for taking the photographs that appear in this book, and for all of her assistance and support during this project.

INTRODUCTION

Hereditary Witchcraft: did it survive the Inquisition or did it ever exist in the first place? Have hereditary Witches hidden themselves so well, and for so long, that no one believes in them even when they finally come forth? Clearly we live in an age of great skepticism, and not without cause, for many false claims have been made. Yet the lure of the hereditary Witch still calls many, and where a witch cannot be found there is always one to be created. Perhaps it's simply that we must believe there will always be one last unicorn, one sole survivor of the elven race, and one last hereditary Witch, lest the Old Ways disappear forever.

This book is about the Old Religion of hereditary Witches, and contains material of considerable antiquity. Some related elements of it appear circa 1896 in books and articles written by such turn-of-the-century folklorists as J. B. Andrews, Frederick Elsworthy, Lady Vere de Vere, Charles Leland, and several others. Though clearly centuries older, we can say with historical certainty that the bulk of this material is *at least* one hundred years old. Therefore we can state with confidence that the concepts and reported practices revealed in this book predate the writings on modern Wicca of Gerald Gardner (circa 1954).

In my previous book, *Ways of the Strega*,[1] I introduced modern Italian Witchcraft, blended together with various elements of modern Wicca. Although I stated this in the introduction, there was some confusion regarding what was traditional Italian material and what was added from other sources. Additionally some book reviewers questioned whether Italian Witchcraft, as I presented it, was not simply a modern eclectic reconstruction based upon Gardnerian Wicca. Such is not the case, as I will establish in this volume.

In 1981 I published a booklet titled *The Book of the Holy Strega*,[2] which focused on a fourteenth-century Italian Witch Queen named Aradia, relating her teachings and her life story. In 1993 Aidan Kelly produced a work titled *The Gospel of Diana*[3] that also dealt with the Aradia figure as a powerful medieval Witch. Despite the fact my work appeared twelve years earlier, there was some suggestion that I based my material on Kelly's *Gospel of Diana*. Concepts in both Leland's material and my own, although published earlier, are both often credited to writers who later wrote on similar themes; the chronology speaks for itself.

I began writing about Italian Witchcraft in 1981 in a magazine called *The Shadow's Edge*. Several years later I wrote for *Moon Shadow* magazine. Unfortunately, due to oaths of initiation, I was constrained to present the Italian material in a "watered down" version, mixed with readily available Wiccan elements. To a lesser extent, this was also true when I wrote for *Raven's Call* magazine. At the time I felt it was better than not revealing anything at all, and therefore I incorporated some Wiccan style formats through which I conveyed Strega concepts.

I first began teaching the Italian Craft at Ye Olde Enchantment Shoppe in San Diego during the summer of 1979. One of the people attending later joined my Tradition and studied under me for three years as a first-degree initiate; Scott Cunningham went on to become a well-known Wiccan author. Although these studies were not mentioned in his biography, *Whispers of the Moon*,[4] I was pleased that Scott acknowledged me as one of his teachers in his book *Earth Power*.[5] Our interests took us in different directions over the years, but our friendship continued, and I kept up-to-date with Scott's life through a

---

1 Raven Grimassi, *Ways of the Strega* (St. Paul: Llewellyn Publications, 1995). No citation appears for subsequent mentions of this work except in the case of direct quotes from the text. Also note: a revised edition of this book, titled *Italian Witchcraft: The Old Religion*, will be published by Llewellyn Publications in 2000.

2 Raven Grimassi, *The Book of the Holy Strega* (San Diego: Nemi Enterprises, 1981).

3 Aidan Kelly, *Diana's Family: A Tuscan Lineage* (Pictish Voodoo Distributing Co., 1993).

4 deTraci Regula and David Harrington, *Whispers of the Moon* (St. Paul: Llewellyn Publications, 1993).

5 Scott Cunningham, *Earth Power* (St. Paul: Llewellyn Publications, 1983).

close mutual friend and former student, Don Kraig (author of *Modern Magick,*[6] Llewellyn, 1989). Like so many others, I was saddened to hear of Scott's untimely death in 1993.

In the period from 1979 to 1986 I continued to teach and to initiate people into the Italian Craft. My teachings were, as they still remain, focused upon structure and formula. Structure helps to ensure survival, and formula contributes to longevity by providing consistent results for practitioners. Structured systems tend to survive the people who practice them, and the keys are passed on for the benefit of future generations. These time-proven keys save students a lifetime of having to discover them for themselves. Therefore students may begin on their path of personal self-development with the knowledge already preserved and provided by previous generations.

In 1981 I created the Aridian Tradition by blending together various beliefs and practices from three major Italian Craft Traditions: Fánarric, Janarric, and Tanarric. The Aridian Tradition was intended to be a reconstruction of the original Tradition as reportedly taught by Aradia during the late fourteenth century. The teachings, as I first possessed them, were considered to be hereditary material. Because I was unable to freely share this with my students at the time

I created an eclectic blend to serve as teaching material for both new students and first degree initiates. It was not until several years later that I released the actual unedited material to my Initiates. Reportedly, the early versions of what I put together are still circulating around in the Craft community. For the sake of clarification, I would like to state for the record that anything I released prior to 1994, though based largely upon Strega concepts, is somewhat eclectic and small portions of it were even drawn from non-Italian sources.

Over the course of the many years during which I taught, I became what we call in my tradition a *Grimas.* A Grimas is the directing elder of the Tradition, and it is his or her duty to ensure its survival. This position allows a person to do whatever is necessary in order to achieve the continuation of the Craft. Accordingly, the position of Grimas can free an individual from the restraints of his or her previous oaths. Therefore I am now revealing a great deal of unabridged material here in this book. Further, this material is originally from the Italian Craft. There is nothing in this book created from, or based upon, any Wiccan traditions whatsoever.

In *Ways of the Strega,* I pointed out that Leland's *Aradia; Gospel of the Witches*[7] (published in 1899) depicted Italian witches

---

6 Donald Michael Kraig, *Modern Magick* (St. Paul: Llewellyn Publications, 1989).

7 Charles Leland, *Aradia, Gospel of the Witches* (London: David Nutt, 1890). No citation appears for subsequent mentions of this work except in the case of direct quotes from the text.

gathering at the time of the full moon. They also worshipped a Roman goddess and god (Diana and Lucifer) and were naked in their rituals. At the end of their rites these witches celebrated with cakes and wine. Gerald Gardner later described English witches in much the same way in his book *Witchcraft Today*,[8] published in 1954. There are those who insist that these aspects of Witchcraft are "Gardnerian elements," not Italian. The fact that these beliefs and practices appeared in writing over half a century earlier than Gardner, and in a description of Italian Witchcraft, has been somehow lost in the debate.

Some people feel that Charles Leland invented the material that he claimed had survived within the Old Religion of Italy. Evidence to the contrary has now arisen, thanks to Professor Robert Matthieson of Brown University, who has studied the original manuscript written by Charles Leland. Through analyzing the handwritten errors and corrective measures evident in the original manuscript, Matthieson concluded that Leland was copying material laid out before him, and was not creating the text as he went along.

The evidence presented by Matthieson appears in a new translation of Leland's *Aradia; Gospel of the Witches* by Mario and Dina Pazzaglini,[90] along with commentaries by author Chas Clifton and a foreword by Stewart Farrar. In several sections of the book it is pointed out by the authors that Gerald Gardner and Doreen Valiente were very influenced by Leland's research on Italian Witchcraft and drew upon his material when expanding and elaborating the Gardnerian Book of Shadows. Curiously, however, the erroneous conclusion is drawn that modern Italian Witchcraft is simply Gardnerian Wicca with Italian seasoning added. Although Leland's books on Italian Witchcraft clearly demonstrate the pre-existence of concepts used later in Gardnerian Wicca, I cannot fault the contributing writers of the new Aradia book too much for failing to understand that the similarities between the two Traditions stem largely from the pre-existing Italian format. Since these writers are not initiates of Italian Witchcraft they are unaware of all that exists as proof.

In July 1997 I was sharing with my mother a few folk spells from a couple of Leland's books, to see what she might think about them. My mother was born and raised in Italy, and is fluent in Italian, French, and English. I also wanted her personal insights, since she was raised in the Italian culture and could therefore better interpret the material in a cultural context. She pointed out several errors in Leland's Italian that I had at first glance attributed to misspellings or differences in dialect.

8 Gerald Gardner, *Witchcraft Today* (London: Rider, 1954).

9 Charles G. Leland. *Aradia or the Gospel of the Witches,* A New Translation by Mario Pazzaglini, Ph.D. and Dina Pazzaglini. (Blaine, Washington: Phoenix Publishing Inc., 1998).

However, she readily identified them as phonetic spellings, casually stating that someone must have been speaking to Leland as he was writing down the person's words (as well as his knowledge of Italian allowed).

One example appears in a magickal spell of good fortune in which Leland writes *"Chuco questo sacchetino per la buona fortuna di me. . . ."* The word "chuco" here should be "cucio," but the Italian pronunciation of *cucio* (chew-cho) is quite close phonetically to the English pronunciation of chuco. Having no personal involvement nor interest in modern Craft politics, she did not realize the impact of her observation as I did. For me, this was further evidence that Leland did not invent his material, but was indeed working with material provided to him by someone else, just as he had always claimed.

As we shall see in following chapters, Charles Leland is not the only writer we can turn to for historical documentation of pre-Gardnerian Italian Witchcraft. I have drawn on articles written in the *Journal of Folklore,* as well as trial transcripts from the Venetian Inquisition. Through such records I will demonstrate that family traditions of the Craft still existed in Italy during the Renaissance period. I will also present evidence to show that they gathered in ritual circles, possessed handwritten books of spells and rituals, and practiced magick of a beneficent nature.

When considering Italian Witchcraft, it is helpful to understand the great antiquity of Italy. Italy is a land in which many of the ancient Roman aqueducts still function and in some cases are still used by some Italians. City festivals and street processions of today can be traced back in unbroken traditional celebrations dating even before the Roman Empire. In some rural areas of Italy everyday life has changed little since the days of antiquity. Preserving traditions is an integral part of the Italian soul, whether we're talking about artisan crafts, regional customs, religious practices, or even a recipe for spaghetti sauce. Therefore it is somewhat shallow to dismiss even the possibility of surviving Witchcraft Traditions in Italy today.

To avoid any confusion for the reader, there are several points that need to be made. First, Italy did not exist as a united country until 1861, but the peninsula itself has long been referred to as *Italia.* Even though the entire region consisted of various regional empires and kingdoms down through the centuries, historians commonly use the term "ancient Italy" when speaking of its past. Second, I want to point out that I use the word "Strega" to denote both male and female witches (although the word actually means a female witch.) The word "Streghe" (witches) is simply the plural form of Strega. "Stregheria" is the Italian word for Witchcraft, the Old Religion. "Stregoneria" is the word for sorcery, or the Craft as a purely magickal nonreligious system.

Additionally, I must announce that the Aridian Tradition depicted in *Ways of the Strega* is no longer under my direction as a Grimas. Therefore it is open to any and all who wish to borrow from it or practice it in whatever manner they please. The former initiate members have reformed under the name "Clan Umbrea," but continue to practice the Arician ways of the Craft. (Aricia is the area in which Lake Nemi lies, the original site of Diana's temple and sacred grove.) This was done in order to avoid confusion between the practices outlined in *Ways of the Strega* versus the initiate level practices of the original Tradition. I am now directing elder

of the Arician Ways and no longer overseeing the Aridian material.

Finally, I want to point out that *Ways of the Strega* introduced different traditions representative of the many regions of Italy. Therefore various god and goddess names were used, along with different mythical aspects. In this present text I am focusing on one structure based upon Diana and Dianus and their myths and legends. This should make it easier for the reader to use this book as the basis for practicing Stregheria. As you will discover in the following chapters, this tradition is based upon very ancient concepts and practices. So let us turn now to Old Italy, and explore the world of Italian Witchcraft.

Figure 1. *Italian Pentagram image found in a wall carving in the Roman city of Spalato, circa A.D. 800.* (Illustration from *Decorative Symbols and Motifs*, Dover Publications, New York, 1986.)

Part One
The Old Religion

WITCHCRAFT
IN OLD ITALY

In 1886 Charles Leland became acquainted with an Italian woman named Maddalena, who claimed to be a Witch. Over a ten-year period she provided him with what she called "The Witches' Gospel." During this time Leland was also heavily involved in the study of Italian folklore. In 1899 he published *Aradia; The Gospel of the Witches,* based on material supplied to him by Maddalena. Unfortunately the work is largely typical of distorted images of Witchcraft common to the era. Upon examination we do, however, discover some valid elements of Italian Witchcraft traceable to actual pre-Christian European pagan practices.

What may be an even more valuable aspect of Leland's book is its presentation of an interesting view of pre-Gardnerian Witchcraft in Italy. Leland gives an account of Witches who gather nude beneath the full moon to worship a goddess and a god. During this celebration they enjoy cakes and wine; the Witches also sing, dance, and make love. For those readers who believe Gerald Gardner invented these concepts, bear in mind this was written in 1899, over half a century prior to Gardner's writings. Some people claim the aspects listed here are "Gardnerian indicators" and argue the Strega Tradition is therefore based on modern Wiccan tenets. However, the time frame does not support such an erroneous assessment, as these concepts clearly predate the Gardnerian movement of the 1950s from which modern Wicca evolved.

It is important to note that Leland is not the only source of information relating to an active Witch sect in Italy circa 1896. In volume three of *Folk-Lore; Transactions of the Folk-Lore Society* (March, 1897) there is an interesting account of Neapolitan Witchcraft. The author, J. B. Andrews, tells us:

> The Neapolitans have an occult religion and government in witchcraft, and the Camorra; some apply to them to obtain what official organizations cannot or will not do. As occasionally happens in similar cases, the Camorra fears and yields to the witches, the temporal to the spiritual.[1]

Andrews goes on to say that the Witches of Naples are divided into "special departments of the art." He lists two as adepts in the art of earth and sea magick. Later he implies that a third specialty may exist related to the stars. Andrews also tells us that Neapolitan Witches perform knot magick, create medicinal herbal potions, construct protective amulets, and engage in the arts of healing.

Andrews concludes his article with information he collected while interviewing Italian Witches. When asked what books these Witches gathered their information from, they replied their knowledge was entirely traditional, and is "given by the mother to the daughter." The Witches also tell Andrews that blood is exchanged from a vein in the arm, and the new member is given a mark under the left thigh. Although the moon is not specifically mentioned, the Witches do report to Andrews that such ceremonies are performed at midnight.

The ancient Roman poet Horace gives us perhaps the earliest accounts of Italian Witches and their connection to a lunar cult. In the *Epodes of Horace,*[2] written around 30 B.C., he tells the tale of an Italian Witch named Canidia. Horace says that Proserpine and Diana grant power to Witches who worship them, and that Witches gather in secret to perform the mysteries associated with their worship. He speaks of a Witches' book of incantations (*Libros Carminum*) through which the moon may be "called down" from the sky. Other ancient Roman writers such as Lucan and Ovid produced works clearly supporting the same theme. From this we can conclude that during this era such beliefs about Witches and Witchcraft were common knowledge.

---

1 J. B. Andrews, *Folk-Lore, Transactions of the Folk-Lore Society* (March, 1897).

2 Thomas Clark, *The Works of Horatius Flaccus* (Philadelphia: David McKay Publishers, 1884).

We know from the writings of Roman times that Proserpine and Diana were worshipped at night in secret ceremonies. Their worshippers gathered at night beneath the full moon and shunned the cities where the solar gods ruled. Diana was a Roman Moon Goddess known earlier in Greece as Artemis; twin sister of Apollo God of the Sun. Proserpine, also known as Persephone, was long associated with the Underworld. In ancient myths Persephone is linked to the Underworld goddess Hecate Triformis of whom Porphyry wrote: "The moon is Hekate . . . her power appears in three forms: Selene in heaven, Artemis on earth, Hekate in the Underworld."[3] Hesiod wrote in the *Theogony* (circa 700 B.C.) that Hecate ruled over the three great mysteries: Birth, Death, and Life.

In *The World of Witches*,[4] anthropologist Julio Baroja reveals evidence of a flourishing cult in southern Europe that worshipped Diana during the fifth and sixth centuries A.D. In the author's notes for chapter four he adds that the cult also worshipped a male deity called Dianum. Transcripts from Witch trials in Italy indicate a connection between Witches and the goddess Diana spanning several centuries. My previous book *Ways of the Strega* contains a lengthy chronology of such trials dating from 1310 to 1647.

In addition to Leland and J. B. Andrews, we also have Italian Folklorist Lady Vere de Vere's accounts of Italian Witchcraft as she encountered it in the Italian region of Tyrol. In an interesting article found in *La Rivista* of Rome (June 1894), Lady Vere de Vere tells us that "the Community of Italian Witches is regulated by laws, traditions, and customs of the most secret kind, possessing special recipes for sorcery." What should be of particular interest here to anyone with an open mind is Leland's, Andrews', and Lady Vere de Vere's use of the present tense when speaking of Italian Witchcraft, circa 1896.

In the *Journal of Social History* (volume 28, 1995) a fascinating article by Sally Scully, Department of History, San Francisco University, details certain aspects of a Witchcraft trial in seventeenth-century Venice. In my exploration of the transcripts of this particular trial I learned that Italian Witches of this period used handwritten spell books and copied from the grimoire known as the *Key of Solomon*. (These transcripts of the Venice Witch trial are the fourth largest in the Venetian Inquisition's records.)

The trial itself focused upon a woman named Laura Malipero. In 1654, her home was searched by the Captain of the Sant'Ufficio, an arm of the Inquisition. Discovered were several crudely written spell books along with sophisticated herbals and copies

---

3 J. Bidez, *Vie de Porphyre*, p. 14.

4 Julio Baroja, *The World of the Witches* (Chicago: Chicago University Press, 1964).

of an occult book known as the *Clavicle of Solomon* (the *Key of Solomon*). This particular book had been banned by the Roman Inquisition in 1640. Laura said in her defense that a boarder in her home left the objects behind. She further claimed to be illiterate and therefore had no knowledge of the contents. However, the Inquisition noted the presence of copies in various stages of completion, and concluded that a copying process was clearly taking place in her home. At her trial a witness testified that Laura was the most famous Witch in Venice.

Laura's lawyer argued that she was a magical herbal healer, well trained in the arts, and that her procedures worked and were valid techniques. He claimed she was instructed by pharmacists and barbers (official guilds of the time) who were licensed by the government. Witnesses came forth to testify to her skills. Unfortunately for Laura, this was her third appearance before the Inquisition on charges of Witchcraft. In 1630 Laura had been sentenced to one year in jail for heresy after her husband divorced her for practicing Witchcraft. She was accused of placing tokens in a shoe, keeping a spell in a purse, and putting holy water in the soup. Laura confessed, but stated that her intentions were beneficent.

In 1649 Laura was again tried by the Inquisition for practicing "stregarie" (love magic, divination, etc.) along with her mother Isabella, half-sister Marietta Bat-

taglia, and thirteen others. Marietta confessed to fortune telling and little works of magic (*piria, cordella, inchiostra*). She herself had also been tried by the Inquisition in 1637 for practicing Witchcraft. In the 1649 trial Marietta alone was sentenced to jail and banishment.

What is interesting in all of this is the historical documentation of seventeenth-century Italian Witches hand-copying spells and manuscripts of a magical nature. If nothing else, this serves as partial evidence that Italian Witches were passing magical traditions through personal handwritten books (what Wiccans would call a Book of Shadows). We can also ascribe secondary importance to the fact that the trial transcripts document magickal texts in Italian Witchcraft of a positive nature. The *Key of Solomon* is not classified as a Black Magick work, and deals in part with banishing evil spirits and demons. This all lends credence to the claims of family Witches that centuries-old oral and written knowledge has been passed down through the generations.

If Laura and her family were involved in such endeavors as described, certainly others were as well. The existence of books hand-copied by Witches is yet another aspect of Italian Witchcraft later appearing in Gardnerian Wicca. In Leland's *Gospel of Aradia* he refers several times to material recorded in writing by Italian Witches. Leland also tells us that the copy of the *Witches' Gospel*

Figure 2–3. *The Book of Ways. An old journal, typical of the type of books passed down through Witch family lines. This book, belonging to the author, dates from the late nineteenth to early twentieth century.*

received from Maddalena was in her own handwriting.

According to legend, Aradia was born in the city of Volterra, in the region of Tuscany. Many Italian Witches believe Aradia was a powerful Witch and teacher who lived in Italy sometime between the mid-fourteenth century to early fifteenth century. She brought about a revival of the Old Religion that swept almost all of what is now Italy. In A.D. 1508, the Italian Inquisitor Bernardo Rategno wrote in his *Tracatus de Stigibus* that a rapid expansion of the Witch cult had begun 150 years earlier. He concluded this from his study of trial transcripts preserved in the Archives of the Inquisition at Como, Italy. If Rategno was correct, his statement may be historical evidence for the life of Aradia.

Oral legends indicate Aradia was the only child of Catholic parents. Her mother wanted Aradia to become a nun, but Aradia refused to accept this and was beaten for her defiance. Unable to control the child, her mother appointed a governess to deal with Aradia. As it turned out the governess was not a Catholic but a Tuscan Witch (according to legend, the governess appears to have been her aunt).

Aradia was initiated into the Old Religion some time later by the governess. Eventually the mother discovered what had occurred and drove the governess off. Fearing discovery, the family fled to central Italy in the Alban Hills region near Lake Nemi. Aradia still refused to obey her parents or to renounce the Old Religion. In desperation, her parents locked her inside a tower cell, but she eventually managed to escape. She put on a pilgrim's dress and traveled to many areas, teaching and preaching the Old Religion.

What Aradia taught was the religion of Diana, the Queen of the Witches and of the Moon; the Goddess of the poor and the oppressed. The fame of Aradia's wisdom and beauty went forth over all the land, and people worshipped her, calling her "La Bella Pellegrina" (The Beautiful Pilgrim). Shortly after the revival of the Old Religion by Aradia, violent persecution of Witches swept through Italy. In order to survive, the cult went underground, meeting only in secret and creating strict laws to ensure they would not be discovered. This secrecy continued until the early nineteenth century when Witches began operating under the guise of Masonic groups and other organizations. This is covered under a separate subtitle later in this chapter.

ANCIENT ROOTS

In *The Ancient Mediterranean,*[5] written by historian Michael Grant, we read a rather bold statement that from the shores of the Mediterranean came, to Western Civilization, almost all that sets us above savages.

---

5 Michael Grant, *The Ancient Mediterranean* (New York: Penguin Books, 1969).

The author goes on to say that we cannot understand our past or ourselves unless we know something of this region that made us what we are. The Mediterranean coast was home to the Egyptian, Etruscan, Roman, and Iberian cultures. Here the Mystery Cults of these civilizations flourished, along with those brought from the Aegean through the expansion of Greek colonies into these regions. These ancient cults formed many of the pagan beliefs later associated with European Witchcraft.

The roots of Italian Witchcraft extend back into the prehistory of Italy. Difficulties arise in attempting to present ancient Italian religion in the same way someone might describe ancient Greek religion. Italy was a mosaic of cultural and social groups scattered throughout the regions of the peninsula. The main ethnic groups included the Latini, Calabri, Samniti, Sabini, and the Etrusci. However, there is marked archaeological evidence between the twelfth and ninth centuries B.C. (Proto-Villanovian) suggesting a unity of sociological structures, ideas, and customs. Examples of this appear in the form of funeral items and the similarity of charms carved from bones that are found throughout Italy.

Archaeological evidence confirms the presence of continuous human life in Italy since the Ice Age. The species known as *Homo Erectus* lived in Italy approximately six million years ago and there is evidence of *Homo Sapiens* present approximately half a million years ago. *The Old Stone Age Man* (Paleolithic Age) lived in Italy during the later stages of the Ice Age when the average annual temperature was around nine degrees centigrade colder than in modern times.

Around 14,000 years ago the ice receded for the last time. *The Middle Stone Age Man* (Mesolithic) emerged—this was a nomadic hunter culture in the same manner as Paleolithic Man. During the *New Stone Age*, humans started to grow their own food in addition to hunting. Approximately two-and-a-half millennia later we see the production of metals such as copper, followed by bronze and eventually iron.

Early outside influences such as the Mycenaean culture (before its fall in twelfth century B.C.) served to change the course of Italian history. The Etruscans, emerging as a power in Italy around 1000 B.C., mixed Mycenaean influences with the indigenous culture of the Villanova. According to the late Professor Marija Gimbutas, the Etruscans were the heirs to the mysteries of the Neolithic cult of the Great Goddess in Old Europe.[6] These mysteries were later to lay the foundation for many of the practices and beliefs of European Witchcraft. Generally speaking, with the advent of the Etruscans, Italian history as we understand it began.

---

6 Marija Gimbutas, *The Goddesses and Gods of Old Europe* (Berkeley: University of California Press, 1982).

The Roman emperor Claudius I composed, in Greek, twenty books of Etruscan history. His first wife, Plautia Urgulanilla, was of Etruscan blood, with old family connections that were still quite strong. Therefore she was able to put Claudius in touch with authentic Etruscan traditions. In his religious policy Claudius respected ancient tradition and he revived the waning old religious ceremonies of Rome. During his reign Claudius established laws protecting the *haruspices* (diviners) and convinced the Roman Senate to establish a library to house various writings on Etruscan religion.

Also preserved in this library were the mystical Etruscan writings known as the Sibylline books—the three legendary books of prophecy sold to the Etruscan King Tarquinius by the mystical Sibyl of Cumae. The Sybylline books were consulted by the Senate of Rome in all matters of great importance. The Emperor Augustus had an additional copy made of them in 18 B.C. as a protection against their loss.

Under the reign of the Emperor Honorius (A.D. 395–423) the Magister Militum (Stilicho) had these books burned as heretical texts offensive to Christianity, along with the entire library of Etruscan texts on religion, magick, and divination. The twenty books written by Claudius were also destroyed. Ancient historians tell us that the Etruscans were the most knowledged occultists the world had ever known, and now lost to us forever is their accumulated wisdom, vanished in the fires set by the early Christian church. When we consider that the Etruscans were the heirs of the ancient Neolithic cult of the Great Goddess, the loss of their knowledge is nothing less than a tragedy.

As with much of Europe, ancient cave drawings and artifacts found in Italy reveal primitive ceremonial beliefs related to hunting and the animal kingdom in general. Over the course of many centuries, ancient shamanic-like beliefs evolved into tribal religion, eventually taking the form we now call *La Vecchia Religione*—The Old Religion. In this religion we find a blend of beliefs common to both hunter-gatherer and agrarian societies. Writers of the Hellenistic and Roman period encountered surviving elements of primitive conceptions and practices in Italy so distant from the rationality of the classical world that they sometimes provoked astonishment and incomprehension.

Most striking were traces of an animistic conception of the supernatural and the omnipresent importance of divine signs and divination. Some writers found what they believed were surviving elements of a former matriarchy reflected in the high social and religious status of women in Etruria and even in early Rome. Encountered also were ancient beliefs in the material survival of the dead in their place of burial, and all the rites implied in such a belief (house-shaped urns and tombs, rich funerary apparatus, funeral games, etc.).

MYTHICAL INFLUENCES

The Old Religion of Italy is rooted in the indigenous Mediterranean/Aegean Neolithic cult of the Great Goddess. In classical mythology the worship of the Moon Goddess was brought to central Italy from Greece by Orestes and his sister Iphigenia. They reportedly fled their homeland after being accused of murdering a provincial king. Iphigenia (a priestess of Diana) aided by Orestes, established a sacred grove at Nemi in honor of the Goddess Diana.

Within the grove grew a certain oak tree of which no branch was normally allowed to be broken. Only a runaway slave was allowed to attempt to break off a branch. Success entitled him to challenge the Guardian of the Grove in single combat. If victorious, he became Guardian and reigned as *Rex Nemorensis* (King of the Woods). Because the Guardian of the Grove was required to be an outlaw, he often wore a hood to obscure his identity while moving about the forest. For this reason, among others, he was also known as the *Hooded Man*.

Legends tell of the first challenger to enter the Grove at Nemi. According to the myth, Diana hid this man (Virbius) from the solar gods in the forest of Nemi, because Virbius had offended Venus by rejecting her for the goddess Diana. In return for the favor of Diana, Virbius became Guardian of the Grove. Although this is all myth and symbolism, the position of Rex Nemorensis/The Hooded Man was actually historical. The rule of succession by combat was observed down to the Imperial Roman times. We know from historical records the Roman emperor Caligula hired a warrior to overthrow the Guardian of Nemi in hopes of disbanding the cult.

In Italian Witchcraft a subcult evolved outside of the classical Rex Nemorensis mythos. The position of the Hooded Man took on many other aspects. He symbolized the God of the Forests and became the Divine King (hence the aspect of ritual slaying). Beyond this he was the people's protector, provider, and their hope. The grove at Nemi was a sanctuary for outlaws and outcasts from patriarchal society. Aradia, a Witch queen of the Middle Ages, lived in the outlaw camps of the woods near Nemi, along with her followers, all of whom were considered outlaws. In Nemi the goddess Diana held the title: Goddess of Witches, outlaws, and outcasts. The main camp of Aradia and her followers lay among the ruins of the Temple of Diana overlooking Lake Nemi.

Lake Nemi was often referred to as *Diana's Mirror*. It was so named because the reflection of the full moon appeared upon the surface waters of the lake when viewed from the temple ruins. The moon, of course, was the symbol of the goddess reigning in the night sky. In early times the moon itself was worshipped literally as the goddess Herself. As the Lunar Cult evolved, the light of the moon became a symbol of divine presence, as it remains to this day.

The Witch Cult and other Mystery Traditions openly flourished up until the fourth century A.D., when agents of the Church looted and destroyed Pagan temples. In this manner the Church disrupted Pagan celebrations and prevented the ancient rites from being preformed upon the traditional sites. In A.D. 324 the Emperor Constantine established Christianity as the official religion of the Roman Empire. The Pagan temples were destroyed or converted into Christian churches. Gradually through the years Pagan customs were absorbed by Christianity. The Old Religion withdrew into secrecy away from the attention of the populace. Only small groups of people continued to gather at the ancient sites and perform the old seasonal rites. The majority feared the attention of the Church. However, the village and townsfolk continued to seek out the local Witch for healing and magical help.

MIDDLE AGES AND RENAISSANCE INFLUENCES

Following the collapse of the Roman Empire in the fifth century A.D., Europe fell into the Dark Ages. The Roman Catholic Church replaced Imperial Rome as the unifying factor in Europe. Latin remained the language of learned scholars and helped to preserve much of the knowledge we now possess about ancient cultures and about magick. Italy led Europe out of the Dark Ages with the Renaissance period originating in Italy during the early fourteenth century. By the fifteenth century the Renaissance spread to France, Spain, England, and the Netherlands. Besides art, science, and literature, the Renaissance produced many books on natural magick and occult philosophy in general. Magick during this period referred to a body of concepts constituting a metaphysical science.

With the Renaissance came the resurrection of the lost Greco-Roman books of magick. In particular the Renaissance produced the great Hermetic teachings that are the foundations for many modern magickal teachings and traditions. The Hermetic books, originally written in Greek sometime around the third century, appeared in a pseudo-Egyptian style or form. These texts preserved the ancient teachings of Persia, Chaldea, India, and the Greek Mystery Cults. As a body of accumulated teachings they were heavily influenced by Neoplatonism, Gnosticism, and Neopythagoreanism (see glossary). The occult manuscripts of the Renaissance period laid the foundation for magickal texts eventually appearing throughout all of Europe.

In 1460 Cosimo de Medici came into possession of many Hermetic manuscripts from Macedonia and the waning Byzantine Empire. He ordered Marsilio Ficino (an Italian philosopher and theologian) to translate these texts; through his efforts we now possess a body of occult knowledge that is still the basis for magickal thought. In the later period of the Renaissance these magickal texts appear in France, England, and Germany.

Neoplatonism, a philosophy based upon the teachings of Plato, greatly influenced southern European occult traditions. Plotinus, a Hellenized Egyptian, brought about its revival circa A.D. 244. Plotinian Neoplatonism was itself revived in fifteenth-century Italy by Marsilio Ficino. John Colet is credited with introducing Neoplatonism into England, which paved the way for the Cambridge Platonists of the seventeenth century. The doctrines of Plotinus became the official teachings of the Platonic Academy and greatly influenced even Christian theology.

Many schools of Neoplatonism, such as the Pergamene, engaged in magickal practices. By the fifteenth century such tenets were firmly established and influenced many friars and monks engaged in the translating of ancient texts. One such example is Tommaso Campanella, a seventeenth century Dominican friar, charged with heresy and imprisoned by the Church for trying to reconcile science and reason with Christian revelation. The monks and friars who, during the Middle Ages, wrote down the Celtic legends we now possess were no doubt knowledged in Neoplatonism, as we find many Mediterranean concepts in Celtic myth and legend. It is likely that as Roman Catholicism passed into such places as Ireland, so too did the Mediterranean teachings influencing Christian theology. In late antiquity and early medieval times philosophies of various religious traditions were attracted to, and influenced by, Neoplatonic thought.

In Italy certain regions held strongly to the Old Religion despite the power of the Church. Tuscany in northern Italy was the strongest center of paganism, followed closely by the region of Benevento in lower central Italy. However, in time even these strongholds fell to the power of the Church. All survivals of Pagan belief, worship, and practice were condemned as demonic and were suppressed by Christian theology and law. The *Synod of Rome* in A.D. 743 outlawed any offerings or sacrifices to Pagan gods or spirits. The *Synod of Paris* in A.D. 829 issued a decree advocating the death of witches and sorcerers, citing the Biblical passages of *Leviticus* 20:6 and *Exodus* 22:18. In 1181 the Doge Orlo Malipieri of Venice passed laws punishing the making of potions and the performance of magick. Although Witchcraft was officially a punishable crime in Italy throughout the thirteenth century, the Witch mania of northern Europe did not sweep Italy until the early fifteenth century.

MODERN WITCHCRAFT

In England, in 1951, the last of the laws against Witchcraft were repealed by Parliament. Soon after this a revival of Witchcraft arose in Great Britain. In 1954 and 1959 Gerald Gardner published his books *Witchcraft Today* and *The Meaning of Witchcraft,* [7] revealing much of the true nature of the Old Religion. Gardner himself was an English Witch, and did much to change the Christianized image of Witchcraft. Oddly enough, the rites that Gardner revealed contained various aspects of Italian Witchcraft such as ritual nudity, wine and cake celebrations, and the worship of a goddess and her horned consort. The name Aradia even appears in the English system, along with segments of the original Italian script found in *The Charge of the Goddess.*

The nineteenth-century Occult Revival that gave birth to the Gardnerian Wicca movement was itself stimulated by the classical teachings revived during the Renaissance. The works of Giovanni Pico della Mirandola profoundly influenced Western Occultism. In 1486 Pico published his work *Conclusiones nongentae in omni genere scientiarum* (*900 Conclusions in every kind of science*) containing everything from natural philosophy, to metaphysics, to the teachings of the Kabbalah.

Oriental philosophy merged with Western Occultism, modifying many of the ancient Aegean/Mediterranean concepts fundamental to Western magickal systems. The later works of Eliphas Levi, Francis Barrett,

Franz Bardon, Aleister Crowley, A. E. Waite, Dion Fortune, and MacGregor Mathers laid the foundation for the inner teachings of Gardner's personal magickal system. This is not to suggest that Wicca is something that Gerald Gardner invented, but rather to confirm that much of what he added to traditional Celtic pagan beliefs came from such sources. Clearly however, modern Wicca is also an evolution of folk magick traditions seen throughout all of Europe.

Masonic Influences

As mentioned earlier, many Italian Witches joined Masonic groups, both to protect themselves and to continue the ancient practices with other Witches. Masonic influences are readily recognized by a simple examination of modern practices. For example, the Italian Masonic group known as the Carbonari (circa 1820) had three degrees of initiation marked by colored cords or ribbons: blue, red, and black. A triangle marked the first degree level. The Carbonari claimed to base their system upon the Roman Mystery Cult of Mithra. One story originating from their order in France states that this particular chapter originated in Scotland during the reign of Queen Isabel, and was befriended by Francis I, King of France. Under his protection the Masonic cult multiplied and

---

7 Gerald Gardner, *The Meaning of Witchcraft* (London: Billing & Sons, 1959). No citation appears for subsequent mentions of these works except in the case of direct quotes from the text.

spread to Germany, France, and England where it was also known as Forest Masonry. There is an interesting similarity here to Italian Witches, who call their own groups "groves" (*Boschetto*).

A Hermetic group in Naples also influenced modern Stregheria. This group was called *Fratellanza Terapeutico-Magica di Myriam* (the Magical Therapeutic Brotherhood of Myriam), and was founded in Naples by Guilian Kremmerz. On March 20, 1896 the Brotherhood of Myriam drew up a constitution and commenced formal instruction. The basic structure of the Order's practices was based on natural magnetic properties found in all living things as well as in the earth itself. The order taught that all things were balanced within a polarity structure. Healing through electromagnetic properties of the body was one of the primary practices of the Brotherhood.

The Brotherhood of Myriam taught the concept of the aura, an energy field surrounding the body. It also instructed its members concerning the *lunar body*. The lunar body was believed to form from the emotional state of an individual, creating an energy body within the aura. The lunar body, in this context, is the occult or spiritual counterpart to the electromagnetic energy field known as the aura. The Order of Myriam also instructed its members on the astral dimensions and various practices associated with astral workings. Although such concepts were previously well known to Italian Witches, the Brotherhood supplied terms and labels later adopted into Stregheria.

DUOTHEISM

In classic Roman and Greek texts we find the divine couple imagery in such matings as Jupiter and Juno, and Zeus and Hera. At the second lectisternium in 217 B.C., for the first time in their history, the Romans selected a dozen deities and grouped them together into divine couples according to the Hellenic pattern. From this celebration arose the Roman version of the Twelve Principle Deities in Roman Mythology. The Aegean/Mediterranean concept of the divine couple had great impact on Celtic deity forms in later centuries.

The Celts of the Iron Age did not usually produce physical representations of deity with enough regularity to constitute an artistic or cultural tradition of such expression. Following Roman occupation in Gaul and then Britain there was a sudden surge of Celtic deity representations reflective of the Roman tradition of iconography. The iconography that preserved Celtic deity forms is owed in a large part to the Mediterranean artist tradition. Some images of Celtic divinities occur for the first time only under Roman rule: the Mother-Goddesses, divine couples, and Ne-halennia specifically. These aspects cannot be traced back prior to

Roman times (described in detail in my book *The Wiccan Mysteries*).[8]

Many people believe that the concept of Witches worshipping a goddess and a god arises from Gardnerian Wicca. However, as I have stated before, this concept appears in the earlier writings of Charles Leland. Leland portrays Italian Witches worshipping the Roman deities Diana and Lucifer. In Roman mythology Diana was the goddess of the moon and Lucifer was the god of the first light of day. Because of this he was also a solar god in the Roman pantheon.

Although a few Strega traditions do include the Roman Lucifer in their pantheon, the majority of Italian Witches employ the names Diana and Dianus. Diana has many other names by which she is known and worshipped among the Streghe. Depending on the aspect of divinity desired, she may be called Tana, Losna, or Atimite. In some traditions she also bears the name Jana. Likewise, Dianus is known by the names Tanus, Poloces (Pollux), or Janus. He is also called *Cornunno*—Latin for "the Horned One."

THE ELEMENTAL TOOL SET

In modern Witchcraft and Wicca the classic set of ritual tools consists of the wand, dagger, cup, and pentacle. The earliest depiction of a magician appearing with all of these tools is found in the fifteenth-century Italian Cary-Yale Visconti deck. This deck is also the oldest-known, extant Tarot deck. The Magician card in this deck depicts the Magician standing before a table. In his left hand he holds a wand. On the table itself is set a large chalice, a sword, and a pentacle. Each of these tools appear in the Minor Arcana of this deck as individual suits called swords, staves, cups, and coins. Stuart Kaplan, acknowledged expert on the Tarot, states that all Tarot symbolism as we know it today evolved from the Italian Tarot.

The Pierpont Morgan Visconti deck of the fifteenth century is slightly different from the Cary-Yale deck. Here the Magician is seated before a table upon which is set a common cup, a knife, and two crude coins of the period. In his left hand he holds a thin rod. As in the Cary-Yale version, the tools of the Magician also appear as individual suits of the Minor Arcana. Therefore we have, in effect, documentation that the four ritual tools of Western Occultism were known in Italy no later than the fifteenth century. The fact that they are used as symbols seems to indicate a previous long-standing mystical tradition connected to these tools in Italy. It is also interesting to note that the oldest known pentagram first appeared in southern Italy circa 525 B.C. It was worn by a mystical group of Pythagoreans in Crotona, Italy. The New Forest coven of Gerald Gardner's era called itself the Crotona Fellowship.

8 Raven Grimassi, *The Wiccan Mysteries* (St. Paul: Llewellyn, 1997).

The Four Elements

In 1609 Francesco Guazzo wrote in his *Compendium Maleficarum* (first book, chapter 18) that Italian witches called upon certain spirits who possessed specific elemental natures: *fiery, aerial, terrestrial,* and *watery.* In Roman mythology the four winds are deities with elemental natures. Their names are Boreas (north), Eurus (east), Notus (south), and Zephyrus (west). They are controlled by another deity named Aeolus who was the guardian of the winds, keeping them in order by chaining them. In this myth we see the four elemental natures controlled by a fifth higher power. This, of course, is the classic symbolism of the pentagram.

According to ancient historians, Empedocles (a student of the teachings of Pythagoras) was historically the first person known to have taught the concept of the Four Elements as a single cohesive doctrine. He was also the first person to introduce the concept of the four elements into astrology, exploring their role in discerning the basic nature of the Zodiac signs. He lived around 475 B.C. in his native homeland of Sicily, where he presented the teachings concerning the four elements as the four-fold root of all things.

In European Occultism these are the traditional assignments derived from the teachings of Empedocles:

Earth: Taurus, Virgo, Capricorn.
Air: Gemini, Libra, Aquarius
Fire: Aries, Leo, Sagittarius
Water: Cancer, Scorpio, Pisces

Earth: cold + dry
Air: hot + moist
Fire: hot + dry
Water: cold + moist

Reincarnation

Reincarnation, which was known in southern Europe as "transmigration of the soul," was one of the mystery teachings in the Orphic Mysteries of ancient Greece and the Roman mystery cult of Dionysus in ancient Pompeii. Reincarnation was known as *Palingenesis,* literally "to have origin again." The Orphic teachings maintained that the soul was preexistent and survived the physical death of the body it inhabited. The departed soul returned again in the body of a human or other mammal until it eventually found release. Once released from the cycles of rebirth, the soul returned to its former pure state in the community of souls dwelling with the gods.

Centuries prior to the Celtic presence in Greece (300 B.C.) the Greek philosophers Pythagoras (sixth century B.C.) and Plato (fifth century B.C.) taught that an immortal soul passed through many incarnations. Some people believe that the Druids taught Pythagoras the doctrine of reincarnation.

However the time frame does not support this, as Pythagoreas was born around 580 B.C. The earliest historical reference to the Druids comes from Diogenes Laertius (circa A.D. 200) who wrote that the Druids were first known in the time of Aristotle (384–322 B.C.). This is almost two centuries after the death of Pythagoras.

The ancient Greek historian Diodorus, along with Ammianus and Valerius Maximus, equated the Druidic beliefs in reincarnation with the "belief of Pythagoras." The ancient historian Hippolytus of Alexandria recorded that the legendary Thrachian Zalmoxis (a student of the teachings of Pythagoras) "instructed the Druids in the Pythagorean faith" during his travels. This was nearly two centuries before the Celts appeared in Thrace. Some historians have mislabeled Zalmoxis as a Celt because he was born in Thrace, but the timeline does not support this.

The Ritual Circle

Old Italian woodcuts like the one appearing in the *Compendium Maleficarum* (1609) by Francesco Guazzo depict Witches gathered in a ritual circle. In Italian Witchcraft the altar is oriented to the north quarter of the ritual circle. The Etruscans who occupied central Italy (from whom the Romans borrowed heavily) placed their deities into quarter associations. To the north was the chief god Tinia (and his consort Uni) who was king of the gods. The north was divided up into four sections that spanned from the north to the east quarter. In the east (the furthest extension of the northeast placement) dwelled the twelve major gods and goddesses of Etruscan religion. In the south were placed the lesser gods and nature spirits. In the west were placed the deities of Death and the Underworld. In this Etruscan view of the Cosmos we have the earliest account of Italic beliefs associated with the four quarters.

The northeast quarter of the circle is considered a sacred portal zone. The east is the quarter associated with deities of light and enlightenment. Therefore the northeast quarter is the joining of divine power and human enlightenment. Thus in Strega ritual circles we always enter and exit our rituals at the northeast quarter. It is interesting to note that the ancient temple of Diana was built on the northeast shore of Lake Nemi.

The Priest, Priestess, and Maiden

In many modern Witchcraft/Wicca traditions we find the inclusion of a priestess, a priest, and a maiden. Sometimes we also find the presence of a guardian. Italian Witchcraft is matrifocal and has its roots in the Neolithic cult of the Great Goddess. Rituals are presided over by a priestess, assisted by her priest and attendant maiden. Over the centuries the function of the priest in ritual circles increased and today we find him presiding over rituals occurring in fall and winter. In ancient times this was not the practice, and all rituals of the Old Religion were under the direction of women, assisted by priests.

Ancient stucco reliefs from the Villa of the Mysteries in Pompeii, Italy (from the Farnesina, 30–25 B.C. Rome, National Museum), depict a woman leading a blindfolded initiate into a ritual. The Priestess is assisted by a silenus priest and a female attendant. The ancient cults of Rome typically involved both priests and priestesses with their attendant maidens. The Mystery Cult of Dionysus at Pompeii is a classic example depicted on murals. It would be difficult to find a Roman Mystery cult that did not employ a priest and a priestess along with their maiden attendants, other than perhaps the Bona Dea, Heracles, and Vestal Virgin cults, which were gender exclusive.

THE DESCENT MYTHOS

The Eleusinian Mysteries, originating in Greece, involve themes of descent and ascent, loss and regain, light and darkness, and the cycles of life and death. Rites associated with these Mysteries were performed at midnight during the Spring and Autumn Equinoxes. The Eleusinian Mysteries spread to Rome and Britain where initiations into this cult were performed in both countries. The Eleusinian Cult contained the Greater Mysteries and the Lesser Mysteries. The Lesser dealt with the abduction of Persephone by the Underworld God, a classic descent myth.

The Greater Mysteries dealt with the Quest for the return of the Goddess, and the rites were performed in honor of Ceres (an Agricultural Goddess who was Patron of the Mysteries). This could account for many of the Wiccan concepts found in the mythos concerning the Descent and return of the Goddess, as well as many themes connected to the Equinox rites.

In the general mythos, Persephone descends into the Underworld and encounters its Lord. The life of the world disappears with Her and the first autumn and winter befalls the earth. The Lord of the Underworld falls in love with the Goddess and wants to keep Her in His realm. Ceres intervenes on Her behalf and pleads with the Underworld Lord to release Persephone. At first He refuses because Persephone has eaten the seeds of the pomegranate, an ancient symbol of the male seed (as we see in the Descent Legend, They loved and were One). Eventually He agrees on the condition that She return again to His realm for half of each year (cycle of the seasons).

THE EIGHTFOLD WHEEL OF THE YEAR

The agricultural year was very important to the agrarian society of ancient Rome, as well as to the Italian farmers of the Middle Ages. The ancient Romans held festivals of one type or another every month of the year and it is easy therefore to find a similar celebration occurring around the same dates as modern Wiccan festivals. Being an agricultural society, Roman farmers were well aware of the Equinoxes and Solstices and their place in the Wheel of the Year. Their significance was also noted in the Greek and Roman Eleusinian Mystery Cult. The rites of the Lesser Eleusinian Mysteries were celebrated at the Spring Equinox and the Greater Mysteries were celebrated at the Autumn Equinox. The focus of these rites was upon the descent of the Goddess into the Underworld and her ascent in the Spring.

Just as we have no historical records to indicate that any specific sect of Celts celebrated the eight Sabbats within any specific cult, so too is it with Italian traditions. We know that the basic themes of each Sabbat are native to Aegean/Mediterranean festivals occurring at the same time of year as northern European festivals. A simple study of Greek and Roman festivals will clearly demonstrate this. To obtain an overview of ancient Italian festivals originating from Etruscan and Roman influences in Italy, let us look at the Wiccan festivals of the year and note the Italic counterparts:

Samhain (October 31/November 1)

In the Italian Tradition this occasion is called *Shadowfest.* According to Italian tradition, the dead return to the human world beginning on the night of November eve and continuing until the second night (three nights in all). In Sicily it is the custom to set an extra place at the table for the return of departed relatives. Sicilian families are also known to set a banquet out before the family tomb as they gather on November 2 to honor their dead.

During the time of the Roman Empire, early Italians associated the fava plant with the dead, due to the single black stain on an otherwise perfect white petal. Romans served fava beans at funeral banquets, honoring the connection of the dead with the fava plant. This association has remained a part of Italian Witchcraft through the centuries; fava bean soup is still a traditional meal served on November eve (October 31). A bowl of fava bean soup is placed outdoors at midnight as an offering to the spirits, and then buried after sunrise on November 1.

In tenth-century Italy, Christian monks searching for a way to assimilate this Pagan celebration decided to cook large batches of fava soup and offer them up for the souls of the dead. Hungry peasants took great delight in the vats of fava bean soup that the monks placed at street corners. The Church allowed this practice to continue because of the conversion opportunities, but it wasn't until the fifteenth century that the Church officially claimed the day of the celebration, November 1, calling it *Ognissanti* or "All Saints Day," and November 2 was designated "All Souls Day."

In modern Italy, celebrants still eat festival treats called *ossi da morto* (bones of the dead) and *fave dei morte* (fava of the dead), sweets that are similar to cookies, but fashioned in the shape of skeletons and fava beans. In Sicily special ritual breads are made in the form of a corpse laid to rest, along with figures made of sugar in the shape of traditional heroes and characters from Italy's past.

Winter Solstice (December 21)

December was marked by festivals to the sun god Sol and to the agricultural god Saturn. The intimate connection between the sun and the growing of crops called for an invocation of both aspects of deity.

Imbolg/Candlemas

In the Italian Tradition this time is called Lupercus. In Gardnerian Wicca it is a time of purification. The month of February was sacred to the Roman god Februus who was a god of purification and death. The purification rites of the Lupercalia were also celebrated in February.

Spring Equinox (March 21)

In ancient Rome the festival of Mars, celebrating his original aspect as an agricultural deity, was held from March 19–22. March also marked the festival of Liberia, who was also known by the name Proserpina (Persephone). Proserpina was, among other things, a goddess of Spring whose ascent from the Underworld was marked by rituals performed in the Eleusinian Mysteries at the Spring Equinox. The ancient Roman Mystery Cult at Pompeii is a good example of the antiquity of this tradition in Italy.

Bealtaine/May Day (April 30/May 1)

In the Italian Tradition this time is called Goddess Day, bearing the name of whatever goddess a group worships, for example, Tana's Day in the Tanarric Tradition. May was marked by the Spring festivals of the Floralia. Flora was the Roman goddess of gardens and flowers. Her week-long Spring celebrations culminated on May 1 with a grand festival marking the occasion. In ancient Roman religion, the spring goddess Maia was worshipped in celebrations occurring in her sacred month of May.

Summer Solstice (June 22)

On June 20, the festival of Summanus was held in ancient Rome. Summanus was an agricultural deity, possibly of Sabine origin, associated with fertility and prosperity. In Celtic tradition this was the time of the

Holly King who defeated the Oak King in ritual combat. The powers of light and darkness battle over the waning and waxing periods of Nature. This resembles the Italian Benandanti sect who at this time of year held ritual battles over the outcome of the coming harvest.

The Roman festival of Vesta occurred in June. Vesta was the goddess of the hearth and goddess of sacred fire, and the Lare (ancestral gods) were under her domain. They were originally spirits of cultivated fields, derived from the Etruscan Lasa who were spirits of fields and meadows. The Lasa are identical to old concepts of fairies throughout Europe. The Mid-Summer festival is connected to fairies and magickal times. In the Roman festival of Vesta, with her Lare, we see the theme of the Queen of the Fairies on Mid-Summer's Eve.

Lughnasadh/Lammas (July 31/August 1)

The festival of Ops occurred in August. Ops was the goddess of the fertility, creative forces and earthly energies. She was the wife of Saturn, the Roman god of agriculture, and thus we have the harvest association. In Roman mythology she was identified with the goddess Fauna/Fatua, the deity responsible for the abundance of plant and animal life.

Autumn Equinox (September 21)

In the Eleusinian rites of the Roman and Greek cults this was the time of the descent of the Goddess into the Underworld. The mysteries of death and rebirth were ritualized themes occurring in both ancient Greece and Rome during this season.

Now that we have looked at some of the general influences upon Italian Witchcraft, we can turn to the inner views of the Italian Witches themselves. Ancient Witch bloodlines still exist in remnants of former priests and priestesses of the Old Religion. Although the Old Religion vanished from its place as a public religion in pre-Christian Europe, the ancient practices and tenets of belief survived among family traditions. Most of these were peasant folk, but a few were noble families. In the following chapters we will examine the beliefs of hereditary Witches and look at the concept they call *being of the blood*.

SECRETS OF
THE BLOOD

An old Strega teacher of mine once told me that the moon is more powerful than the sun. She said this is because the moon can appear both at night and during the day, but the sun can only show itself during the day. I dismissed this, of course, as a quaint peasant view from an unsophisticated era in our history. She later told me that the sun and moon will not rise if there are no Strega to practice the Old Ways, and again I listened with a patient smile. I dismissed much in those early days of my training, but what I wouldn't give to believe now, as she did then.

Hers was an ancient faith, basic and solid, without question. When confronted, she simply grinned or chuckled quietly at those who belittled her views. She was Strega, and she knew who she was. This she taught me long ago, and I have only come to know it now myself after a long, painful, and lonely journey. I once watched as a Christian evangelist attacked her pagan beliefs, trying to convince her of the hell awaiting her. She smiled at him as he pressed his points even harder. His face was red with anger as he delivered the account of how she would suffer in hell. Finally she looked up at him and said, with a cute little Italian accent: *"No, no a' hell, you a' silly."* A look of astonishment swept over his face. It was a great moment.

From her I learned about Aradia and the Witches of Benevento. I learned that modern Streghe are the descendants of those Witches who once gathered beneath the full moon at lake Nemi, and worshipped under the branches of the sacred walnut tree at Benevento. Some are spiritual descendants claiming a heart-felt connection to the ancient ways of their ancestors. Others come from bloodlines and family traditions in which the Old Ways have been preserved for countless generations. From the solitary Witch who lives in a remote mountain village to the secret clans that gather still in the ancient cities of Naples and Benevento, the Old Religion in Italy remains a living legacy of pre-Christian worship.

In this chapter we will examine the belief among hereditary Witches concerning the importance of *Witch Blood,* and we will uncover the true meaning behind *being of the blood.* If we look back far enough in time, we are all descended from Pagans who practiced magical rituals (although the Hebrew people might feel otherwise).

Among Strega family traditions there is a deep inner connection with lineage and bloodline. It is difficult to communicate this concept to others, especially when many people today do not believe that hereditary Witches actually exist. In *Ways of the Strega* I

presented considerable evidence as to the forces behind the survival of hereditary Witch families, therefore I will not belabor the point here. It is important only to note that some of the old Witch clans are still with us today.

Many hereditary Witches will not discuss the Old Ways with anyone who is not "of the blood," or not married into a Witch family. This is not an attitude born of elitism or egotism as some people choose to believe, but instead originates from a sense of simply being different from others. This difference is not viewed as better or special, but as something unavoidably separating the Strega from many other types of people.

In essence this difference is actually an occult quality within the blood, predisposing the Strega to heightened psychic and magical abilities. Just as a soul is an indwelling entity contained within a physical body, so too is this *occult quality* contained within the blood of hereditary Witches. If indeed the soul is the accumulation of all its past-life experiences, then it may be that the soul carries this occult essence with it into the next incarnation, regardless of what bloodlines it may be born into. Nevertheless, among the Strega, rites have been designed to ensure the return of the soul within the same family bloodlines for the good of the Craft Community as a whole.

Strega children are watched for signs of possessing that certain *quality,* sometimes called *the gift,* which will later be nurtured and developed by their parents or grandparents. This is why the Church sought to destroy not only captured Witches, but their offspring as well. No doubt the widespread persecution of Witches throughout all of Europe is an indication that this *quality within the blood* was not unique to Italy alone.

According to old family lore, the strega bloodlines originated from a mysterious people, known as the Enu, who founded the Etruscan Civilization. The Strega still maintain remnants of a language and alphabet unlike Italian, said to originate from the time of the Enu. Today the alphabet is referred to as the Tuscan Runes, or simply the Tuscan Script (Figure 34, p. 141). Many Strega today will claim Tuscan heritage, whether it be the case or not. It is not that they are liars, it is just that they are Italians (and if you're not Italian, no one can ever explain the difference to you!).

Growing up Strega is not something anyone normally talks about to *outdwellers* (a term denoting anyone who lives outside of the *Old Ways*). This silence stems from generations of persecution and discrimination which, in turn, are founded upon the stereotypes commonly formed through ignorance and bigotry. The Strega view the world quite differently than does the general public. Being different can be an open invitation to ridicule and mistreatment, especially among children. Therefore a child is never at liberty to tell outdwellers anything about family traditions or religious beliefs. Most Strega families appear to be Catholic to the general observer. Attending the Catholic church, and having statues of Mary and various other saints in the home is quite common among Italian family Witches. This is not hypocrisy, for the Strega simply view the saints as pagan gods in Christian garb.

In attempting to communicate the following perceptions about the Strega Elders, I can only draw upon how I viewed my own teachers, and what I have heard other students say. Mainly, there is something within the Elders that goes beyond their training and breeding; there is something unknown that can be seen in their eyes or felt in their presence. I have heard this described by non-hereditaries as "a quiet strength" or "the feeling that comes over you when you enter a library or a museum." Perhaps it is simply the sense of antiquity that emanates from them as they speak of the Old Ways. Or perhaps it is the accumulation of centuries of knowledge, effortlessly flowing in their teachings, as they draw upon a seemingly endless source of magical and ritual material. To gain an understanding of what this might actually be, let us look back through the magical mist of the past.

THE BLOOD SECRETS

In early tribal states, hunters and warriors held a very significant place in society. The bravest and most cunning of these was honored among the tribe, and looked upon as a leader. In many cases the *well-being* of this individual affected the *well-being* of the tribe. Even today, our national leaders' ailments are always minimized and they are always "recovering well." To understand this ancient relationship, we must look at certain aspects and connections.

Before humans learned to farm and herd, the hunt was essential to life. Without successful hunters, the clans would perish. Hunting was dangerous, as humans had not yet risen above the food chain. Primitive weapons such as a club or spear required the hunters to get close to their prey, and injuries were very common. Many hunters lost their lives or became lame as a result of the hunt. In time, the hunter became the warrior, risking his life for the sake of his tribe. The needs of the tribe, whether for food or defense, required sending out the best hunter or warrior the tribe had to offer.

Over the centuries this concept formed and evolved along with humankind's religious consciousness. The concept of deity and its role in life and death began to be reflected within clan ritual and dogma. Eventually the idea arose of sending the best of the tribe's people directly to the gods to secure favors. This was the birth of human sacrifice. Those who went to their death willingly were believed to become gods themselves. The concept of making offerings to the gods was nothing new at this stage. The custom of laying out food and flowers or game was already an ancient practice. To offer one of your own was considered the highest offering the tribe could make. Among human offerings the sacrifice of a willing human was the height of all possibilities. Surely, it was believed, the gods would grant the tribe anything if someone willingly laid down their life.

The Cult of the Slain Offering gave birth to a sacred lineage of blood lines. The rulers of ancient Rome and Egypt were considered by their people to be descended from the gods, or even as gods themselves. Specific members of the tribe showed some evidence of genetic lines leading back to the *Old Blood* originating from outside this Earth altogether. This led to the practice of sacrificing kings (the best of the clan) and royal blood lines became extremely important. This is the concept known in pre-Christian European religion as the Slain God or Divine King.

Once sacrificed, the blood and flesh of the king were distributed among the clan and into the land. Parts of the body were buried in cultivated fields to ensure the harvest. Blood and flesh were consumed by tribal members, a form of burial in the stomachs of the clan. A similar concept is also found in the Christian rite of communion, associated with the body and blood of Jesus.

Once human sacrifice was abolished, the custom remained to burn slain offerings on a funeral pyre. Remnants of this practice still appear today in the effigy burning of Befana in Italy as described in *Ways of the Strega*. Blood lines are still very important among hereditary witch families. Witch blood, or being of the Blood as it is called, is essential to the passing on of Craft secrets within the old family traditions. Most families in the Old Country will not even discuss the Craft with someone who is not of the Blood. This is one of the most difficult obstacles in trying to teach (and to maintain) the Old Religion. Guarding secrets of the Blood is something that one grows up with as an integral part of understanding *self*.

In the Divine King/Slain God Mythos, sacrifice is only part of the story. Retrieving the best member of the tribe after dispatching him or her in sacrifice was of equal importance. To accomplish this, rituals were designed to bring about the rebirth of these *slain gods* and blood lines were carefully traced. Special maidens were trained and prepared to bring about the birth. These were typically virgins who were artificially inseminated so that no human male could be said to be the actual father.

As human consciousness matured and evolved, human sacrifice evolved into animal sacrifice. This has been termed the *scapegoat*

ritual of killing an animal. Eventually this practice became the plant sacrifice associated with harvest rituals. The same essential Mythos applies to plant sacrifice—today we still find the "eating of deity" in the ceremony of cakes and wine (flesh and blood) within our rituals.

In the ancient tradition it was through the connection of the body and blood of the Slain Offering that the people were made

Figure 4. *Ritual Moon Bowl dating from the 2nd–3rd century B.C. Given to author by Mel Fuller in 1993, the bowl disappeared from Mr. Fuller's apartment following his death in 1994, where experiments were being conducted on the use of the bowl. This piece originally contained a companion bowl placed inside to receive menstrual blood and semen as part of ancient Italic fertility rites. (Photo by author.)*

one with deity. This is essentially the concept of the Christian rite of Communion or Eucharistic Celebration. At the "Last Supper" Jesus declares to his followers that the bread and wine are his body. He then declares that he will lay down his life for his people, and bids them to eat of his flesh and drink of his blood (the bread and the wine).

Blood was believed to contain the essence of the life force. The death of the king freed the sacred inner spirit, and by the distribution of his flesh and blood (in the people and the land) heaven and earth were united, and his vital energy renewed the kingdom. Remnants of these practices can still be clearly seen in the Old Religion, although they are veiled and highly symbolic. The Divine King/Slain God appears in various aspects throughout the ages. His image can be seen in the Jack-in-the-Green, the Hooded Man, the Green Man, and the Hanged Man of the Tarot. He is the Lord of Vegetation, he is the Harvest, and in his wild (or free) aspect he is the Forest.

THE DIVINE KING PRINCIPLE IN MODERN TIMES

You may be wondering about the relevance of this concept in modern times. The principles of the Divine King/Slain God may seem alien or anachronistic at best in our so-called *Enlightened Age.* It may surprise you to find that we all still live in a society with this same ancient *mindset.* Consider the relationship between fans and celebrities of any kind, as an example of this mentality.

I was first struck by this ancient principle in modern times when I observed people talking about *their* football teams. One person would say "Yeah, we kicked your butt in the play-offs . . ." and another would recount the previous victories of *their* own team. They were identifying themselves with the victors in their use of the term "we." I began to notice how people would display their collection of autographed objects, once the former property of someone famous. This seemed to elevate *them* in some fashion, and others were moved to admire them for the remnant they possessed. This applies as well to fans of rock stars and movie stars.

The person who owned the object had not changed or improved from the day before he purchased the object, so why was he or she now the focus of admiration? The answer lies in the fact that he or she now possessed a piece of the modern folk hero. A portion of power had been transferred to him or her through connection with the object formerly in intimate contact with the hero. This is the basis of the ancient principle: something deeply embedded in the group mind and in our ancient genetic memories.

This concept can be taken even further when we stop to consider the effects of having the *number one* team be from one's own city. I observed this phenomena arise when a team from a certain city went to their first Super Bowl game. The community came alive and was united in a way I had never before seen among its people. Banners appeared everywhere, and almost everyone was wearing symbols of the team. Everywhere I went, people were saying "we're going to win," or "we're the best," as if the actions of the team would somehow prove the community itself to be the best.

In ancient times, the Divine King/Slain God was given the best that his community could provide for him during the last year of his life (while in his prime). Today, our sports heroes are given millions of dollars and great admiration for playing a game. Are they really worth millions of dollars just to provide us with a season's entertainment, or is it that we are drawing more from them than we fully realize?

Whether we see our own *higher selves* in an actor's portrayal of some dashing hero or we are winning prestige through the victories of our athletes, what we are really doing is connecting with a very ancient principle. We are, in those moments, an ancient hunter-gatherer standing in awe of our most powerful hunters or warriors, and wanting very much to be just like them. In them we perceive that quality which is greater than the sum of its part. It is, perhaps, something of another world or another realm; perhaps it is even something of the gods themselves.

The ancient processions given to kings and queens are carried on today in our victory celebrations. In many ancient cultures a ruler was believed by his people to be a god, or descended from a god. Since the rulers represented the spiritual base of power of the clan itself, it was therefore necessary to preserve the *purity* of their bloodline, ensuring it was passed along through successive generations. Identifying with them, being one with them, was a principle empowering individuals. It made them somehow closer to that *something* which was *of the Blood.*

In the early days of the Witch Cult, it was taught that the *gifts* of psychic abilities were transmitted and maintained through a direct blood link with the priestesshood/priesthood. They themselves were considered to be either direct descendants from the Ancient Bloodline, or indirectly descended by virtue of having consumed the *Royal Blood* during their initiation into the priestess/priest class.

In a metaphysical sense, anyone who consumed the *essence* of such a *descendant* would then themselves possess the occult principle. This empowered them to be able to pass on the indwelling etheric energy into the ritual cakes and wine that later replaced the actual bodies of the Sacrificial King. The passing on of power through the exchange of sexual body fluids, later replaced certain aspects of the blood rites, and can be found today in some Third Degree Initiation ritual aspects, commonly known today as the Great Rite.

THE BLOOD SEED

What are the qualities that make someone cunning, brave or heroic? What attributes are there within someone who is a natural leader, and what generates *charisma?* Are these things merely genetic traits, simple chemistry, DNA codes? Or do these things emanate from another related *quality* carried from one generation to the next? I am certainly no expert on genetics, but I venture to say that the traits I've mentioned are not merely genetic programs activated here and there as needed. Often the most timid individuals can perform the bravest of deeds, and even obscure individuals can rise to powerful positions of leadership.

Among the Strega, it is believed that an occult property is passed within the blood, down through the generations. It appears more pronounced in some individuals than in others, thus it is called *The Gift*. This quality can appear in any individual, regardless of nationality, and I believe it to be the empowering force behind anyone who achieves their dreams or their place in history. A great many famous people state they always felt destined for fame or fortune. From the time they were young children, they heard an inner voice, or felt they were meant to be someone special.

Laying dormant within the average person is the ancient seed containing the power to become great things. This is easily seen in small children as they mimic superheroes in play. It is glimpsed in the daydreams of teenagers and in those unique people who "march to the beat of a different drummer." In time, many people lose sight of this *seed of potentiality,* eventually surrendering to the service of others in their jobs and families. Yet, laying deep within them (just like a seed beneath the winter snow) is the sleeping current of a different age, in which the world was new and magick was alive.

This ancient current is like a river flowing from the past. It is, in part, the Spiritual Consciousness of our ancestors that can be tapped by magical techniques explained later in this book. But it is also the remaining Consciousness of the Great Gods themselves, waiting there in the shadows for someone who will place before them the old familiar offerings. The memory is there within your own bloodline, carried for untold Ages by your own pagan ancestors. It requires only a slight shift in consciousness to access your ancestral current, along with a simple focal point known as a shrine.

THE LARE HOUSE/LASA SHRINE

Lare (pronounced lar-ray) are ancestral spirits who have evolved beyond the need for physical existence within the world as we know it. They can assist us in this lifetime, and traditionally serve as protectors of home and family. A small shrine, resembling the front of a Roman temple, was placed in either the East or West portion of the home. In early Roman times, the Lare house was set above the hearth—the honored place of family gatherings and meal preparations.

An image of the Lare spirit was placed within the shrine, along with an offering bowl. Typically, the image of a Lare was that of a Roman youth clad in a tunic, holding a cup and bowl (see Figure 5). Lare are invoked on all important family occasions, such as departures, marriages, births, and funerals. Traditionally at such occasions their shrines are decorated with a garland, and offerings of incense, fruit, and wine are placed before the shrine. In Roman times, a new bride, when carried across the threshold of her new home, gave offerings to the Lare and placed a coin upon the shrine.

The Lare evolved from earlier spirits, known in Etruscan times as the *Lasa* (pronounced loss-ah). Lasa were known as the first spirits, and were believed to have existed long before humankind. They are the spirits of the Old Religion, the essence of what it is that we feel when we look at the beauty of Nature. In effect, they can be thought of as the animating and empowering forces behind Nature. This is why we sometimes refer to them as the Old Ones, or as the spirits of the Old Ways.

Instructions are provided in this section for erecting a shrine to either the Lare or the Lasa. If you are of Italian ancestry, you may wish to set up a Lare House. If you have no connection with Italian ancestry, you may wish to set up a Lasa Shrine. Either object is fine, regardless of ethnic background, so chose whichever feels right for you.

Figure 5. *Lare Spirit. A modern replica of a Roman statue depicting an ancestral spirit. From the author's collection.*

PREPARATION OF A LARE HOUSE OR LASA SHRINE

Select a suitable shrine structure in which to house the Lare or Lasa spirits. Place it on a wall (or over a mantel) in the west or east alignment of the home. Place within the opening of the temple structure (doorway/portal) an image representing the spirit. Lay a small offering bowl on the ledge of shrine, and next to this place an uncooked fava bean if selecting a Lare shrine—or a sprig of rue, a key, and some salt if selecting a Lasa shrine.

Light some incense of either pine, sandalwood, or a similar "earthy" scent. Pass the smoke beneath the shrine so that the smoke rises up through and around the shrine. While doing this say:

Spirits of the ether, awaken, gather the ancient ones here, who were of Old called Lare (or Lasa). Bless this shrine in the names of (give deity names of god and goddess), *as it was in the time of our beginning, so is it now, so shall it be.*

At this point the shrine has been blessed and consecrated. Give an offering to the spirits, placing it in the offering bowl. Sit quietly before the shrine and visualize a small, soft, blue light around the Lare or Lasa image. In time you will actually see this light come and go within the shrine, and perhaps there may be even more than just a single light. This is assuming that you give an offering at each full moon and all family occasions such as birthdays, marriages, and so forth. Light a candle each time you sit before the shrine. Make requests or ask for assistance in personal matters, and work to establish a rapport.

Figure 6. *The author's Lasa shrine, set with an offering of fava beans in a walnut shell, a white candle, and a cord of folk charms.*

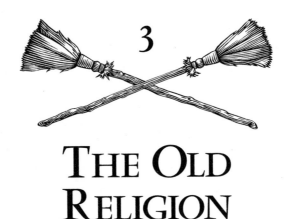

THE OLD
RELIGION

The earliest known use of the term *The Old Religion* first appears in Roman Senate records in the first century A.D. Here it was used by the emperor Claudius I, and the orator Seneca when speaking of Etruscan religion. It was also used by these same individuals when speaking of the occult arts practiced by the Etruscans—in particular, the art of divination and omens. Charles Leland recorded in his nineteenth-century writings that the Italian Witches of Tuscany refer to their beliefs as *La Vecchia Religione,* the Old Religion. Gerald Gardner later used the same term when writing of Witchcraft in his mid-twentieth century books.

The elements comprising the Old Craft, or Hereditary Witchcraft, differ in many regards from modern Witchcraft. It is a blend of what today we call Ceremonial Wicca and Shamanic Wicca. Hereditary Witchcraft employs primitive practices such as drumming and trance techniques not unlike Shamanic Wicca. It also incorporates ceremonial aspects such as the construction of ritual circles and the use of ritual tools. However, the older hereditary systems did not originally possess the same formal full-scale *Treguenda* (Sabbat) rituals found in the modern Craft. In my opinion, it is probably not until around A.D. 600 that we find Hereditary Italian Witchcraft resembling the current structure of contemporary Craft rituals. The primary exception to this would be lunar rites.

The full moon ritual and the rites of initiation predate the Treguenda and comprise the bulk of original ancient hereditary material. However, we do find in addition what constitute simple fertility rites designed to bless plant and animal life. Naturally such rites were performed as would be appropriate to the season. Therefore, many of these rites mark the solstices and equinoxes, and contain surviving elements of ancient European Mystery Traditions. Religious rites associated with the dead, personal purification, herd production, and crop yield marked the cross quarters (periods of the seasons falling exactly between the solstice and equinox). However, these rites resembled more the simplistic blessings of a priest or priestess, and primitive, mimetic, magickal practices, than they do the type of formal ritual structure seen in the rites of modern Witchcraft.

Hereditary Witches are all that remain of the ancient priest(ess)hood lineage of the Old Religion. By the early Middle Ages we find elements of both hunter-gatherer and agricultural communities expressed in the practices and beliefs of Hereditary Witches. The Old Religion of the Pagan populace, and that of the priests and priestesses, were two slightly different religions. To the populace, the Treguenda were times to ensure abundant crops and herds as well as occasions for festival fun. To the priests and priestesses they were times to align with the forces of Nature, and to redirect the currents of energy in order to manifest the needs of the community. We can liken this to the differences experienced between a Catholic priest and his congregation during the Mass. Both are doing different things during the same ritual, and are therefore experiencing the same ceremonial worship somewhat differently.

If we isolate the two Catholic factions here, we find two very different structures of worship. Imagine what might evolve separately if these two factions were cut off from one another due to a violent persecution such as existed during the Inquisition. Then envision each faction continuing to practice independently in secret. The Priest persists in setting the altar, manipulating the tools, invoking deity, and so forth. The populace continues to gather, appoints a facilitator who tries to remember what the priest did at the altar (and why), and everyone kneels and stands at whatever cues seem familiar. Within a few generations you would find many differences and yet a similar thread running through both surviving factions. In effect, you would end up with two somewhat different religions based upon the same foundation. This is similar to what happened to the Witch Cult and is the basis for differences between Hereditary Witchcraft and many modern Wiccan traditions.

WITCH BLOOD DURING THE MIDDLE AGES

The Old Witch Blood of Europe dates back to the days of priestesses and priests who served the pre-Christian European Pagan community. According to legend, Aradia of Tuscany was initiated and taught by a woman of Witch Blood descent. Aradia was most likely of Witch Blood herself, as the legends claim it was her aunt who initiated her (this is covered in more detail in chapter 12).

In chapter six of the *Compendium Maleficarum* (an Italian Witch hunter's manual published in 1609) we find several references to a hereditary tradition within Witchcraft. The writer, Francesco Guazzo, states that Witchcraft is passed from parents to their children. Guazzo also writes of Witchcraft that there are many examples of "this inherited taint in children." Another aspect of the Old Craft is revealed by Guazzo in several accounts wherein adolescent offspring are initiated into the Witches sect through sexual union, typically with the male or female leader of the Boschetto. While this may be shocking to modern sensitivities, in part this act ensured that the adolescent's first sexual union was with someone older and more experienced who would take the time and care necessary to make the experience a positive one. The surrendering to something so intimate was also an act of full and complete devotion to one's religious path on the part of the initiate.

The Tradition of the Old Craft employed certain peasants who were loyal to the old Witch Bloodlines of pre-Christian Europe. These people guarded the ritual sites and performed various mundane tasks as well. They were given red sashes to wear as a sign of their service to the Old Religion. In other words, these sashes symbolized acceptance by the Witch Blood Clan, and granted certain rights and privileges. Red fabric was not commonplace and this limited the chance appearance of someone wearing a red sash.

Those who were of the old bloodlines wore short red cords around their thigh. This practice eventually evolved into wearing red bands, typically on the left arm or around the left thigh. A series of gestures was established to test anyone who might be presenting themselves as a Witch. The proper exchange of signs assured the correct identity of the person. Therefore the cord or sash was not enough by itself. During the festivals those who wore red sashes around their waists were identified as *Affine* (kindred). Those who wore red cords were identified as *Parentado* (being of Witch Blood). Elder Witches wore green cords around their waist as a sign of their initiatory experience within the Craft. A white bead, shell, or strip of linen attached to the green cord identified the Witch as a priest or priestess of the Old Religion. The Elder directing the rites wore a ritual mask in order to be identified during the night rituals.

The inclusion of masks and other items contributed to some very serious misunderstandings of Witchcraft practices. When viewed at night, highlighted only by flickering torches, ignorant observers of the rituals misinterpreted many of the things they viewed taking place. Small effigies used in folk magick rites for fertility and healing were most likely mistaken for human infants. The ritual leader clad in stag or goat guise was perceived as the devil. However, other charges made against Witches, such as sexual intercourse, did take place, although not for the reasons claimed by the Inquisition. It is important to remember that the Old Religion evolved from an ancient pagan fertility cult.

It is not implausible that some Witch groups made members step on a cross, or defile it in some other manner, in order to safeguard against Christian spies infiltrating the cult. Religious fervor was intense during the Middle Ages and into the Renaissance; it is highly unlikely that any Christian would risk defiling the cross, even to ferret out Witches. If we give the Witch hunters of this period the benefit of the doubt, we can assume that instead of making up stories about various Witch gatherings for their own agenda, they reported gross misunderstandings, born of fear and ignorance.

To illustrate this and other aspects of Italian Witchcraft, some Italian woodcuts of the period appearing in the book *Compendium Maleficarum,* written in 1609 by Francesco Guazzo, are reproduced here (Figures 7–14, p. 40–43). The woodcuts deal with the theme of initiating new members into the Witch Cult. First let us see the presiding demon figure as a misinterpretation, and gross exaggeration, of the ritual facilitator dressed in horned god disguise. Then we can examine the settings of the woodcuts from the perspective of the Old Religion, and obtain a more realistic view of the Witches' microhistory. Once we change the demon figure into a priest of the Old Religion, in animal costume, then the entire feel of the woodcut is transformed. It is in perceiving the horned figure as a devil that the Witch hunters erroneously colored their own perceptions of Witches and their rites.

In Figure 7, we find a group of Witches gathered in a circle marked on the ground. This is one of the earliest depictions associating Italian Witchcraft with ritual circle sites. Figure 8 shows a man being touched upon the forehead, reminiscent of the act of first degree Initiation in which the psychic senses are awakened through this center.

Witches declare their disassociation with Christianity in Figure 9 by stepping on a cross. No doubt this was an important act for new members to perform during an era in which agents of the Church were hunting down Witches to be tried and executed. This practice no longer exists in any groups that I am aware of.

In Figure 10, we find a family of Witches presenting themselves at their first Treguenda. This woodcut is interesting from our aforementioned perspective because the family is not sacrificing its children (a popular accusation made by the Inquisition.) The mother appears to be smiling, older children are present instead of just infants, and no one appears to be in fear. In other words, we find nothing here to indicate the ritual sacrifice of babies in this woodcut.

In Figure 11, two books appear in what seems to be an act of comparison or the passing out of a book. Are we seeing copied books being handed out to new members of the Cult? As mentioned in chapter one, handwritten copies of private occult books were found in the home of a Witch in Venice. Yet, if we are going to use these woodcuts as evidence for our alternative history, then in fairness we must also look at the less benign woodcuts.

There are three specific woodcuts that create an image problem for Witches. One depicts a female Witch apparently in the act of kissing the posterior of the horned figure (Figure 12). We do know that the Old Religion was an ancient fertility cult incorporating images of male and female genitalia. The base of the spine (sometimes called the tail bone) has long been regarded as the residing center of the Kundalini, or serpent power of sexual energy. Perhaps what we see in this woodcut is the placing of a kiss of reverence

on the sacred center of the horned god, the Lord of Fertility. According to the Inquisition, all of the Witches performed this act upon the horned figure. In our scenario, this would make sense because the Witches are empowering the Horned God, passing their united energies to him and linking themselves to the primal fertile power he bears on their behalf.

The second troublesome woodcut shows a nude infant laying on the ground in front of a group of Witches (Figure 13). Guazzo states that here the Witches promise to sacrifice children to the devil. First we must consider whether the child figure was actually real or was a puppet employed in folk magick. In the case of the latter, the puppet may have symbolized the Child of Promise, a mystical pre-Christian European entity appearing in many Witchcraft ceremonies (see glossary). If instead the child was real, could this not have been simply a presentation of the infant for a blessing by the horned god priest? Perhaps this was simply a form of "baptism" into the ancient sect.

The third negative woodcut image depicts what appears to be a child being roasted over an open fire (Figure 14). I assume the Witches are using a puppet as a symbol of death and regeneration in a ritual slaying context. The burning of effigies is quite common in folk magick and is associated with rituals of death and renewal throughout much of Europe. At night, highlighted only

Figure 7. *Witches gathered in a circle marked upon the ground. Italian woodcut by Francesco Guazzo, from the* Compendium Maleficarum, *published in 1609.* (Reprinted by arrangement with Dover Books, New York.)

Figure 8. *A Witch being initiated into the Craft. Italian woodcut by Francesco Guazzo, from the* Compendium Maleficarum, *published in 1609.* (Reprinted by arrangement with Dover Books, New York.)

Figure 9. *Witches declaring non-allegiance to the Christian Church. Italian woodcut by Francesco Guazzo, from the* Compendium Maleficarum, *published in 1609.* (Reprinted by arrangement with Dover Books, New York.)

Figure 10. *A family of Witches present themselves to two horned figures at their first Treguenda. Italian woodcut by Francesco Guazzo, from the* Compendium Maleficarum, *published in 1609.* (Reprinted by arrangement with Dover Books, New York.)

Figure 11. *Books presented to a new Witch. Italian woodcut by Francesco Guazzo, from the* Compendium Maleficarum, *published in 1609.* (Reprinted by arrangement with Dover Books, New York.)

Figure 12. *A Witch giving the ritual kiss on the base of the spine. Italian woodcut by Francesco Guazzo, from the* Compendium Maleficarum, *published in 1609.* (Reprinted by arrangement with Dover Books, New York.)

Figure 13. *Witches presenting a child for a blessing of fertility by the Horned God. Italian woodcut by Francesco Guazzo, from the* Compendium Maleficarum, *published in 1609.* (Reprinted by arrangement with Dover Books, New York.)

Figure 14. *Witches preparing puppets for symbolic ritual of death and rebirth. Italian woodcut by Francesco Guazzo, from the* Compendium Maleficarum, *published in 1609.* (Reprinted by arrangement with Dover Books, New York.)

by torch light, the limp puppet figure probably appeared to be a dead human infant. The puppet was presumably attached to a small scaffold and placed in the fire, the imagery being mistaken for reality by a horrified onlooker hiding in the woods.

In Hereditary Witchcraft we also find the inclusion of "the man in black," whom the Inquisition believed was the devil. In Hereditary Italian Witchlore, the man in black was an emissary from the Old Religion to the peasant folks. He was known as the *Capinera* (pronounced, cap-ee-near-ah). The priest-(ess)hood of the Old Religion still existed and periodically sent out such figures in an attempt to ensure survival of the Witch Cult. The Capinera scouted out villages and observed individuals who sought solitude in the woods or other isolated places. Generally, they were only approached if their behavior suggested an interest in old folk beliefs, or if they were seemingly outcasts of the town or village.

A *Boschetto* (a coven) was sometimes formed from such individuals, organized and led at first by the emissary. The members wore masks to conceal their identity, in order to minimize betrayal to the Inquisition. If the members proved worthy of trust, and were open to the primitive practices involving costumes, phallic cult objects, fertility themes, and other pagan practices, they were eventually initiated into the Craft by a priest or priestess of the Old Religion.

THE CULT OBJECTS

The cauldron, skull, broom, stang, and phallus all figure prominently in Hereditary Witchcraft. Many modern Witches shy away from such objects due to stereotypical images of Witchcraft common today. The image of the sterile old hag performing superstitious spells over a bubbling cauldron arose during the Middle Ages. I always found it curious that such a poor figure was so feared by the Church that it became necessary to hunt Witches down and kill them.

The pre-Christian image of a Witch, such as Medea or Circe, was quite different. In this era the Witch was proficient in the arts of magick as well as sexually seductive. By 30 B.C. this image was shifting, as reflected in the *Epodes of Horace* written during this period. Here the Witch was physically unattractive but still proficient in her magickal abilities. Horace notes, for example, that Italian Witches had the power to "draw the moon down from the sky." However, as patriarchal power became more and more firmly implanted, the once self-empowered female figure was transformed into an old woman muttered spells and cackling in the night. It is interesting to note that male Witches bore no such stigmas, but almost always appeared as powerful mysterious figures. Curiously though, certain elements of Circe and Medea persisted into the Middle Ages in such characters as Morgan Le Fay of Arthurian mythology.

In the old Craft, the skull symbolized the principle of death and rebirth, and also represented the Slain God and Lord of the Underworld. The cauldron complimented this imagery as a symbol of the womb, the portal of life itself. As such the cauldron was also a symbol of the Great Goddess, being both the womb and the tomb. The broom evolved into a composite of both male and female fertility. This was due in part to the fact that it was made from plants of the field, but also because it symbolized male and female genitalia. The shaft was the male's phallus and the foliage was the female's pubic patch. The ritual broom was not tightly bound and the shaft was easily removed for ritual use as a wand.

Within the Old Craft, the ritual phallus was both symbolic and operative. Ancient fertility rites often called for multiple sexual acts designed to return life essence into the fields and forests. Since males are limited in the successive frequency of performing sexual unions, the phallus was employed as a substitute. This allowed the rites to continue uninterrupted by any mundane circumstances that might occur.

The stang was a symbol of the goddess. A forked branch from a fruit tree was chosen, representing the mother image. The forked "Y" shape symbolized the sacred vagina of the goddess. A oak or walnut stang was used to symbolize the god, in which case the forked branches were not trimmed back into two single forks. Instead they were left with several shoots to symbolize the horns of a stag. The ritual stangs were placed at various quarters of the circle depending on the theme of the season. The east quarter was employed for themes of gain and the west for themes of loss. The north or south quarter (typically north in the winter and south in the summer) were often incorporated for times of power.

To a lesser degree, other ritual items such as ivy, rue, salt, and wine also served as cult objects, traditionally carried in the Nanta bag. Each of these is linked to a ritual tool (respectively, needle, twig, coin, and thimble). The needle is associated with ivy because of its winding and weaving motion in sewing. The twig is linked to rue because of its stalk. Salt is symbolic of the coin because both are taken out of the earth itself. The thimble, which is a cup-like object, represents the wine. Each of these small items represents the classic ritual tools of Western Occultism depicted in the Italian tarot as early as the fifteenth century (Cary-Yale Visconti deck). The needle is the ritual blade, a twig is the wand, the coin is the pentacle, and the thimble is the chalice.

GODS OF OLD EUROPE

Hereditary Witchcraft has preserved many of the old Neolithic deity forms of Old Europe. The old gods of Europe originated from a pre-Indo-European culture that contrasted sharply with the ensuing patriarchal proto-Indo-European culture. The later superimposed on all of Europe except the southern and western fringes. Between 4500–2500 B.C. three waves of infiltration from the northeast swept across Europe, replacing (in many cases) the goddesses of old Europe with the gods of the Indo-Europeans. What developed from this merging of traditions was a mixture of the two mythic systems of old European and Indo-European religious cultures.

As early as the 7th millennium B.C., villages were established in southern Europe that depended upon the domestication of plants and animals for continued survival. The inhabitants of southern Europe 7,000 years ago were not the primitive villagers of the incipient Neolithic Era. During the periods from the 7th to the 5th millennia, the farmers of southern Europe had developed an agricultural system (and corresponding cultural associations unique to themselves) that was contemporary with similar developments established in Mesopotamia, Egypt, Anatolia, and Syro-Palestine. By the 5th millennium B.C. this culture had reached its peak in old Europe.

In old Europe the ancient Mythos of Deity was not polarized into feminine and masculine power, per se, as it appears to have been in the Indo-European peoples. Both aspects of Deity were manifest side by side, or pictured with their opposite genders in animal companion forms, serving to affirm and strengthen their respective forces (such as the goddess Diana with a stag or with hunting hounds). In the agricultural communities people began to more closely observe the forces of nature than did those of the hunter-gatherer communities, for obvious reasons. Deities began to be reshaped into gods and goddesses of the fields and crops. They retained their ancient hunter-gatherer associations of both a magical and religious nature but often the figures were renamed and appeared in a domesticated form (such as the horned stag god of the hunter-gatherer reappearing as the horned goat god of the agricultural community).

The late Marija Gimbutas (former professor of European Archaeology at UCLA) writes in her book *The Goddesses and Gods of Old Europe* (see note 6, p. 10):

> Significantly, almost all Neolithic goddesses are composite images with an accumulation of traits from the pre-agricultural and agricultural eras. The water bird, deer, bear, fish, snake, toad, turtle, and the notion of hybridization of animal and man, were inherited from the Paleolithic era and continued to serve as avatars of goddesses and gods. There was no such thing as a religion or mythical imagery newly created by agriculturists at the beginning of the food-producing period.

We can easily see that the earliest forms of those deities which we readily recognize as the gods and goddesses were originally powerful animal totems. Some of the most ancient and enduring of these animal forms are as follows:

The Bear

As early as 4500 B.C. images of bears appear in ancient carvings and religious artifacts. The bear was a powerful image of the Mother Goddess—strong, nurturing, and protective. As noted earlier, the bear was associated with Artemis/Diana as one of her cult animals.

The Stag

As early as the 6th millennium B.C., carvings of deer appear in religious artifacts. In the 4th millennium B.C. images of stags appear with lunar crescent symbolism associating the deer with the moon in early religious belief. The association of the stag with Diana originated from this early connection. The stag is also the fertile impregnating consort of Diana, dwelling in her wooded domain.

The Boar/Pig

Images of pigs are known from all parts of Europe and date from every period. The fast-growing body of a pig came to symbolize the earth itself. The pig became a sacred animal probably no later than 6000 B.C. It was also strongly linked to the Underworld and appears as an animal totem to many Underworld deities, including Demeter and Persephone.

The Wolf

Images of dogs and wolves appear in carvings and paintings as early as the 4th millennium B.C. Much of the symbolism is connected with themes of protection and hunting. Wolf heads were worn by shamans, and some Roman standard-bearers, symbolic of an atavistic connection with this ancient animal spirit. Wolf cults flourished for centuries, comprising both warrior and priest classes (remembered now only in legend and folklore as distorted stories of werewolves).

The Goat

Goats have long been symbols of fertility and sexual virility. During the Middle Ages, female Witches were accused of having sexual intercourse with goats (an ancient practice in certain mystery cults originating in the regions of Egypt and Chaldea, and seen also in some Greek Mystery Traditions). Early forms of goat deification can be seen in the god Pan, as well as in the legends of satyrs. In Italy, legends arose that Witches rode on the backs of goats, unlike the Witches of northern Europe, who were said to fly on broomsticks.

FAMILIAR SPIRITS

The concept of a familiar spirit among Hereditary Italian Witches is related to the Lare or Lasa. It is the ancestral spirit of the clan, the animal guide from the Other World. The early Italic people were migratory and took sacred animals as their guides. Typically each clan named themselves after their guardian animal. The Piceni were guided by the woodpecker, known in Latin as *picus*. The Lucani chose the wolf, known in Greek as *lukos*.

The animal guide was viewed as the ancestor, feeder, and protector. The practice of integrating the animal guide into the clan structure was widespread throughout prehistoric Italy. Evidence of this, and its survival into pastoralism, is abundant in the so-called Apennine Bronze Age. The Etruscan she-wolf of Rome is one example of an Italic animal spirit guide stemming from the ancient Italic rite of *ver sacrum*, the sacred springtime. It was the tradition for each clan to divide and establish new colonies each spring. The founding of Rome by Romulus and Remus, who suckled beneath the Etruscan wolf, is an interesting reflection of the ver sacrum concept. Etrusca was the original clan, the mother, and Rome became the new clan.

The concept of the guiding and protecting animal spirit shifted into the ancestral spirit when humans settled into towns and cities. The first stage of this evolution became the Lasa spirit, originally the spirit of fields and forests, reflective of the animal spirit of the woodlands. Following Roman conquest of Etrusca, the Lasa became the household spirit known as Lare. Even in this humanoid image we still find the animal spirit appearing in the drinking horn held by the Lare. The drinking horn is typically designed as a stag's head, or some other horned animal. This vessel is symbolic of the ancient animal nature of the Lare.

The Witches' familiar spirit, well known to us from the Middle Ages, is the atavistic resurgence of the ancient animal guide of the early Italic tribes. Today this concept is most commonly associated with Witches' pet cats, birds, snakes, and so forth. As we can see, the physical pet familiar is a relatively new concept. During the Medieval period non-Witches believed that the devil's agents came to Witches in the form of animal servants. The physical pet is a totem extension of the familiar spirit aiding the Witch.

Familiars are used for magickal purposes in Witchcraft. They can carry the energy of a spell to someone, or some place, if you desire. They can obtain information for you on the planes (physical or astral) or serve as guardians and so on. In the recommended reading list at the end of this book, I have selected several books on how to obtain and employ a familiar spirit. If you are interested in experimenting you should find the list useful.

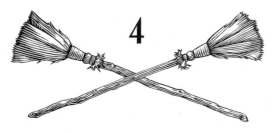

ITALIAN FOLK MAGICK

A very rich legacy of magick and primitive religious belief originates from old Italy. To the early Italic peoples, the universe was controlled by a host of spirits and deities. Humans, as users of tools, assembled objects believed to exert influence over entities inhabiting the *supernatural* world. Most ancient pagans were poor, common folk, with little access to the type of tools associated with modern Witchcraft such as the silver chalice, ritual bell, altar cloth, and so forth. Instead they employed material and items readily available to them.

The basic tools of Folk Magick in Italy are antique keys, colored ribbons, scissors, thread, rings, horseshoes, and pins. The mortar and pestle and certain types of cookware are also incorporated in spell casting, along with sewing items such as thimbles and needles. Such common items were customary to the home during the time of the Persecution and would not bring suspicion upon anyone who possessed them.

Old keys of the *skeleton key* type (commonly found in antique shops today) are considered amulets for good luck. They can be carried on your person in a pocket or purse, or may be hung from a red ribbon near a window or doorway. When you find a key it is considered bad luck to pass it by. One should always pick up the key and say the following as you take the key in your left hand:

It's not a key that I have found
nor one that I shall bear around
but fortune that I trust will be
ever my friend and near to me.

Keys are often used to gain success in relationships with women. The word *chiave*, which means "key" in Italian, symbolizes the phallus, and the phrase "to key" is an old slang term for sexual intercourse. The key also symbolized "hearth and home," and is believed to attract a future spouse when employed magickally. Its magickal properties may be traced back to its association with the dwelling place and therefore to household spirits known as Lare. The Lare are ancestral spirits of family and home, commonly venerated in ancient Roman times.

Folk lore reveals that if you blow through the opening on a key, or whistle through it, you can call forth spirits or fairies to assist you in any magickal undertaking. This technique is employed especially in matters of love. Magickal *binding* is used in key magick as well as in other forms of magick. Attaching a lock of your lover's hair to a key is believed to ensure fidelity. Locking a padlock while pronouncing a couple's names is believed to stop all intimacy between them.

Ribbons possess magickal correspondences and are often used in divination. A color code, established centuries ago, is referred to when seeing a ribbon in dreams, or encountering one laying about somewhere:

Red: Good fortune, prosperity, and
    success in matters of love
Scarlet: Passion
Green: Healing at work
Yellow: Jealousy, gossip
Blue: Blessings
Orange: Misfortune
Silver: Spirits or spiritual forces at work
Gold: Material success and gain
Gray: Calm, neutrality, content
Black: Hidden forces, secrets, possible
    plots

The belief in the magickal power of the color red (especially red wool) dates back to ancient Roman times where it symbolized blood and fire (the sacred liquid of life and the heat of the sacred flame). Blue was the color of the spirit flame, associating it with divine blessings. Silver, as a lunar color, held power over spirits of the Astral World. Black was associated with things hidden in the night, and gold became the common symbol of wealth.

Many tools and symbols continue to retain their ancient connections and still evoke time-honored responses. The old spirits can still be stirred by ancient calls and gestures when performed with time-proven techniques. Italian

Witches have continued to perform them since the days of antiquity and therefore the connections have never been lost.

In Italy, Folk Magick is retained within the ritual/magickal structure of The Old Religion, and is connected with the non-physical realms where the spirits of Witch-craft dwell. The Craft in Italy did not suffer as violent a persecution as in northern Europe, therefore much of the ancient knowledge was preserved. Due to relatively little fragmentation in the Old Religion of Italy, the Strega Tradition still exists as one of the most complete systems today. [Note: For the convenience of interested readers, the original Italian text for many of the spells contained in this chapter is reproduced in Appendix 5, beginning on page 239.]

When using the Folk Magick tools and paraphernalia of Italian Folk Lore, you are using living connections with the Spirits of Old. The Elder Streghe say that never has there been a time when the old rites have not been performed. Never has there been a time when the ancient offerings to gods and spir-its have not been placed. One of my teachers once told me that if the Old Ways were to disappear, then the spirits of Nature would withdraw from humankind. The sun and moon would no longer rise, the seasons would not return, and the world would wither and die, but as long as one Strega still kindles the Spirit Flame, all will be as it was in the time of our beginning.

FOLK MAGICK SPELLS

I am presenting the following spells, and lit-tle works of magick, out of a love of ancient tradition and lore. The source of power for these spells appears to be either personal power or the intervention of a spirit or deity. The majority of these particular spells are quite old and it is my wish to preserve them here in this book. The form of Italian used in most of the following spells dates to at least the late nineteenth century. This is also confirmed by similar spells recorded by Charles Leland in several of his books on Italian Witchcraft, circa 1896 (see bibliogra-phy and suggested reading lists).

Knot magick

Knot magick is the art of using cords, or string, to focus energy for the purpose of influencing a person or situation. Knots can be tied accordingly, to bind something or prevent something from happening. They can also be used to fix magickal energy into place, saving it for later release. Some sys-tems of magick refer to this as cord magick.

Binding can be used to stop someone from harming another person, spreading lies and rumors, or from disrupting a commun-ity. It can also keep someone away from you or your property, in which case you would carry the cord or fix it to your property. As you will see from the following spell, the spirit of Terminus guards the intent (and woe to he or she who violates his charge).

The Strega of Old Italy compiled magickal correspondences which serve as guidelines to employ various colored cords. The basic correspondences originate from their *elemental* connections, through which Nature magick is performed. The following colors and their ritual associations are the most commonly used ones in knot magick:

Red: (Fire) Energy, aggression,
　destruction, passion, etc.
Yellow: (Earth) Craftsmanship, skill,
　endurance, etc.
Blue: (Air) Joyfulness, intellect, mental
　activity, creativity, artistic expression
Green: (Water) Emotions, love,
　relationships, family, etc.

The basic method for binding the spell is to hold the cord, one end in each hand, while facing North. Lift up the cord, as though presenting it to someone, and say:

> *Hear me, you spirits of this world*
> *　and beyond,*
> *I call upon you now in the name*
> *　of Diana,*
> *She who is the Queen of all*
> *　witches and fairies,*
> *for I am one of Her chosen ones,*
> *and I bid you to so aid my spell.*

Next, you turn facing South and begin to raise your personal power. To do this, coil the cord around your left hand and then place the fingertips of both hands together (similar to "praying" hands, but the fingers are not interlaced). It should appear as though you are holding a sphere between your hands. Turn the left palm upward and begin to press your palms together, resisting with firm fingertip pressure, and do not allow the palms to actually touch.

Push, and release pressure again, repeating this action to a count of thirty-six times. If you are doing it correctly, you will feel a *presence* begin to form between your fingers. It will feel very much like a sheet of glass. One of my teachers called this "a spider doing push-ups on a mirror" (this may help you to visualize the hand positions and actions). Count out each compression as you perform this technique, and move your hands at a quick, easy pace.

Once you finish your count, place your hands back in the "sphere holding" position. Face the East now, and state what it is you desire this spell to do. Gaze steadily upon the cord and begin three more compressions (visualize the desired effect of the spell). This time your compressions will be slow and more forceful (as though you are *packing* in the power). Just before you perform each of these final compressions say the following:

> *Spirits of Matter,*
> *bind, twist, and fix!*
> *Spirits of Fire,*

burn, bind, and mix!
Spirits of Ether
move now in betwixt!

Now the cord is ready to be tied in order to fix your spell. Remove the cord from your hand and tie a knot in one side, saying as you do so:

Terminus be.

Terminus is the guardian spirit of bindings and boundaries.

Do the same with the other end of the cord, and repeat:

Terminus be.

Now take hold of a knot in each hand, and tie a third knot into the center of the cord, saying:

Here to bind Thee.

Pull firmly as you force the knot. You want to concentrate your magick here, so be as focused as you can when you pull the knot into place.

When you wish to release the magickal effect, you will want to be near the target of the spell. Simply untie the end knots first, saying:

Terminus free.

Then untie the middle knot saying:

So to free Thee.

Complete the spell by whirling the cord over your head three times and letting go of it, so that it is thrown free of you. The power of the spell is then released. If you do not wish to release what you have bound, then place the cord into a pouch and hide it in a secret place. Bear in mind always that you are fully accountable for forcing your will upon another. Make sure that the cost is worth the gain, but believe me, it rarely is.

Another aspect of cord magick appears in the so-called Witches' Ladder. Leland mentions in *Etruscan Roman Remains in Popular Tradition*[1] that he showed a drawing of the Witches' Ladder, which had appeared in an 1886 issue of the *Folk Lore Journal,* to an Italian woman in Italy who readily identified it and went on to describe its use in Witchcraft. In Gardnerian Wicca we also find mention of a Witches' Ladder. Please note its reference by Leland half a century prior to Gardner's writings, as this is not a Gardnerian invention (however, a similar object was found in the belfry of a church in England near the close of the nineteenth century, as reported in the *Folk Lore Journal* referenced by Leland).

Essentially, the Witches' Ladder is a cord used for binding. It is also employed to keep a count by sliding one's fingers along a knotted cord while performing ritual acts

---

1 Charles Leland, *Etruscan Roman Remains in Popular Tradition* (New York: University Books, 1963).

for spell casting and other works of magick. If a spell requires the repetition of a name spoken ten times, then ten knots are made in the cord. For binding, a knot is made in the center of the cord flanked by three knots on each side. The center knot is tied around a link object to the person or situation requiring the binding spell. The flanking knots are tied around the feathers of a black hen, or a crow or raven. As each knot is tied, recite:

> *Feathers here as black as night,*
> *bind the villain with magick tight,*
> *and in darkness actions quell,*
> *until such time I release this spell.*

The cord is then delivered to the person or to the site of the situation. The spell can be countered when the Witches' Ladder is returned to the sender, who must untie each knot and toss all of the items into flowing water.

Ring Magick

Ring magick is used for spell casting, divination, protection, healing, and binding in matters of love. One of the oldest uses of rings in magick is sigil magick. This form uses soft clay that is imprinted by rolling a ring across the surface, leaving certain magickal symbols etched in the material. The clay is then allowed to dry, and thus becomes an amulet, talisman, or charm.

For healing purposes the ring is purified by holding it in an open flame. Allowing it to cool, the ring is then held between the fingers as one would hold a pen. Various symbols, denoting the desired effect, are then traced over the area to be healed. A number of circles which delimit the sickness are traced with the ring, followed by some radiating lines which start from the injured area and move outward from the body. The movements must be decisive and quick in order to drive out the sickness from the affected area. This tracing of circles and lines is performed three times.

The practitioner repeats certain words during this operation, and the entire process is repeated for three days. At the end of the three days the ring is washed and then dipped in salt water to discharge the negative energy. A final rinse of spring water is applied to the ring, and then all is considered normal again. Rings can be used for skin ailments such as eczema, rashes, burns, warts, and herpes.

Spell of the Triple Flame

The purpose of this spell is to discover who has cast a spell against you (i.e., is causing you misfortune) or is working against you in some manner. If you feel that something is happening to you due to unseen forces, or to anyone you know, then perform the following:

On a square table in your bedroom, place three votive candles in a triangle. In the center of the triangle arrange a sharp knife and three straight pins, with the blade of the knife pointing North, and the pins pointing to the East, West, and South.

If you suspect someone in particular, then write his or her name on one of the candles. If you feel that it could be any one of several people, then mark the other two candles with a name also. As you will see, the first candle to burn out will bear the name of the person involved. If the first candle to burn out does not contain a name, then the misfortune is not being caused by anyone.

At midnight, sit in a chair beside the table and gesture the *jettatura* over the items. Turn to each quarter of the room and do the same. Then say the following:

> *Hear me, O Great Mother. If the misfortune which I sense comes from the ill works of another, I ask that you speak to me as I sleep this night. I pray that this misfortune shall be lifted away by you and that good fortune shall come in its place. If another has cast an ill spell, then I ask that one of these candles be extinguished, and that you reveal this person to me in my dreams tonight. Then shall their power be diminished in your name, and pass away with the burning of these candles.*

At this point you go to bed and allow yourself to sleep. You will awaken at some point to find one or more of the candles extinguished, and so you will have your answer. The next day burn away any remaining candles and pour the wax into a hole dug in the earth. Bury the wax and do not disturb it further. The spell will then be broken.

The Spell of the Holy Stone

This spell originates from the folk belief that looking through the hole of a sacred object can allow the viewer to see into the world of fairies and other spirits. In Tuscany it is believed that this *other sight* can be obtained by looking through a consecrated ring or a wreath made of verbena.

To find a stone with a hole through it is a powerful talisman, sacred to the goddess Diana. There are several versions of this spell and so I will share two of them here.

A). To seek for a holy stone, arise at dawn and go out upon the road toward a meadow or into the hills. Take with you a red wool pouch and gather some herbs of rue and vervain. If, in your search for the herbs, you should come upon a stone with a hole through it, then pick it up and say:

> *I have found a Holy Stone upon*
> *the ground.*
> *O Destiny, I thank you for the*
> *joyful find.*
> *And also the spirit who upon this*
> *road has given it to me.*

*May it prove to be for my true
good and fortune!*

Now it is time to ask the spirit to enter the stone so that it will be an object of power. To do this, toss the stone up and catch it three times, place it in your pocket, and then say the following:

*Good spirit of omens
    who has come to my aid
believing I had need of you,
spirit of the red fairy
since you have come to aid me in
    my need,
I pray that you will not abandon me!
I beg you to enter now this sphere
that I carry in my pocket,
and when I have need of anything
that I can call upon you,
whatever need it may be,
and neither by night or day
will you ever abandon me.*

After this, place the stone and the herbs into the wool pouch, give thanks to Diana, and return home.

B). If you find a stone with a hole in it, on a beach or in the sea, it is a powerful talisman for seeing into the spirit world.

The stone is consecrated in the same manner as the first spell.

Once properly prepared, take the stone with you to a cemetery and stand just before the burial grounds. Hold the stone up to your left eye and look through the hole, while keeping the right eye closed. Then say the following:

*In nome di San Pietro,
E di San Biagio,
Fate che da questa pietra
possa vedere che forma
Fanno gli spiriti.*

*De profundia clamao
In te Domine, Domine!
Et Domine, et fiantatis,
Bugsein et regina materna,
Edognis Domine!*

Folk belief has it that you will see the spirits of the departed. You may also see the Crone aspect of the goddess walking with a lighted torch.

Spell against Malocchio (the Evil Eye)

To avert or exorcise the evil eye, perform the following. Extend the index finger and little finger of your left hand while bending the others inward (resembling two horns). Then speak the formula:

*Horn, big horn, twisted horn;
red the cloth,
crooked the horn,
I mock you:
I go and return,
Horn! Horn! Horn!*

Another spell involves the use of fire. Light a fire, then take a piece of paper and draw a symbol representing the evil done to you. Drop the paper into the fire and as you watch it burn say:

> *O blessed fire,*
> *you who burns so immensely*
> *you who warms all mankind*
> *I pray you to burn this evil spell*
> *and the one who smote me*
> > *with it!*

The Herb Magick of Rue

When someone suffers with sore eyes take a branch, a *coccha,* of rue, and tie it round in a wreath, *in forma di una corona,* with a red ribbon. The patient should be in bed and not see the garland being made; it must be always prepared by a woman in another room, and it must not be seen by children or even by any animal. She who binds it must say:

> *I prepare this wreath*
> *To place it on the eyes*
> *of that sufferer,*
> *That her sight I may restore*
> *And she may never suffer more!*

When she gives it to the invalid. he or she must look through it three times, and say:

> *Saint Lucy, Saint Lucy, Saint Lucy!*
> *Make me recover from the evil eye!*

Then the invalid must spit through it three times.

Santa Lucia, the modern Catholic saint of light, is the direct descendant of the Etruscan Losna, goddess of the moon, also of the sun (*Vide Losna*), which again gives further credence to rue's association to sight and vision. The medieval cult of the Benandanti invoked Lucia before going out to battle the Malandanti at night. Lucia gave the Benandanti night vision, providing them with an advantage over their enemy.

Good Luck Spells

The following is an old good luck spell known in Italian as *le quattro cose della buona fortuna.*

Take a small red bag made of wool. Inside the bag place a crumb of bread, a pinch of coarse salt, a sprig of rue, and a pinch of cummin. Sew the bag closed with a red woolen thread, and while sewing repeat the following words:

> *I sew this little bag*
> *for my good fortune,*
> *and also my family,*
> *that misfortune be held far away.*

After this the bag must be carried on the person's body night and day. According to tradition the bag cannot be used by more than one person.

Another good luck spell involves a certain chant spoken when catching sight of a firefly. In Italian, fireflies are called *lucciola,* which means "little lighted ones." Upon seeing a firefly, speak the following chant to bring good luck:

> *Firefly! Firefly!*
> *come to the competition!*
> *Put the bridle*
> *to the mare,*
> *put the bridle*
> *to the king's son,*
> *so that fortune*
> *comes with me,*
> *my firefly,*
> *come to me!*

Healing Spells

Take a silver coin that has been set beneath the full moon from midnight until 1 A.M. Anoint the coin with olive oil that has also sat beneath the full moon. Place the coin face down on the afflicted area. Move the coin in a counterclockwise circular manner (sliding the oiled coin around the area). As you perform this task, speak these words:

> *Pain that hits*
> *with the fury of dragon's blood,*
> *for the love of all spirits*
> *leave this body,*
> *remove your stain.*

For the magickal healing of any ailment there is a Sicilian Witch prayer that must be spoken. Its words are passed from teacher to student on the morning of the Winter Solstice. To pass this on causes the teacher to lose the ability to heal with this prayer. This is the prayer:

> *Maizina'd bo, maizina'd vaca*
> *chi la mal a slu grata.*
>
> *Maizina'd vaca, maizina'd bo,*
> *chi la mal, le tut so.*

DIVINATION

Divination is commonly thought of as the foreseeing of future events through the use of various tools, such as crystals, tarot cards, runes, and so on. In the Italian system we view divination as foreseeing what is likely to occur if nothing changes the patterns currently forming. The Strega do not believe that future events are fixed in time and space. We believe that the role of divination is to foresee the outcome of forming patterns, allowing us to make the necessary changes to alter the likely results.

If the future is fixed and unchangeable, then divination would be rather pointless, other than simply allowing you to prepare for your fate. Fortunately, the powers-that-be are much kinder and more compassionate than that, and have given us the means by which to alter our course. Astrology, palmistry, crystal gazing, and other types of divinatory arts all serve to reveal the astral patterns forming around us.

In this section we will look at several different ways in which currently forming patterns can be revealed, and future events can be foreseen. The oldest form of divination still used by the majority of Strega is divinatory runes. Second to this is the use of cards, followed by the use of oil and water. Certainly the observation of omens and signs in Nature predates these techniques, but I am not specifically addressing those techniques in this text.

The Streghe believe that everything first forms on the astral planes, before it manifests within the material world. On a mundane level we can liken this to a thought arising before an action takes place. From an occult perspective, energy patterns stimulate the astral substance and forms begin to take shape, reflecting the desired result. *Thoughts* literally become *things* within the astral dimension. Through the arts of divination we can look at these patterns and discern the images that are forming and, therefore, moving toward manifestation.

In Italian Witchcraft, astrology reveals the stellar imprint upon a soul at the time it is born in a physical body. In Streghe mythology, the realm of Aster is the stellar dimension in which the gods dwell. Here also resides the community of souls that have completed the cycle of rebirth within the physical world. The astrological imprint is a reminder to the soul of the lessons awaiting within the current physical existence in which it finds itself. The astrological chart depicts the strengths and weaknesses that the soul carries with it in one particular life experience. However, among the Strega, free will supersedes the patterns of one's stars. Therefore, astrology becomes a tool for personal reflection and correction in Stregheria.

Palmistry, among the Strega, is related to psychometry (the art of receiving impressions through physical contact). Energy patterns form in the aura of an individual, influenced largely by power centers in the body. In the modern Craft, these centers are often referred to as chakra centers. This chakra system originates from Eastern Mysticism. Each chakra—there are seven—is linked to one of the seven dimensions of the occult universe (see Figure 15, p. 60). The chakras send and receive energy flows to and from the dimensions with which they are associated, and therefore, the aura contains information concerning the patterns that exist in any given dimension relating to the individual.

Holding a person's hands while "reading" their palm allows the palm reader to draw upon the energy imprints within the person's aura. Impressions arise as the reader focuses upon the individual for which he or she is divining. The lines formed on the palm are actually energy patterns—the symbols of past, current, and future manifestations. These lines provide the palm reader with an overview of the person's experiences in this lifetime. From an occult perspective, however, the palm reader is accessing the astral memories, current energy imprints, and future patterns, all through physical contact with the person's aura and physical body. See Figures 16 and 17 (p. 61) for both the Old Ways and the traditional occult associations of the hand.

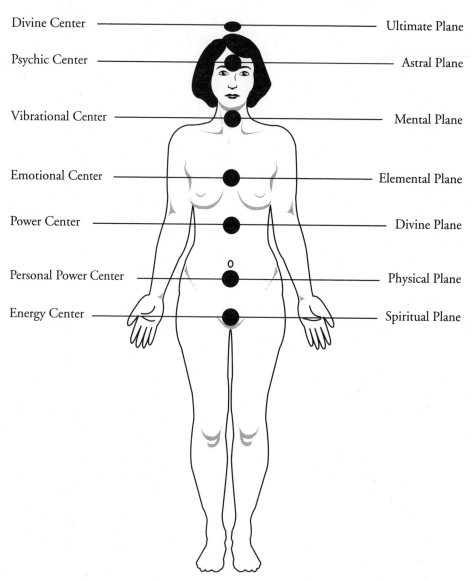

Divine Center — Ultimate Plane
Psychic Center — Astral Plane
Vibrational Center — Mental Plane
Emotional Center — Elemental Plane
Power Center — Divine Plane
Personal Power Center — Physical Plane
Energy Center — Spiritual Plane

Figure 15. *Modern Chakra System with gateway associations to the seven dimensions.*

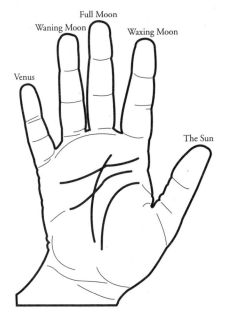

Figure 16. *Old Occult Associations of the Hand.*

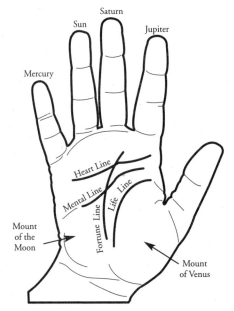

Figure 17. *Modern Occult Associations of the Hand.*

Neapolitan Card Reading

In Naples the use of playing cards for divination is quite common among the Streghe. One might call these cards the poor person's tarot deck. For simple yes or no answers, five cards are dealt out. The reader simply looks at the abundance of suits among the cards. Pentacles and cups signify yes, swords and clubs indicate no.

A person might wish to know, for example, how long before he or she finds a job. The reader would deal out two parallel horizontal lines of six cards, face down. Each card is then turned up from left to right, beginning with the top line of cards. This entire procedure is repeated until the ace of clubs appears. Each card turned over represents one month.

To divine a particular situation, seven cards are dealt out in a vertical line. The middle card is turned over and this represents the situation (what everything is centered around.) Next the cards are turned over in pairs, beginning with the top and bottom cards. Each pair is discerned in the context of how they relate to each other and to the center. This is continued, in the top and bottom card pairing, until all cards have been turned over. For a lengthy reading the cards may be dealt out five times. Cards having no meaning are used either numerically or symbolically to add to the meaning within a pair. In other words, the numbers can indicate periods of time and the face cards can indicate other people influencing the situation. Cards turned upside down are read with reversed meaning just as they are in Tarot readings:

Ace of clubs: Joy, sex, happiness, pleasure, fertility
Reversed: No children, sadness, indifference

Two of clubs: Communication, notification, letter coming from nearby
Reversed: Bad news, a person who is a long distance away

Three of clubs: Mortification, bad news, agitation
Reversed: Change for the better

King of clubs: Young man, a student, powerful
Reversed: A person who dislikes study; a person who wants to get out of his or her current situation

Knight of clubs: Anxious, anxiety, upset.
Reversed: Everything is all right

Page of clubs: Whore, evil woman, unknowing, jinx, makes mistakes often
Reversed: Fortunate woman, looking for a husband with money

Ace of cups: Home, family
Reversed: Thinking of home, returning home soon

Two of cups: Triumph, good friends, union, justice
Reversed: Bad times quickly passing, a couple breaking up but reuniting soon

Three of cups: Crying, sadness, discontent, broken-hearted woman, unpleasant times
Reversed: Sad man, bad news from a distance

Four of cups: Work, a person with an active mind, a person without problems, a dreamer
Reversed: Indecision, day dreaming, failure

King of cups: Teacher, commercial, clear ideas, mathematician
Reversed: Studying, student, artist, creative

Knight of cups: Good trip, long trip, looking for new work in the future
Reversed: Difficulties, bad trip, looking for work soon

Page of cups: Young woman, brown hair, red hair, virgin, honesty
Reversed: Anxious woman, seeking marriage, abortion

Ace of pentacles: Bed, sickness, marriage.
Reversed: Virginity, marriage to come, recovery soon to come

Two of pentacles: A lot of money, change for the better, a person nearby

Reversed: A little money, fantasy

Three of pentacles: Creativity, money
Reversed: Coming into money, good
news

King of pentacles: Blond man, money,
good financial position, comforts
Reversed: Looking for work, looking for
a new home soon

Knight of pentacles: Change for the
better, a financial trip, a person from
the outside who brings money
Reversed: A trip that cannot be made,
lack of money

Page of pentacles: Rich woman, old,
anxious, married
Reversed: Preoccupation, widow

Ace of swords: Meaningless conversation,
broken heart
Reversed: Looking for love, solitude

Two of swords: Union that is a mistake,
mistaken friends, bad news, robbery,
a thief
Reversed: Need for medical attention,
bad news

Three of swords: Sadness, desperation,
death, sickness, melancholy
Reversed: Slow convalescence, bad
friends

King of swords: A wealthy man (usually
married), a doctor, lawyer, judge

Reversed: A man desperate for work, a
possible marriage soon

Knight of swords: A bad or sad trip,
loneliness when traveling, bad news
Reversed: A person traveling well,
change

Page of swords: Evil woman, a particular
person, bad language, young
unmarried girl
Reversed: An unhappy marriage soon
to come, marrying for money

Dream Magick with Cards

When preparing for bed, place under your
pillow a prayer book open to the matrimonial service. On the page place a key, a ring,
a flower, a sprig of willow, a small heart-shaped cake or cookie, and a crust of bread.
Lay the following cards on top of the items:
10 of wands, 9 of cups, ace of swords and
ace of pentacles. Wrap the collection in a
linen cloth or cheese cloth. Place this under
your pillow, lay down cupping your hands
together over your heart and say:

> *Luna, every woman's friend*
> *to me thy magick pray thee send*
> *let me this night in vision see*
> *symbols of my destiny.*

Vision Symbols:
1. Key: Power, status in community,
prosperity
2. Ring/Ace of pentacles: Marriage

3. Flower: Joy

4. Willow: An unfaithful lover

5. Cake/cookie: A prosperous life

6. Bread: An industrious life

7. Wands: Far away places await

8. Cups: Children born out of marriage

9. Swords: An untimely death

10. Pentacles: Wealth

11. Bad weather: A troubled life

12. Birds: A large family

13. Rooster: More than one marriage

Divination by Fire

The lighting of a fire, and the way it burns, can be used for divinatory purposes. Before lighting the fire it is traditional to say the following:

> *Fire, blessed fire!*
> *My house waits for fortune,*
> *and always comes to you in hope*
> *that the wish of good fortune*
> *you will devote yourself to!*

To begin, you state the nature of what you wish to divine, or ask to receive an omen concerning a certain matter. This is performed in a fireplace with common wood. If the fire is difficult to light, or burns with little weak flames, then this is a negative sign.

To divine a situation, you study the flames as you think upon the matter in question. As the fire burns well or poorly, so too will the situation go. Generally speaking, if the fire burns with a single attractive flame it is a sign of good fortune. Several flames shifting position or jumping about, with a snapping, means that friends or relations are coming to visit you.

Another type of divination by fire employs an effigy of Befana. A wooden puppet figure of Befana is constructed, and in her hands she holds a spindle and distaff. The hollow figure is stuffed with grapes, dried figs, chestnuts, pears, apples, carob, with *sapa* and *cotnognata.*

A pyre is then built in a conical stack, six to seven meters high. Chopped wood is placed on the bottom of the stack. Next brambles are laid, then horse chestnuts and finally straw. When all is ready, Befana is sawed open and all her ingredients are dispersed to the celebrants. Following this the image is burned on the pyre. Yes and no questions are asked as the fire burns, and exploding chestnuts indicate a positive response. The resulting shower of sparks is also divined by its patterns and how the sparks fall. Upward bursts indicate abundance, downward sparks mark decline, right side bursts indicate something coming into one's life, while the left side means a loss. A shower of sparks directly toward a person means he or she will be in danger.

Part Two

Myths and Lore

THE GODDESS AND
THE GOD

Anthropologist Julio Caro Baroja[1] tells us that as late as the sixth century A.D. the cult of Diana and her consort "Dianum" still flourished among southern European peasants. St. Martin of Braga wrote of the goddess Diana and spirits called the *dianae* during his travels in southern Europe. The temple of Diana[2] once stood on the northern shore of lake Nemi, Italy. Historical references indicate that a great forest covered the Alban hills there, consisting of oak, beech, elms, chestnut, walnut, and other trees. Hidden in this forest at Nemi stood the sanctuary of *Diana Nemorensis* (Diana of the Woods). As we noted earlier in this book, a guardian called *Rex Nemorensis* patroled Diana's wooded sanctuary.

Votive offerings discovered at Nemi indicate that Diana was worshipped as a goddess connected with fertility, childbirth, and the abundance of wild game. Her annual festival was held on August 13 when in honor of Diana her grove blazed with hundreds of torches. At night the light of these torches reflected upon her sacred lake, sparkling magickally upon the

---

1   Julio Baroja, *The World of Witches* (Chicago: University of Chicago Press, 1975), pp 65–66.
2   Rebuilt around 500 B.C. following an earthquake.

surface of the water. Diana was also known as "Diana Vesta." Lamps similar to those used by vestal virgins for perpetual fire have been found with images of Vesta at Nemi.

The sanctuary of Diana was also home to a goddess nymph named Egeria. Egeria was the Lady of the Lake at Nemi, intimately connected not only with the lake but also with streams and waterfalls. Vestal virgins in Rome collected water from a stream sacred to Egeria, and used this water to wash the temple of Vesta. This is an interesting connection between water and fire, and may be linked to the concept of the spirit flame of the Streghe. The ancestors of those people who founded Rome once lived in the Alban hills, bringing Egeria and her connection to sacred springs with them when they settled on the banks of the Tiber river.

Egeria was intimately connected to Virbius, a son born from a tryst between Diana and Hippolytus. Virbius was the first guardian of Diana's grove at Nemi, and was appointed Rex Nemorensis (King of the Woods). The well-being of the King of the Woods was attributed in part to his relationship with Egeria. According to James Frazer, in *The Golden Bough*,[3] Egeria's stream bubbled up from the roots of the Sacred Oak at Nemi. Because oak burns at higher temperatures than most other wood, it was used in ancient times to heat the forge from which swords were produced. Primitive magickal

belief held that the spirit of the Oak God was passed to the flames and therefore to the sword carried by the King of the Woods. In addition to his sword, the King of the Woods also carried a staff carved from the broken oak branch taken from the sacred tree at Nemi. The sanctuary of Diana at Nemi saw a long succession of grove guardians, recorded even up through the reign of the Roman emperor Caligula. History tells us that Caligula hired a skilled warrior to kill the reigning Rex Nemeorensis, in hopes of abolishing the cult at Nemi.

The myth of Rex Nemorensis presents some very interesting similarities between the sword of King Arthur and the staff of the King at Diana's sanctuary on lake Nemi. Only a person bearing certain strengths could draw the sword from the stone or break the branch from the oak tree at Nemi. To do so in either case bestowed kingship. The Sacred Oak represented the sun god and was under the protection of the Guardian of the Grove. This mythos is not unlike the Celtic legend of King Arthur and the sword Excaliber. In the earliest myths Arthur's magickal sword is given to him by Nimue, the Lady of the Lake, whose arm rises up from the water bearing Excaliber in her hand. Later versions of this mythos have Arthur drawing the sword from a stone in which it has been embedded. It is interesting to note the likeness between the names

---

3   James Frazer, *The Golden Bough* (New York: Macmillan Company, 1922).

Nimue and Nemi, both connected to a similar mythos related to a lake.

At Nemi, Rex Nemorensis was required to break a branch from the sacred Oak in order to be worthy of his reign. The branch was a challenge of combat to the Guardian of the Grove, a position fought over down through the centuries at Nemi. The branch was part of the tree rooted in the earth, filled with the water bubbling up from Egeria's stream. It is not difficult to see the sword Excaliber rising from the Lake, and the Oak Branch ascending from the Sacred Tree within the stream of Egeria, as one and the same image.

A tradition of great antiquity connected to kingship in ancient Latium centers around the oak tree. It was the custom to crown Latin kings with oak wreaths and to perform mock marriages to Egeria. The first such reference in ancient times relates that King Numa consorted with Egeria in the woods at Nemi. The legend of Numa and Egeria recounts the affair between the two and has been likened by some writers to the marriage of the King and Queen of May. We know that the ancients believed in an intimate connection between the King and the land, reflected even in the Celtic mythos of King Arthur and the Fisher King. The sacred marriage of Latin kings to Egeria strongly suggests a purposeful union between humankind and a goddess of Nature, to ensure the vitality and fertility of the king.

DIANA AND DIANUS

At Nemi, Diana was a goddess of the Green Wood, and of the oak tree in particular. Naturally her consort would share these associations as well. Diana's consort Dianus also bore the attributes of a higher god named Jupiter, who was likewise linked to the oak. Some folklorists feel they were the same deity, on different levels. Ancient legends support this, especially the legend of Rex Nemorensis itself. In this mythos, the guardian of the Grove impersonated the oak god and thus drew upon the god's power to protect Diana's Grove. His intimate relationship with Egeria, from which the ceremonial marriage of Latin kings evolved, is symbolic of mating with Diana herself in the woods. In many cases ancient writers equate Diana and Egeria.

The famous image of Diana of Ephesus contains a visual history of the ancient cult of Diana from Paleolithic times. Covering her body are images of various animals, all of which are sacred within the Witch Cult of Old Europe. The farther back we go in our research of Diana the nearer we come to the animal totems that predate her human form. From archaeological and anthropological studies of ancient clans we know that the first deities to be worshipped appeared in animal form. The earliest form of Artemis/Diana seems to have been a bear, and it was not until much later in time that images of her human form appears. In ancient art Diana is pictured appearing with either a dog (domesticated wolf) or a stag. The stag and the wolf are symbols of the waxing and waning forces of Nature, affecting both the plant and animal life over which Diana reigns.

Archaeological findings indicate that the first moon deity was an animal, followed by the spirit of deity in animal form (in other words, a supernatural being). Later the deity is attended by these same animals who have evolved into cult animals of the specific god or goddess. Later still, animal attendants are replaced by humanoid figures wearing animal masks and performing animal dances. The animal attendants and animal emblems surrounding the goddess in deity shrines reminded the cult followers of the former aspects from which the nature of the gods had descended. This type of symbolism became the key to understanding the inner secrets of the cult, and of the gods themselves. To merge with the animal nature through imitation is to invoke the primal force of the god or goddess reflected within.

The classical image of Diana in Rome was that of a young woman dressed in a hunter's tunic. She is a young powerful virgin; a huntress and a warrior. In early statues, Diana is portrayed standing with a stag; her bow in one hand and the other reaching to retrieve an arrow from the quiver on her back. The stag is, among other things, symbolic of her forest-dwelling horned consort Dianus. In later art forms, Diana appears with hunting dogs (a remnant of the wolf

that slays her lover in the Wheel of the Year). From these ancient symbols we can conclude that these animals are reflections of her primal power and her spirit animal nature, dating back to Neolithic, if not Paleolithic, times.

In southern Europe it was observed that vegetation flourished for the most part due to the coolness of night and the accumulation of dew. The dew provided a substitute for the lack of rain during the dry months. Ancient people were aware that the dew was most plentiful when the sky was clear and moonlight fell upon the fields. This, in part, served to connect the moon goddess with fertility of the crops. It also linked the moon goddess with wetlands, lakes, wells, and other bodies of water. The effect of the moon upon the tides was also noted, of course, as was the moon's influence upon menstrual cycles.

In Italy, Diana never lost her early association with the hunter-gatherer era. Even in the agricultural communities, myths persisted of Diana roaming at night through fields and forests with her nymphs and satyrs. The presence of the full moon gave light to the darkness, and therefore Diana was viewed as the protector of travelers and herds (as wild animals were more easily observed and defended against by moonlight than by fire light). However, the moon was dark at times, so accordingly a dark side was also attributed to Diana. Therefore, she was the goddess of the wild animals as well.

In Arcadia the goddess was known as Calliste, and was worshipped in the form of a bear. As the Bear-Mother she nursed, reared, and protected her children. Young girls were sometimes called bears, in allusion to their patron goddess. When they reached puberty it was customary for them to dedicate their girdles to Diana. The soft pure light of the moon suggests the idea of modesty, or an "unblemished" nature, and by extension Diana was also viewed as the "chaste" goddess in her maiden aspect.

Well-bred Athenian women of marriageable age danced as bears in honor of Artemis of Brauronia, and during the rites of cult initiation *became* bears (wearing animal masks and mimicking the beasts). The girls and women of Lacedemonia performed orgiastic dances to glorify Artemis, and were later joined by the men in a fertility dance. Offerings to Artemis included phalli and all species of animals and fruits, for she was protector of all life, bestowing fertility upon humans, animals, and fields. Goats and stags were highly valued as offerings to the goddess, as was the hare.

The early Italic people knew Diana as Leukothea, and also as Atimite. Leukothea was the goddess of the ocean and all tides, and was worshipped by sailors. As Atimite she was the goddess of the forests and wild animals, chaste and untouched by men. These were both aspects of Diana as the goddess of the moon, whom the Etruscans called Losna. Atimite has been characterized as a goddess of free wildlife; as a huntress she dominates the animal world. This is a symbolic projection of her role as ruler over the unconscious powers that still take on animal form in our dreams. Diana still rules the night when we dream, just as Dianus still rules the day during which we labor.

In the Old Religion of Italy, the god-force is considered to have three aspects. These are commonly known as the Horned One, the Hooded One, and the Old One. Each of these aspects pertain to the religious concepts of the Old Ways. In the early days of clan life people were nomadic hunter-gatherers. Hunting game was extremely dangerous because primitive weapons required a hunter to get very close to their prey. The bravest hunter wore the skin of a stag, attempting to move very close to the herd. In order to accomplish this he had to act like the very beast that he hunted. His bravery was much revered by his tribe and he became a symbol of power. Out of this evolved the concept that he must be in touch with, or favored by, a great spirit of the animal world. This was well reflected in his ability to *become* the stag that he hunted.

The first male deity of the early Witch clans in Italy was the Horned One, which in Latin is *Cornunno*. The god is known by many names: Faunus, Silvanus, Dianus, and many others. He was the god of the forests, providing food for the clan and animal hides

72

for clothing and shelter. He was portrayed as part human and part beast, typically bearing stag horns upon his head. In this manner he represented the power of the hero-hunter, a human who could merge with the animal world and become One with the beasts. Therefore, the god was a great spirit who could merge with humans and become One with them as well. Thus the clan was under the protection of a greater power than themselves, a god.

The second aspect of male deity was the Hooded One, Rex Nemorensis, the King of the Woods. He evolved out of the Horned One, as religious concepts began to mature in human spirituality. The Hooded One is therefore considered to be the son of the Horned One, and represents the plant kingdom in very much the same way that Dianus represents the animal kingdom. The Hooded One is said to be hooded-in-the-green, literally covered with the greenery of the forest. As humans began to rely more on plants, learning to grow and harvest crops, the god who provided for their needs began to change as well. He evolved from the Lord of the Woods to the Lord of the Harvest.

Figure 18. *Nineteenth-century bronze figure of the god Pan. From the Clan Umbrea collection.*

Figure 19. *Early twentieth-century bronze figure of the mythical character Actaeon, changing into a stag. From the Clan Umbrea collection.*

The third aspect of the god is the Old One. This aspect encompasses the other two, representing yet another stage in the evolution of human spirituality. The Old One is more human in appearance, and is portrayed as an Elder. He carries a staff that sports a pair of antlers, and around which is entwined a living vine. He does not appear as a man in the decline of old age, but rather as a powerful, experienced, and wise man, transformed by the years he has lived. He has earned his beard, but has not passed his prime.

LUNAR ASPECTS OF THE GODDESS

In the Old Religion of Italy the feminine aspect of Deity is viewed as having four individual aspects. Since the Old Religion is a lunar cult, each of these aspects is associated with one of the four phases of the moon. These are the names used by most Hereditary Italian Witches:

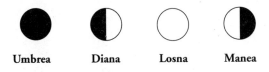

Umbrea   Diana   Losna   Manea

Figure 20. *The Moon Phases.*

When the moon is dark and unseen (for three days) we associate this phase with the goddess Umbrea, whose name means Shadow. When the moon is new, a waxing crescent, we associate this phase with the goddess Diana. When the moon is full, we associate this phase with the goddess Losna, who is Diana as the Great Mother. When the moon is a waning crescent, we associate this phase with Manea (who is a goddess of night spirits, and of departed souls).

Umbrea is the name of the goddess in the Underworld. She is the wife of Dis, the god of the dead. She is goddess of shadows and secrets and all things that are hidden and obscure.

Diana is the most common name associated with Italian Witchcraft. She is the goddess of the poor and oppressed. She is the goddess of outcasts and all those who are rejected by society (those who do not "fit in" within the mainstream of society). Diana is a moon goddess and is viewed as the chaste maiden aspect of feminine divinity. She is the huntress, and the Amazon warrior. An entire cult of Witches, devoted exclusively to Diana, flourished in Italy up through the Middle Ages. They viewed her as the only goddess and acknowledged three aspects within her. She was the maiden, mother, and crone. In each aspect they pronounced her name differently in order to evoke a separate aspect:

Maiden: Die-anna
Mother: Dee-ah-nah
Crone: Dea-nah

The Romans believed that Diana was present at all births and they called her the "Opener of the Womb." Through this association with the lunar goddess Diana, the Great Mother aspect became linked to the moon. Porphyry wrote that Hekate was Artemis (Diana) on the earth, and Hesiod tells us in the *Theogony* that Hekate rules over the three great mysteries: Birth, Life, and Death. The Great Goddess was also associated with the moon, due to the swelling of the moon and its subsequent decline, reflecting the changes in a woman's body during pregnancy.

Losna is an old Etruscan name for the Moon Goddess in her mother form. The Etruscans also knew her as Tana and Leukothea. Losna was literally the moon itself, and the early Etruscans believed it to be a living goddess. Therefore Losna is the moon as a living entity, rather than a goddess of the moon. Leukothea was an aspect of the moon goddess associated with the ocean and the tides. Therefore, Leukothea is a goddess of the power of the moon, or the light of the moon (to the Etruscans, this was the same thing).

When the moon is full, we associate this phase with Losna. Tana is the name used to denote the Great Goddess who encompasses all aspects. Therefore, Tana is the universal aspect of the Goddess. In early Etruscan times she was called *Uni*, which means "The One Goddess."

Manea is the goddess of night spirits and spirits of the dead. In classical Roman mythology she is the goddess of the dead, and the mother of the Lares and the Manes. The Lare are collective ancestral spirits, and the Mane are individual ghosts of the dead. Manea is the crone aspect of the goddess and rules over decline and death. When the moon begins to wane, following the full moon, we associate this phase with Manea.

The ancient Romans made festival loaves called *maniae* that were fashioned into the shape of people. These loaves represented the *manii*, or spirits of the dead, and were part of ritual elements dating to the indigenous Neolithic Cult of the Dead. One loaf was always larger than the others and was called *Manea*. Human effigies made of wool were dedicated at the Roman festival of *Compitalia*, during which the effigies were hung in the homes. In effect, these effigies were offerings to the dead. This dedication was performed in the hope that the spirits of the dead wandering the earth at this season would take away the spirit of the effigy rather than the spirit of the person who lived in the home.

The Moon Goddess, as the bringer of Life and Death, sends rain, storms, and floods, and moves the tides of the ocean. The rain that she sends to earth in order for life to exist can also become the storms through which she removes life. This is reflective of her dual lunar nature: Light and Dark, Waxing and

Waning. Darkness is the Mother of the Moon. It is the first primal power, and therefore was approached with both fear and reverence under the name *Anthea,* the Underworld Queen. Her name meant "The Sender of Nocturnal Visions." Later she was known as Hecate Triformis, a Greek moon goddess associated with the powers of darkness and the moon. Just as the moon was viewed as having power over the forces of the outside world, it was also believed to have power over the forces of the inner world of humankind, the mind and the spirit. Therefore the Moon Goddess could bestow psychic visions to an individual or insanity, as she pleased.

In ancient times the light of the moon itself was literally the power of the moon. This is why the ancients depicted Hecate and Diana with torches in their hands, wielding the power of the light itself. From this concept arose the ritual practice of employing candles, torches, and bonfires in lunar ceremonies. This was designed to encourage the light of the moon, as seen in the ancient rite of carrying torches around a newly planted field at night.

In ancient Greece, the torches of Hecate were placed in a circle around freshly sown fields to aid in the germination of the grain. Italian Witches employ an invocation during the time of the full moon, requesting that the light of the moon impart occult knowledge to them in their dreams. In ancient Italy, on the festival day of Diana (August 13), a multitude of torches were lighted to honor the moon goddess, and to secure her favor not to send storms that might harm the coming harvest.

In *The Wiccan Mysteries* (1997), I mentioned the connection between Diana and the fairy kingdom. I also demonstrated that fairies evolved from the Cult of the Dead, during which time they were simply spirits of the dead. The old Etruscan Lasa spirits were entities of the fields and therefore of the grain. They also appeared in tomb art connecting them with ancestral spirits. Roman Lare spirits later evolved from the Lasa figures. In the next chapter we will explore further the place of the fairy in Italian Witchcraft.

THE FAIRY FAITH

6

Like most European countries, Italy has a rich legacy of fairy lore and folk practices. In the Old Religion, fairies are an integral part of the belief system. Author Italio Calvino, in his book *Italian Folktales*,[1] tells us that Italian fairy tales (*fiaba*) from the oral tradition were recorded in literary works long before those from any other country. The book *Piacevoli Notti* (by Straparola) was written in Venice during the middle of the sixteenth century. From the seventeenth century came the fairy tales of Naples, retold by Giambattista Basile in his book *Pentameron* (*Entertainment for the Little Ones*).

Prior to 1637, Giambattista Basile traveled around the Mediterranean, Venice, and Crete listening to the old tales told by Italian peasants. Italian fairy tales differ from other European tales (especially the French and Germanic) in that they are less violent and more humorous. Themes of family love and loyalty permeate every Italian folk tale, demonstrating the importance of family and cultural tradition among the Italian people.

---

1   Italio Calvino, *Italian Folktales* (New York: Pantheon Books, 1980).

Another theme often seen in Italian fairy tales is the adoption into the family of a small tree or animal character as a child figure or surrogate. Typically this is because a child died or the wife is barren.

Italian fairy tales are rich in metaphor and robust in nature. Deeds are set in real towns and villages where fantastic encounters occur between wandering fairies and humans who have been wronged in some fashion. Fairies also appear to the broken-hearted and those in despair. The tales of Pinocchio and Cinderella are two good examples. In the original Italian version of Cinderella, the fairy godmother is actually the deceased birth mother of Cinderella returning in fairy form to help her daughter. Cinderella's father brings her the gift of a small date tree taken from the Grove of the Fairies, that he has obtained during his travels in Sardinia. After several days of caring for the tree it grows to full size, and out steps a fairy helper, the spirit of Cinderella's dead mother. In the case of Pinocchio, the fairy is the deceased wife of Geppetto, the toy maker. In the Pinocchio character we again find the ancient connection of the tree (wooden puppet) and fairies.

In *The Fairy Faith in Celtic Countries* by W. Y. Evans-Wentz (who holds a doctorate in folklore from Oxford University) we find that the words *fatua, fata* (respectively, Greek and Roman for fairy) and *fee* (English for fairy) are all the same word. In chapter 3 of this book we read:

> . . . the race of immortal damsels whom the old natives of Italy called Fatuae gave origin to all the family of fees . . . .[2]

The origin of what can be called Italy's fairy faith dates back to Etruscan times. Ancient pottery and burial tomb art of Etruscan culture depicts fairy creatures known as Lasa. The Etruscan Lasa were originally spirits of the dead, eventually evolving into spirits of the field and forest. The ancient Romans absorbed Lasa beliefs into their own religion, calling these spirits "Lare."

The Lare were protectors of fields and crossroads. Each home had a Lare shrine because the Lare were also protectors of the household. In Roman religion the Lare were associated with ancestral spirits. Offerings were made to the Lare for each family event such as a birth, death, or marriage. Traditionally, these offerings were of grain, connecting the dead with rebirth and renewal. This is still the practice among the Streghe. Veneration of one's ancestors is an honorable practice found in many cultures. Roots that receive nourishment produce a healthy tree, which in turn produces fruit and healthy seeds for the future.

In Italian Witchcraft we also find spirits known as *Fata,* or *Folletto.* The Fata are the

---

2   W. Y. Evans-Wentz, *The Fairy Faith in Celtic Countries* (New York: University Books, 1994. Original publication 1912).

old Nature spirits predating humankind. They are the inner mechanism of Nature and they bestow vitality into plant and animal life. In folklore we find a long-standing relationship between fairies and Witches. The Witches' goddess Diana is also known by the title "Queen of the Fairies." Fairies and Witches both share a reverence for Nature and a respect for all living things.

On the island of Sicily we find perhaps the purest form of fairy worship in southern Europe. The island suffered very little foreign influence over the centuries, compared to mainland Italy. Sicily was, however, part of the Spanish Empire from 1282 to 1713, and the Spanish Inquisition took up residence in Palermo from 1487 to 1782. From 1547 to 1701, transcripts concerning the indigenous practice of magick and Witchcraft are recorded in 3,188 cases preserved by the Inquisition. Included in these records is a well-documented study of the Sicilian fairy faith.

The fairy sect in Sicily was known as the *Donna di fuora.* The sect was divided up into groups called companies, and its members included both fairies and humans. Each company was comprised of an odd number of individuals, generally ranging from seven to nine members, headed by a woman called the Queen of the Fairies. She was also known as *La Matrona* (the Mother), *La Maestra* (the Teacher), or *Donna Zabella* (Lady wisdom/ Lady Sybil). Only one man

was allowed in any company. The recorded names of these companies appear in Inquisition records under these titles: the Company of Nobles, the Company of the Poor, the Company of Palermo, the Company of Table and Distaff, the Company of the Mother, and the Company of Ragusa.

The main purpose of the Donna di fuora was to serve as healers within the community. They practiced an ancient form of fairy magick by which they could either harm or heal. The Donna di fuora also served as mediators between humans and fairies. Serious accidents and sudden illnesses were often attributed to angered fairies. Members of the Donna di fuora could be persuaded to aid afflicted members of the community by appeasing the fairies. Only the Donna di fuora knew the required spells and offerings to appease the fairy folk, on a case by case basis. According to the records of the Inquisition, members of the Donna di fuora possessed a power called *Tocadura de brujas* (Witch-touching), by which they could cure or harm through a laying on of the hands.

Like the Witches of mainland Italy, the Donna di Fuora claimed to attend ceremonies beneath the walnut tree in Benevento. They professed to travel in a spirit body in order to fly to Benevento for their ceremonies. According to the Inquisition, the Donna di fuora claimed to attend the *games of Diana* held at Benevento. Mainland Witches in Italy "confessed" to being members of the Society of Diana, despite the Inquisition's attempts to make them confess to worshipping the devil.

OFFERINGS, MAGICKS, AND RECIPES

Even after the rise of Christianity and the decline of Paganism, Italian peasants still honored the sites once sacred to the fairy folk. In the book *Legends of Florence,* written in 1895 by Charles Leland, there are several beautiful tales of fairy encounters. In Italy, fairies are believed to inhabit fountains, bridges, wells, towers, woodlands, and beautiful gardens. In legends they always reward humans who honor them and bring misfortune to those who insult them.

Offering to Appease the Fata

In the Old Religion it is believed that if someone should ever offend a Fata, he or she will become very ill. If a person is under the spell of a Fata, the following offering must be made so that the spell can be removed. This offering does not force the Fata to remove the spell, but instead appeases them and thereby restores their friendship or goodwill.

On a Tuesday, Thursday, or Saturday decorate the sick person's room with flowers (dainties). Set a table with jugs of water and wine, sweetmeats, five loaves of bread, five napkins, a honey-cake, a drinking cup, and eating utensils. Cover the sick person's bed with a red cloth and perfume the entire room with sweet-smelling incense.

Once everything is set in place, leave the room quietly without looking back. The old legends tell us that one should never look back over one's shoulder at a fairy. Fairies are said to be offended by this act, as it displays a lack of trust. Some legends say that the fairies perceive a backward glance as an attempt to catch a glimpse of them. Fairies are said to prefer appearing to humans on their own volition, and are offended when humans try to trick or trap them.

Offering for the Blessing of a Child by the Fata

On the third night following the birth of a child you must perform the following to obtain a blessing from the Fata. Chain the dog, and either unlatch the house door or leave it open. Inside, keep a light burning, and in the center of the child's room place a low table with three cushions or short stools on the floor around the table. On the table set an open container of honey, three white almonds, a loaf of bread, and a cup of water. In the center of the table place the most expensive piece of jewelry the family possesses.

Offerings to Fairies and Nature Spirits

Modern Strega still believe in the same spirits of rock and river, foundation, cavern, and forest as did their Tuscan ancestors from ancient times. Therefore, the same offerings continue to be made to them in accordance with the ancient ways preserved in the Old Religion.

If someone passes by a grove or a rock where folletti or fairies live, he or she will put three coins (or pins) into the ground to please them, and say:

> *These things I bury*
> *that I may gratify*
> *spirits or witches*
> *that they may never*
> *such things be wanting*
> *or go against me,*
> *changing my fortune*
> *from good unto evil!*

(If a person passes a fountain or a stream inhabited by fairies, then he or she will throw his or her gift into it and repeat the same words, adapting the words.)

Sometimes a spirit called a *Linchetto* may come by night into a house and cause annoyances or nightmares. Legends say that such a spirit may sit on the chests of sleepers, stifling them. If an individual shows fear, the folletto will tear all the coverings from the bed and pull him or her out onto the floor, departing with a roar of laughter.

To prevent the type of acts described, legends prescribe that an offering be made to the spirit. The Linchetto are fond of flowers.

The best offering is to place three sunflowers outside the windowsill, and say:

> *In the window sunflowers three*
> *I put; and may the spirit be*
> *here no longer to torment me*
> *and with that I will content be,*
> *if so long as the sun goes round*
> *he may ne'er in my house be found,*
> *let at least his troubling cease*
> *so that I may sleep in peace!*

When this is done and said, the spirit will cease troubling the home and the weary household members will be at rest.

The tradition of laying sunflowers on the windowsill, according to ancient symbolism, is to detect or discover the offender of any act against the home or its inhabitants. Long ago it was the custom to place three sunflowers in the window as a sign to the offender that their identity was known. In the Folk Magick tradition, if anyone is robbed, the offender will appear in a dream if their victims sleep with sunflowers under their pillow. This flower has long been an emblem of the sun that shines on the world. Therefore the spirit of the sun who sees all in his journey across the sky imparts to his symbol the power to see and search out all things. As a symbol of the power of light it also frightens away the spirits of darkness.

Tooth Fairy Magick

Required Items:
  newly lost Tooth
  a small Glass (such as a juice glass)
  a pinch of Glitter (star confetti)
  Colored Sand (green is best)
  a small Box to save the fairy dust in
  a sleeping Child

The tooth is placed under the upside-down glass, which is set on the window ledge. This is what the child sees before going to sleep. When he or she is asleep, then you may go in and replace the tooth with some coins, wrapped candy, or some type of treat. Next, sprinkle the item(s) with some of the glitter and sand (fairy dust), replace the glass over them, and sprinkle some of the glitter and sand over the glass, whispering these words:

> *Fairies of the mantle, the*
> *basement, and roof*
> *bless now this mixture of dust for*
> *the tooth.*
> *Fairies of field, meadow, and tree*
> *may all my child's wishes, turn out*
> *to be!*

In the morning, have the child collect the fairy dust and put it in the small box. Then the child may have the present(s).

The magick here is two-fold. First, you have the magickal thinking of the child, and the beauty that arises from his or her joy.

Secondly, if the child saves the fairy dust, he or she will have a magickal talisman. The magickal belief of the child is imprinted upon the fairy dust. Later in life, the fairy dust can be used for a wish or in spell casting. Traditionally it was later carried in a small bag as a good luck charm. Should the child grow up and lose his or her sense of magick someday, then the fairy dust can be used to restore it. Here the person would sprinkle themselves with the dust and say:

> *Fairies of time and long-faded belief,*
> *remember the child who once*
> *waited in sleep.*
> *Fairies of dreams fragile as the ember,*
> *help now my heart and my soul to*
> *remember.*
>
> *Awaken the child who now sleeps*
> *within me,*
> *who once gathered the dust of the*
> *ol' tooth fairy,*
> *believed that dreams and wishes*
> *could be,*
> *with a sprinkle of dust my eyes*
> *then could see.*
>
> *Come now again to reclaim what*
> *was lost*
> *for the price I paid here is too*
> *dearly a cost.*
> *come now from the meadows, the*
> *fields, and the trees,*

*and grant me the heart that once
knew the fairies.*

Old Fairy Dust Recipe

Required Items:

> contents of three ripe Foxglove seed pods
> pinch of scrapings from the stone
> Rhyolite
> (a fine grain of volcanic Granite)
> pinch of Pollen
> (from Selenetrope or Evening Glory)
> seven Vervain blossoms
> pinch of Lavender blossoms
> pinch of Sand (west shore)

On the night of the Full Moon, mix the foxglove seeds with the sand and Rhyolite grains. Then sprinkle the tiny Vervain and Lavender blossoms over the mixture. It is now ready.

Fairy Sight Stone

Required Items:

> a pinch of Myrtle leaves
> a pinch of Moon Flower pollen
> 3 Vervain blossoms
> soft Clay

On the night of the full moon, mix the ingredients together and fashion the clay into a disk shape. Form a hole through the center. Fire the clay so that it becomes permanently hard. Paint the disk black and then paint four white lines, equally spaced, at the edges of the hole (similar to compass points). Legend says that Fairies can be sighted by looking through such a disk.

FAIRIES AND ITALIAN FOLKLORE

According to Italian Folk Tradition, the first spirits were the *Fauni* and the *Silvani*. The Fauni were guardians of fields and forests and the Silvani were protectors of all animal wildlife. Eventually these two races married and produced offspring known as Folletti, the fairy folk of old Italy. A third race of female spirits arose known as the *Aguane*. The Aguane were the first spirits of hills and mountains, as well as of the streams and rivers crossing through them. The Aguane mated with the Silvani and produced offspring called *Salvanelli*. The name "Salvanelli" (also known as *Sanguanello*) refers to light sparkling on the surface of water, or reflecting off a mirror. Folk traditions speak of beings known as *Salbanelli*, who are the offspring of Streghe and Salvanelli matings. In Italian Witchlore, the Strega and the fairy share an intimate bloodline relationship.

The Streghe view Nature filled with spirits that inhabit objects and places. The Fauni and Silvani are spirits who dwell in the woodlands. The *Monachetto* are gnome-like spirits associated with caves, crevices, valleys, and tunnels. The *Linchetto* are elven spirits, creatures of the night and all dark places. They are said to cause nightmares and odd noises in the night. The Linchetto are native to Tuscany, once the region of the Etruscan civilization.

In Hereditary Tuscan Witchcraft the North quarter is a place of great power. Elemental spirits known as Pala (or Palos) are associated with the North. The East quarter is linked to spirits called *Bellarie.* In the South are the *Settiano* who are spirits of Elemental Fire. In the West are the *Manii* (a type of Lasa) who are spirits of Elemental Water. Through the interaction of all these spirits, vegetation flourishes, rains fall, and life continues. The Elemental spirits are the inner forces of Nature.

There are many different types of spirits in Italian folklore, although most belong to the general race known as Folletti. The Fata are spirits of the woods and water. They are beautiful, gentle, and kind. They also are excellent shape-shifters and often appear in human or animal form. There are many legends in which a person has stopped to help an animal or an old person, only to discover it was a Fata. Those who helped a Fata in disguise are always richly rewarded, but anyone who is cruel to them risks grave danger. The *Lauru* is a folletto spirit with black twinkling eyes, long curly hair, and clothes of the finest velvet. Lauru are said to be mischievous, but when treated with respect they may reveal hidden treasure or winning lottery numbers.

All Folletti travel in the wind, and often appear as swirls of dust, known in Italy as "Knots of winds." The Folletti may also appear in the form of butterflies, one of their favorite tricks. Traditionally, the Folletti are known to be friendly toward humans, but can be mischievous and annoying. It is not uncommon for a Folletto (a male Folletti) to lift up a woman's dress in the wind, or knock over objects with a sudden gust. In northern Italy certain Folletti are called the *Basadone* (woman-kisser) and their kiss is disguised as a breeze passing against a woman's face. The female spirits are known as *Folletti,* which is also the term for the entire race as a whole.

A more somber or darker aspect of the fairy spirit are the *Fouchi Fatui* or *Fiammetta.* These spirits are often seen in cemeteries or swamps, appearing as drifting spheres of light. They are not unlike the will-o-the-wisp of Celtic lands. The Fouchi Fatui are also said to be lost souls of the dead. The Fiammetta is a spirit that leads the dead (or those about to die) into the Otherworld. Such spirits are remnants of the ancient Cult of the Dead indigenous to southern Europe.

FAIRIES AND THE CULT OF THE DEAD

The region that encompasses Italy, Greece, Czechoslovakia, southern Poland, and the western Ukraine archaeologists call "Old Europe." In this region originated what is now called the Cult of the Dead. Here we find the emergence of distinctive burial customs including the placing of personal items and tools with the corpse. These practices reflect a belief among early humans of an existence beyond the grave.

The Cult of the Dead produced certain cult objects that appeared as universal symbols everywhere the cult rooted and spread. Tomb entrances associated with this cult were aligned with the position of the moon at the Winter Solstice. Tomb symbolism reflects both solar and lunar images associated with the measurement of time. Other symbols also appear such as serpents, plants, and mystical forces controlled by goddesses, but the main symbol of the cult was the human skull. All of the tomb symbolism addresses the cult's belief in the regeneration of life.

This ancient cult spread from southern Europe to the Mediterranean coast of Spain and across to Egypt sometime around 4000 B.C. From Iberia it spread into western Europe and northward to the British Isles. Around 3000 B.C. the same symbols appeared in Britain that had been found earlier in the Mediterranean region. Along with the custom of burial mounds, the belief in the spirits of the dead also spread into Gaul and the British Isles. The spirits were connected to the tombs, coming and going through a small opening left for this purpose.

In the Cult of the Dead, wells, bogs, and all openings in the ground were considered sacred passages into the spirit world. These sites were often marked as sacred by erecting standing stones or stone enclosures at their location. This was especially true if the offering site had a reputation for producing the desired results. The burial mounds of Old Europe, connected to the Cult of the Dead, and the fairy mounds of Celtic lands are one and the same.

In the Etruscan mythos, fairies are associated with tombs, vegetation, and the secrets of Nature. In art they are depicted nude and winged, carrying a small vial of elixir. The liquid contained in the vials could produce any of three results. One drop could heal any malady, two drops opened the eyes to the secrets of Nature, and three drops transformed matter into spirit or spirit into matter. Such transformations were necessary in order to pass from the fairy world into the physical world and vice versa.

The magickal abilities of fairies is a constant theme in fairy myths and legends. The ancient power of fairies to transform physical matter is still recalled in such Italian fairy tales as Pinocchio and Cinderella. Myths and legends preserve many ancient beliefs and practices of the Old Religion. In the next chapter are retold the myths of Stregheria, several of which are intimately connected to the fairy race.

MYTHS OF THE
OLD RELIGION

This chapter presents the complete mythos of one of the oldest sects of Italian Witchcraft. The majority of English translations that appear here date from the late nineteenth century. For the sake of preservation, and the feel of antiquity, I have left them in the quaint style in which they were originally presented. The only myth that seemed to not exist individually from ritual references is the myth of Lupus and Cern. In Italian Witchcraft, Lupus is the wolf god, representative of the waning forces of Nature. Cern is the stag god, symbolizing the waxing forces of Nature. These gods are also referred to as the powers of Light and Darkness.

If we examine the ritual material and extract all references to Cern and Lupus, we can put together the following mythos. On the day of the Spring Equinox, while hunting a deer, Lupus is struck by a bolt of lightning shaped like an arrow, and he seemingly perishes. The next morning he rises up from the Underworld as the Sun. Having learned of the death of his brother Lupus, Cern becomes the god of this world and reigns in his place on earth. The only physical remnant of Lupus is his wolf skin, found in the forest by another hunter. The pelt turns out to be magickal and has the power to transform men into wolves. The first man to wear the wolf pelt of Lupus became a priest of Lupercus and founded the society of the Luperci.

Lupus represents Fall and Winter, the waning seasons of the year, even though he appears as a sun god in the ritual material. His brother Cern (the stag god of the forest) represents Spring and Summer, the waxing seasons. In this mythos we find the rivalry of Winter and Summer, Spring and Fall; opposing forces and yet related, "brothers," necessary balances in the scheme of Nature. Lupus is slain during the hunt, in which Cern is the hunted. He is slain by a centaur who is given a bolt of lightning for his bow by Dianus (having been persuaded by his sister Diana). Cern is later slain as well, but on the Autumn Equinox by Mars during another hunting incident.

It is interesting to note that the centaur in the constellation Centaurus is aiming a bow at the constellation Lupus, the wolf. In mythology, the centaur was beloved by Apollo and Diana, who instructed him in many of the ancient arts. Diana and the stag are strongly associated in the Witch cult, and in her classic Roman statue she is portrayed standing with a stag. It is also interesting to note that the wolf was sacred to Mars, and perhaps we see some sort of "vengeance" slaying in the myth of Cern.

The story of Lupercus is a tale of our own journey and our struggle with our higher and lower natures. In the cycle of the sun god born in darkness, growing into the fullness of light, slain, and descending back into darkness only to be reborn again, we find the journey of our own soul. It is a myth of transformation, renewal, challenge and accomplishment. In the ritual of Lupercus we release the wolf within us; that which is untamed and unowned (even by ourselves). Through this purging of the contaminations of modern life, and the imposed restrictions of an oppressive society, we realign ourselves to the nature within, and out of this we can then refocus upon our journey toward enlightenment. In this hunt for ourselves we are "struck by lightning" and we are transformed into a new light.

THE OLD MYTHS AND LEGENDS

In this section I have collected an old body of myths once designed to explain the origins of various aspects of Witch beliefs. I have always treasured these myths because they indicate a complete and cohesive system of Witchlore clearly stemming from a thriving Witchcraft tradition. Some of the myths appear to unfold in a chronological order. Others seem to overlap and sometimes even repeat various themes. To me this indicates the evolution of concepts, that in turn indicate a span of time. In other words, what we have here is a living tradition rooted in the past.

Fragments of old legends also point to the antiquity of a Craft Tradition. One example relates to the cult of the Benandanti and their use of a fennel stalk. The Benandanti fought against evil Witches (Malandanti) by using stalks of fennel in ritual combat. In ancient Greek mythology, the hero Prometheus stole fire from the gods and brought it to humankind concealed in a bundle of fennel stalks. Thus we find the connection of fennel and the Forces of Light. Fennel stalks were also used as candle-like torches because the inner pith burns very slowly, producing a small flame on the end of the stalk. In ancient times, fennel was used to transport fire from place to place. Greek and Roman sailors stocked it on their ships for these uses as well. To find fennel appearing in Italian Witchcraft myths and rituals centuries later further confirms the antiquity of the Old Religion.

I must point out that some of the following myths appear in other Italian traditions and some do not. The names of the deities and entities sometimes differ in these myths from tradition to tradition as well. To my knowledge there are only two Italian Traditions in which all of the following myths appear together. Italy has a diversity of Witches and Traditions just as many other European countries do. It is unfortunate that I cannot present every Italian tradition in this book. Some Traditions, such as the Sicilian, would not share openly with me, nor

did they wish to be included in a published book. Out of respect for their wishes, I have not included what little I know of their inner beliefs and practices.

In the old myths and legends we find the ancient beliefs and mysteries that breathe life into the Old Ways. The very soul of *La Vecchia Religione* resides in these timeless tales. What Witches have whispered to one another through the ages still resounds in the voice of the wind. Therefore, let us turn now to the old stories passed from generation to generation.

How the Universe Came to Be

In the days before the People roamed the land there dwelt upon the earth those spirits of the elements. And with them were the spirits of the trees and meadows, streams, and stones and mountains. Yet before all of this had come to be, there was nothing but the Darkness. Within this Darkness there dwelt the Mist, who was alone brooding in Solitude. Now the right hand of the Mist held Desire for Creation and the left hand held the Source for Creation. And the Mist stretched forth both hands into the unending Darkness, uttering the Divine names upon the Darkness and thus were born the Great Ones, Tagni and Uni, born upon the breath of the Mist.

Then the Goddess moved through the night and Her scent aroused the Passion of the God. And He put forth His hand and drew Her to Himself. Such was his love for the Goddess that He took His Divine Flute of seven reeds and played for Her. And the Worlds formed upon each note that He played.

They loved and were One beneath the sacred stars. And from their Union a silver and golden mist appeared bearing Life to the four winds. Then together they fashioned the Earth.

How the Sun and Moon Came to Be

Many centuries ago there was a Folletto who was in the company of a god called Teramo. This god, known for his powers of speed and quickness, was much pleased with the Folletto, so much so that he bestowed upon him the gift of running like the wind, so that whatever he pursued (be it spirit, animal, or human) he would certainly overtake and catch.

The Folletto had a beautiful sister, who like him ran errands (not for the gods but only for the goddesses). Diana gave to this fairy, on the same day, the power to never be overtaken by anything that chased her.

One day the brother saw his sister speeding like a flash of lightning across the heavens, and he felt a sudden strange desire in rivalry to overtake her. So he dashed after her as she flitted on, but though it was his destiny to catch her, she was fated never to be caught, and so the will of one supreme god was balanced by that of another.

So the two kept flying round and round the edge of heaven, and at first all the gods roared with laughter, but when they understood what had happened, they grew serious and asked one another how it was to end.

Then the Great One of the Mist said: "I will change the sister into a moon, and her brother into a sun. And so shall she ever escape him, yet will he ever catch her with his light, which shall fall on her from afar; for the rays of the sun are his hands, which reach forth with burning grasp, yet which are ever eluded."

And thus it is said that this race begins anew with the first of every month, when the moon, being cold, is covered with as many coats as an onion. But while the race is being run, as the moon becomes warm she casts off one garment after another, till she is naked and then she stops, and when she has once again dressed, the race begins again.

How the Spirits of Nature Came to Be

Long ago after the Creation of the Old Gods, the Beings of Light were brought forth. There was strife among these spirits and they began to take sides against one another. One day as they prepared for battle their legions gathered to take up their positions. The Old Gods looked down from Aster upon the spirits and beheld what was about to take place. In their anger, the Gods caused Time itself to stand still, and all of the spirits were frozen wherever they stood.

Some were in the sky and some were in the sea. Others were upon the mountains, in caves, and in the woods. Some were down in the very depths of the earth. The Gods told them that they would not be released until they agreed not to battle against one another. They who were frozen agreed, upon the condition that Time would never again have any power over them. The Gods conceded and all the spirits were released. This is why Time does not affect spirits as it does mortals.

But the Gods, in their wisdom, did not allow the spirits to return to their original abodes. Instead it was ordained that each would dwell within the realm to which Time had once bound them. This is why spirits now inhabit streams, caves, lakes, forests, and all other places. Such was the origin of all fairies and other Nature spirits.

How Diana Came to be Queen of the Fairies

All things were made by Diana, the great spirits of the stars, men in their time and place, the giants which were of old, and the dwarfs who dwell in the rocks, and all who once a month worship her with cakes.

Diana had not made herself known to the spirits and fairies and elves who dwell in deserted places. One day she hid herself in humility and became a mortal, but by her will she rose again above all. She had such passion for magic and became so powerful therein, that her greatness could not remain hidden.

And thus it came to pass one night, at the meeting of all the spirits and fairies, that Diana declared that she could make the darkness of the heavens sparkle with many lights. All the fairies replied: "If you can do such a wondrous thing, having risen to such power, you shall be our Queen."

Diana went out into a clearing in the woods. She took the bladder of a bull, and with a charm of silver she cut the earth, and filled the bladder with soil and many mice from the field. Then Diana blew into the bladder until it burst.

And there came a great marvel, for the earth which was in the bladder became the round heaven above, and for three days there was a great rain. Then, when the rain had ceased, all of the mice had turned into stars twinkling in the night sky. And having made the heaven and the stars, Diana became the Queen of the fairies. From then on was she known as the cat who ruled the star-mice, the heaven, and the rain.

After this there were men and women upon the earth. One night a young woman, who was poor and had no family, sat in a lonely place beneath the full moon. Although she was lonely, she thought how beautiful the moon was above her. Then there appeared a thousand little fairies, shining white, dancing in the light of the moon.

"What are you?" she asked of the fairies.

"We are moon-rays, the children of Diana," replied one of them. Then they all began to sing: "We are children of the Moon, we are born of shining light, when the Moon sends forth a ray, then it takes a fairy's form."

Then one of the fairies came to her and said: "You are one like us because you were born when the Moon, our Mother Diana, was full. You are kin to us and belong to our race. For children who are born under a full Moon are sons and daughters of the Moon."

Then the fairies gave to her an enchantment sent by Diana upon the light of the Moon, and the woman became the first of all the Strega.

How the Seasons Came to Be

In the earliest of times Diana and Dianus lived in the ancient forest of Nemi. Diana was the Lady of the earth and mistress of the moon. Dianus was Lord of the earth and the sun. Diana loved Dianus and one day she seduced him as they lay together in a beautiful meadow at dawn. And there did she receive the Sacred Seed of the God from which all things sprout.

Then together they ruled over the world and all that dwelled within. But Dianus knew not the secret that only the Goddess would soon understood, for she had drawn the life from him. And the world was abundant with all manner of creatures and that which grows from the earth.

Now there came a time when all things grew to their fullness and were gathered by hunter and fieldsman alike. One day as Dianus was chasing Diana in the woods, the gods mistook him for a deer and shot Dianus with a golden arrow. Then Diana appeared and took him into a field to rest while she sought the god Paeon, that he might heal Dianus. Now a fieldsman was working in the field harvesting fennel, and did not see the god as he labored. By great misfortune Dianus was cut up into seven pieces.

When Diana returned, so great was her grief that she left the world and made her journey to the Hidden Realm of the Shadows, where all the dead are carried by Dis, so that she could find her departed lover. But the world grew cold and lifeless and the sun did not give warmth, the world grew harsh and unyielding. So the people made offerings to the Gods and went before the Old Ones who held council over the world and pleaded with them to restore Diana and Dianus. So the Old Ones departed into the Underworld in search of the missing God and Goddess.

In time the Grigori returned bearing the son of Dianus which they placed in the sky, saying "Behold the newborn Sun God." Then it came to pass that the new god grew strong and matured. Such was his splendor that the Goddess returned from the Underworld, saying "How like my Lord is this new god of the heavens." So they dwelled together in the forest at Nemi and the Goddess desired the new God, and so she plotted to seduce him. Humming a song that was like the sound of bees, she cast a spell causing the god to fall asleep and dream of love. And as he slept, the Goddess lay with him and she received the Sacred Seed of the new God.

The Myth of Diana

Diana was the first created before all creation; in her were all things. Out of herself, the first darkness, she divided herself into darkness and light. Dianus, her brother and son, herself and her other half, was the light.

And when Diana saw that the light was so beautiful, the light which was her other half, her brother Dianus, she yearned for it with exceeding great desire. Wishing to receive the light again into her darkness, to swallow it up in rapture, in delight, she trembled with desire. This desire was the Dawn.

But Dianus, the light, fled from her, and would not yield to her wishes. He was the light which flies into the most distant parts of heaven, the mouse which flies before the cat.

Then Diana went to the Fathers of the Beginning, to the Mothers, the Spirits who were before the first spirit, and lamented unto them that she could not prevail with Dianus. And they praised her for her courage; they told her that to rise she must fall; to become the chief of goddesses she must become a mortal.

And in the Ages, in the course of Time, when the World was made, Diana went on Earth, as did Dianus, who had descended, and Diana taught magic and sorcery, from whence came Witches and magicians, and all that is like Man, yet not mortal.

And it came thus that Diana took the form of a cat. Her brother had a cat whom he loved beyond all creatures, and it slept every night on his bed, a cat beautiful beyond all other creatures, a fairy (but he did not know this).

Diana prevailed with the cat to change forms with her, so she lay with her brother, and in the darkness assumed her own form, and so by Dianus became the mother of Aradia. But when in the morning he found that he lay by his sister, and that light had been conquered by darkness, Dianus was extremely angry; but Diana sang to him a spell, a song of power, and he was silent, the song of the night which soothes to sleep, and he could say nothing.

So Diana with her wiles of Witchcraft so charmed him that he yielded to her love. This was the first fascination; she hummed the song which was as the buzzing of bees, and the spinning of a wheel; the spinning wheel spinning Life. She spun then the lives of Men, and all things were spun from the Wheel of Diana. And it was Dianus who turned the Wheel.

The Myth of Diana and Dianus

In the time that was before Time, when our Lord and Lady had bodies, before the veil was between the Worlds and in the age when the Grigori held council over the Earth, does our myth begin.

Now Dianus, our Lord and Creator was young but knowledged in many ways. And in his youth he rejoiced in the spirits of Nature with whom he spent his days. For he loved them because they were of the blood of he and his sister.

Diana, our Lady and Goddess, thought her brother Dianus to be of splendid and fine beauty and she desired him. But Dianus took her advances as sport and would run from her as she took chase.

Diana was lonely and desired the company of others. And so she decided to seduce her brother and thereby obtain his offspring. So while Dianus slept, she came to his bed and seduced him in secret while he dreamt.

Now Dianus loved his sister, but he was angry at being deceived in such a manner. So he set a veil between the Worlds, between him and his offspring, which was humankind. And over the Earth he placed the sun and the moon as symbols of himself and Diana, saying: "Ever shall she the Moon follow and seek he who is the sun." Then he departed.

Now Diana loved the Earth and her children, but her love for Dianus caused her great sorrow. So she sent messengers to seek him out and proclaim her love for him. One day he returned and told her: "I love you as well, but I cannot stay with you." Then Diana took him and showed him all the beauty of the Earth and all of her children and he was moved with compassion. "I will remain with you for a time each year and for a time I will depart," he said, "for our children have need of my essence and of our Union, and of our love." And so for a time he stayed, and then he fell upon a field and departed into the soil.

Thus came the time when Death appeared upon the Earth and Diana did not understand. So she went before the Grigori that they might give council. But the Grigori could tell her nothing of Death, but said to her: "If you would know and understand Death, then it must be that you should surrender yourself to the cold of its embrace."

Diana thought to herself: "It is true. I will descend to the very depths themselves for I must have knowledge of all things. Then with such knowledge I shall return my beloved Dianus to life again." So Diana prepared herself for her search for Truth. And the Grigori prepared her body and fashioned a Great Vessel in which she could journey through the Night Sky, among the very stars, and to the greatest depths. When the time had come, Diana arose and entered her boat in search of Dianus and the Mysteries.

The Myth of the Descent of the Goddess

Diana, our Lady and Goddess, would solve all mysteries, even the Mystery of Death. And so she journeyed to the Underworld in her boat, upon the Sacred River of Descent. Then it came to pass that she entered before the first of the seven gates to the Underworld. And the Guardian challenged her, demanding one of her garments for passage, for nothing may be received except that something be given in return. And at each of the gates the goddess was required to pay the price of passage, for the guardians spoke to her: "Strip off your garments, and set aside your jewels, for nothing may you bring with you into this, our realm."

So Diana surrendered her jewels and her clothing to the Guardians, and was bound as all living must be who seek to enter the realm of Death and the Mighty Ones. At the first gate she gave over her scepter, at the second her crown, at the third her necklace, at the fourth her ring, at the fifth her girdle, at the sixth her sandals, and at the seventh her gown. Diana stood naked and was presented before Dis, and such was her beauty that he knelt as she entered. He laid his crown and his sword at her feet, saying: "Blessed are your feet which have brought you down this path." Then he arose and said to Diana: "Stay with me I pray, and receive my touch upon your heart."

And Diana replied to Dis: "But I love you not, for why do you cause all the things that I love, and take delight in, to fade and die?"

"My Lady," replied Dis. "It is age and fate against which you speak. I am helpless, for age causes all things to whither, but when men die at the end of their time, I give them rest, peace, and strength. For a time they dwell with the moon, and the spirits of the moon; then may they return to the realm of the living. But you are so lovely, and I ask you to return not, but abide with me here."

But she answered: "No, for I do not love you." Then Dis said: "If you refuse to embrace me, then you must kneel to death's scourge." The goddess answered him: "If it is to be, then it is fate, and better so!" So Diana knelt in submission before the hand of death, and he scourged her with so tender a hand that she cried out: "I know your pain, and the pain of love."

Dis raised her to her feet and said: "Blessed are you, my Queen and my Lady." Then he gave to her the five kisses of initiation, saying: "Only thus may you attain to knowledge and to joy."

And he taught her all of his mysteries, and gave her the necklace which is the circle of rebirth. And she taught him her mysteries of the sacred cup which is the cauldron of rebirth.

They loved and joined in union with each other, and for a time Diana dwelled in the realm of Dis.

For there are three mysteries in the life of man which are: Birth, Life, and Death (and love controls them all).

To fulfill love, you must return again at the same time and place as those who loved before. And you must meet, recognize, remember, and love them anew. But to be reborn you must die and be made ready for a new body. And to die you must be born, but without love you may not be born among your own.

But our Goddess is inclined to favor love, and joy, and happiness. She guards and cherishes her hidden children in this life and the next. In death she reveals the way to her communion, and in life she teaches them the magic of the mystery of the Circle (which is set between the worlds of men and of the gods).

Figure 21. *Amber crystal bowl with silver overlay, custom made in the late 1930s for the author's grandfather, and later presented as a gift for the author's mother. The only surviving item of an eight-piece set depicting mythical themes of the Old Religion. The bowl is decorated with nine identical images of the goddess standing in the Underworld river of descent, holding up the necklace of rebirth. The top of the bowl is a silver handle, representing the full moon.*

The Myth of the Ascent of the Goddess

Now the time came in the Hidden Realm of Shadows that Diana would bear the Child of the Great Dark Lord. And the Lords of the Four Corners came and beheld the newborn god. Then they spoke to Diana of the misery of the people who lived upon the World, and how they suffered in cold and in darkness. So Diana bid the Lords to carry Her son to the World, and so the people rejoiced for the Sun God had returned.

And it came to pass that Diana longed for the Light of the World, and for Her many children. So She journeyed to the World and was welcomed in great celebration.

Then Diana saw the splendor of the new god as He crossed the heavens, and she desired Him. But each night He returned to the Hidden Realm and could not see the beauty of the goddess in the night sky.

So one morning the goddess arose as the god came up from the Hidden Realm, and She bathed nude in the sacred lake of Nemi. Then the Lords of the Four Corners appeared to Him and said: "Behold the sweet beauty of the Goddess of the Earth." And He looked upon Her and was struck with Her beauty so that He descended upon the earth in the form of a great stag.

"I have come to play beside your bath," He said, but Diana gazed upon the stag and said: "You are not a stag, but a god!" Then He answered: "I am Cornunno, god of the forest. Yet as I stand upon the world I touch also the sky and I am Lupercus the sun, who banishes the Wolf Night. But beyond all of this I am Dianus, the first born of all the Gods!"

Diana smiled and stepped forth from the water in all Her beauty. "I am Fauna, goddess of the forest, yet even as I stand before you I am Jana, goddess of the moon. But beyond all this I am Diana, first born of all Goddesses!"

And Dianus took Her by the hand and together they walked in the meadows and forests, telling their tales of ancient mysteries. They loved and were One and together they ruled over the World. Yet even in love, Diana knew that the god would soon cross over to the Hidden realm and Death would come to the World. Then must She descend and embrace the Dark Lord, and bear the fruit of their Union.

The Myth of Lupercus

There came a time upon the land of the People, the Time of Great Sorrow, the Time of the Wolf. For Dianus, Lord of the sun, had journeyed a great distance away and all withered in his absence. So the Grigori of the Four Winds went forth to seek him out, that they might bid him to return.

Now it came to pass that the Grigori were brought forth before the throne of Dis, the Dark Lord of the Shadows. And they spoke, saying: "Do we find you here in this Realm of Shadowed Life?" "Yes," Dianus replied, "now have you truly seen my two faces." Then the Grigori pleaded with Dianus to return, revealing the sorrow which he had left behind him in the world. But he declined, saying: "The Gods of the Mists, who are greater than I, have ordained that this time must be, and I am powerless to change that which must come to pass."

But Diana had overheard them speaking and she took the Grigori aside in secret. "You must take my son Lupercus, who shall be born of Dianus, that he might give life back to the world." So when the time came the Grigori took the newborn god and began their journey from the Realm of Shadows. Now as they journeyed they spoke of how to prove the worthiness of this new god to the People of the World. So they decided to test him with twelve Sacred Labors. And these were the Twelve Labors of Lupercus:

1. To carry the sacred ram and set him among the stars

2. To purify the hide of the sacred white bull

3. To tame the twin serpents of Teramo

4. To carry off the Great Sea Crab to the western horizon

5. To free the sacred lion

6. To fashion a bow for the goddess Diana

7. To forge the Great Scales of Justice for the Gods

8. To seal the giant Scorpion back within the Earth

9. To make a golden arrow for the King of the Centaurs

10. To fashion two golden horns for the Great Goat Fish

11. To purify the jugs of water which are borne to the Gods

12. To leash the two Great Fish of the Sea and set them among the stars

Bravely did the young god complete the tasks given to him. Then was he received by the People of the World in all his brilliant splendor. Now because of the absence of the sun, in his time there were many wolves who nightly attacked the herds and flocks, and the people were in despair. So Lupercus descended from Aster and dwelt among the wolves, and having transformed himself into a powerful golden wolf he became their King. Before him all wolves would flee into the woods and hills at his anger. Then the People rejoiced crying "Great is Lupercus, Lord of the Sun, King of the Wolves, banisher of the Dark Wolf Night."

So each day Lupercus would rise up and journey across the heavens, bearing his fennel torch. As he went, Lupercus would gather the souls of those who had died during his absence in the sky, and deliver them unto his Father Dianus in the Great Hidden Realm, which lay beyond the western waters. Here they were given refreshments and were prepared for a new life, then Grigori would escort them to the realm of the Goddess in Luna to await rebirth. Each night Lupercus rested in the Hidden Realm, to again make his journey across the world of mortals.

The Myth of the Raven

In the Time, which was before time, when the Gods ruled in the Realm of Aster, there was war between the powers of Light and Darkness. But not all of the Gods had declared their allegiance, and one such God was Raven. Raven was the son of the Goddess Telete, and the God Teramus. When war broke out in Aster, Raven journeyed to the Island of the Moon to discern his place among the Gods. Here Cata told him that he must pass through the pool of Umbrea, and retrieve a pearl which lay on the bottom, if he desired a true knowledge of Self.

The pool of Umbrea was filled with a still, dark liquid, the depth of which was unknown. Gathering his courage, Raven dove into the pool, his white feathers looking for a moment like the Moon against the Night Sky, then he disappeared into the depths of Umbrea. He did not reappear for three days, but on the third night Raven came up out of the pool, bearing the pearl. His feathers were now stained black, and he could see as clearly in the darkness as he had been able to see in the light. This is why Ravens are black today, and why they collect various trinkets, for they are all His children.

Because of his new sight, Raven would not join in the battle between Light and Darkness. Instead, he would journey between the two camps, serving as a messenger. Neither side trusted Raven, and threatened him each time he was to deliver a message, to ensure that it would be as they had ordered. Cata took pity on Raven, and taught him how to use the pearl to gain insight into the hearts and minds of others. She also taught him the arts of magic, so that he could protect himself.

Upon the Earth, Raven found worshippers and a home. He left the company of the Gods for many years, and dwelled upon the Earth. One day the Oracle of Tanes spoke to him and revealed that the Powers of Darkness were prevailing, and that the world of Humans would next be in danger. Raven then collected many of the Earth Gods and other Spirits together, under his banner which was blood red, bearing upon it a Raven descending in flight.

Raven brought his army down upon the Forces of Darkness, as they were assaulting Aster itself. Because of his intervention, the balance between Light and Darkness was restored. Raven then returned to his Kingdom upon the Earth.

The Myth of the Raven (Part Two)

In the days of Aster, when the worlds had been formed, Raven was the first of the gods to descend upon the world of Humankind.

Raven went about the world, and looked upon all of the creatures, which had been created there, and he was very pleased. But when he saw the men and women who lived in this world, he was greatly concerned. For he said to himself: "These poor creatures have no claws for digging roots, nor can they run as fast as the other creatures, and they have no feathers or fur to protect them from the elements." Raven found them to be very poor creatures indeed.

Raven asked the People if they were hungry, and they said they were very hungry. So Raven taught them how to hunt, and how to fashion clothes. He taught them to take care of the world, and to not abuse anything that had been created there. Then Raven gave them one of his feathers, the power of which gave them Knowledge, and they became more intelligent than any of the other creatures in the world. The People were happy and so was Raven. But Raven noticed, on his many trips back to the world of the People, that they were beginning to change.

People were beginning to fight with each other, and to abuse the animals and the lands that had been given to them. So Raven went to the Gods and Goddesses of Aster, and asked for their assistance, but they were busy with the other worlds they had created, and told Raven to come back at a later time. So Raven returned to the world of the People, dividing them into different clans, separating all those who were fighting between themselves. Then he taught them how to grow crops for food, so that they would not meet one another as they traveled in their hunts.

Raven was unaware that other gods had also come and visited with the People while he was away. The People began to separate themselves into groups that worshipped different gods and goddesses. Raven called together all of the gods and goddesses who were upon the world in those days. And these were the nine; Dracos, Lupus, Cern, Catta, Canus, Civetta, Falca, Ursa, and Raven. Once they had assembled, Raven spoke to them and pleaded with them to keep peace between all of the People who lived in this world. But each of the Nine favored a certain clan of people, and they could not agree upon anything in common.

Raven then flew back to Aster, and once again went before the Great Gods, asking for their assistance. Once again, he was told to come back at a later time. While Raven stayed in Aster, he began to think of a way to trick the Great Ones into coming to the World of the People. So he went to each god and each goddess, when they were alone, and told them that he thought that they were the most beautiful of all the gods. Now because the gods and goddesses had never seen themselves, there was much arguing now in Aster, as to who was the most Beautiful. So Raven told them that there was a mirror in the world of the People, and that they should each come, and judge for themselves, by looking into the mirror. The Great Ones agreed to come, and Raven said that he would go to make the necessary arrangements.

When Raven returned to the world, he told the gods upon the earth that the Great Ones had somehow heard that the Nine had created a beautiful mirror for them, and that they were coming to see it. "What are we to do now?" they said to each other, for they were very concerned that the Great Ones would be angry. "I have a plan," Raven said, at long last. "We shall make them a great mirror, and I will show you how." So Raven had Dracos breathe out flames to clear a place in the forest. In the clearing he had Ursa, Canus, and Lupus dig a huge hole in the ground. Then Raven, Falca, and Civetta flew to the seas and gathered up water in their beaks, so that they soon filled the hole completely with water. Then Cern hooked a piece of the Moon's light with his antlers, and drew it down upon the lake. Catta kneaded the Moon's light into the water, tucking it all around the edges of the hole. Thus was the first lake formed, which to this very day is called the Mirror of the Goddess.

When the Great Ones descended upon the world of the People, they held a contest to see which of those who lived in Aster was the most beautiful. After much debate, Uni, the Great Goddess, was chosen, and the People of the world gave Her the mirror as a gift of their love and respect. The People then lived in peace between themselves, and were left under the care of the Nine. From those days forward, the Great Gods never forgot the world of the People, and visited there often, from Time to Time.

Wheel of the Year Mythos

Below and on the following pages are reproduced images that reflect the Wheel of the Year Mythos. These illustrations first appeared in Charles Leland's work on Italian Witchcraft, *Etruscan Roman Remains* (1892). The original engravings were made from rubbings of the backs of ancient brass mirrors collected by Leland.

Figure 22. *Beginning of the Mythos. The God and Goddess in the Underworld Realm, known as Achru. Here they love and are as One. From this union will be born the new Sun God of the year to come. His name will be Lupercus, son of Dis and Umbrea. Note that Tagni holds the Moon Disk, the staff of power belonging to Uni. This is symbolic of the reign being passed from the Goddess to the God at the Time of the Shadows: Festa Dell' Ombra.*

Figure 23. *The second stage of the Mythos. The new Sun God is born. It is Manea who gives him birth at the Winter Solstice, although it was Umbrea whose womb bore him to full term. Note the appearance of the fruit of the moon tree upon the pillar. The new Sun God sits at the feet of the Moon Goddess, and the solar disk is seen near his own feet, just as it is seen at the right shoulder of the former Sun God. Note that he raises his left arm to the crescent moon, and the three points of manifestation appear at his gesture. They also appear flanking the fruit of the Moon Tree.*

Figure 24. *The third stage of the Mythos. The new Sun God Lupercus is prepared to reign as the God for the Year. In his left hand he bears the Thunder Bolt of Tagni, the symbol of divine reign. In his right hand he holds the Staff of the Sun. Behind Teramo are the spirals, signs of the Labyrinth and of return. The Quest, and the trial of 12 labors, now lie before Lupercus.*

Figure 25. *The fourth stage of the Mythos. The Goddess departs from the Underworld and returns to the world of the living. Budding trees and other signs of new life signal Her return. The Lord of the Underworld holds the pomegranate, a symbol of the life essence: the seed of the male and the blood of the goddess. Not only is the juice of the pomegranate the blood of the hymen, but also the blood of menstruation. The blood of the Goddess links all souls to the source of rebirth.*

Figure 26. *The fifth stage of the Mythos. The God courts the Goddess and they become lovers. The swan placed between the two is a sign of divine seduction, meaning this union is destined and directed by the High Gods of Aster. The bird perched on the God's lyre is the goddess Carmen, in disguise, singing the song of enchantment. The deer is a symbol of the Stag and the Doe, the primal courtship.*

Figure 27. *The sixth stage of the Mythos. The God and Goddess wed at the Summer Solstice, the Time of the Promise of Plenty. Here on this day the forces of Light and Darkness come together. This time is also marked by ritual battles, such as those fought between the Benandanti and Malandanti, a Summer festival theme since ancient times.*

Figure 28. *The seventh stage of the Mythos. The Time of Plenty, and the anticipation of Harvest. The World has produced in abundance to celebrate the Union of the God and Goddess. Spirits of the fields have blessed the grant, and all that bears. All is fertile in the World, and the gods have rewarded the labors of all men and women. It is the time of Cornucopia, the Horn of Plenty.*

Figure 29. *The eighth stage of the Mythos. The God of the Year is slain, harvested at the peak of his power. His spirit is bound up in the bundles of the Harvest so that it does not escape the land as the fields are put to the sickle. Note the spirit at the base of the drawing. He holds a fish, the symbol of abundance, and his legs form into serpents, symbols of regeneration and fertility. The serpent also moves between the World of Humankind and the Underworld (crevices and burrows), just as the Sun and Moon disappear beneath the horizon, only to return again from the other side.*

Part Three

The Rituals

8

SOLITARY RITUAL

The rituals presented in this chapter are based upon the group rituals presented in my previous book *Ways of the Strega*. They are drawn from the Aridian system of the Strega Tradition, employing the deity names of Diana and Dianus, and are modified for solitary practice. We will begin with the basic altar setup, and the method of casting a ritual circle. The chapter concludes with the full moon ritual and the seasonal rites. Performing these rites consistently and consecutively will align you with the harmonious patterns of Nature actively flowing at the times of the year marked by each ritual.

It is important to put yourself fully in the moment as you perform each ritual. Keep the symbolism of the prescribed actions in your conscious mind at all times. Most importantly, do not regard the rituals as a mechanical process. These rituals are guidelines and specific steps in the unfolding of a spiritual experience. Feel free to add to each rite as your intuition leads you. However, be sure to not omit a prescribed step as you perform the ritual.

Rituals are the physical forms through which spiritual energies flow and manifest. Just as the soul requires a physical form to function fully in the material world, so too do the spiritual beings and principles with which we seek relationship in this lifetime. Familiar rites allow our consciousness to move beyond the moment. We can liken this to learning to drive a car. At first the acts of steering, working the pedals, and so forth, fully occupy our consciousness. We cannot enjoy the journey because we are caught up in operating the vehicle. Soon however, everything becomes a familiar ritual, and we no longer have to think about the act of operating the machine. Instead we are free to experience the higher nature of the transportation itself.

THE ALTAR ARRANGEMENT

The altar is always oriented to the north quarter of the ritual setting. In other words, you will be facing North when standing in front of the altar. The North is considered the place of power. Traditionally the altar is round in shape, however a rectangle or square table may be used as well. Setting up the altar is an important part of any ritual. It should be performed with focus and concentration upon the inner meanings as each item is placed on the altar. In effect, you are creating your own microcosm of the Universe as you set the altar and cast the circle. Everything that you will create in this magickal work establishes your own reality.

First, place a black cloth over the table to symbolize the darkness of "procreation" from which all things manifest. Set a green candle (representing the goddess) at the northwest corner of the altar. Place a red candle (symbolizing the god) at the northeast part of the altar. Statues of the goddess and god are placed next to the candles. This represents their presence as they oversee the process of creation reflected in your altar setup.

Lay the altar pentacle on the center of the altar. Set the spirit bowl, containing flammable liquid, directly upon the pentacle. This liquid is the spirit fluid, which will burn a beautiful blue flame, representing the presence of Divinity. Next, place the elemental bowls around the pentacle, representing the creative elemental substances from which all things are made manifest. Place the bowl containing sand or small stones, representing earth, in the North position. To the East, lay the bowl containing incense (smoking) to represent air, to the South set a bowl with a red votive candle for fire, and to the West place a bowl of purified water.

The ritual wand is set on the altar next to the air elemental bowl. The spirit blade is placed to the South by the votive candle, and the chalice to the West by the bowl of water. Mundane tools such as a utility knife, candle snuffer, and so on, may be placed at the north. With this arrangement the altar is now complete.

Figure 30. *The author's ritual tools are laid out in traditional formation upon this outdoor altar.*

PREPARATION OF THE RITUAL CIRCLE

When the moon is full, or when a treguenda occurs, you will want to cast a ritual circle for celebration and union with deity. Mark out a work area by forming a circle on the ground for your ritual circle. Then perform the following steps:

1. Purify the ritual area with salted water.

2. Set up the altar as described earlier. Trace the gesture of power (see Figure 31) in the air and light the Spirit Bowl, reciting the invocation:

Awaken now, O Spirit of the Old Ways,
with your reaching blue arms,
wake now soundly, very soundly,
I who tend the ancient fire call to you,
awaken, Spirit Flame, awaken.

3. Light altar candles once the blue flame is burning, and recite the altar calls:

(To the Goddess): *Beautiful Diana, goddess of the moon and beyond, think even for a moment upon we who gather in your name.*

Figure 31. *Ritual Gesture of Power*

(To the God): *Dianus, god of the sun and beyond, think even for a moment upon we who gather in your name.*

4. Conjure the Elementals: Ring the bell over each elemental bowl three times, beginning at the North and circling clockwise, and recite:

I call out into the mist of Hidden Realms, and conjure you spirits of Earth and Air and Fire and Water. Gather now at this sacred circle, and grant me union with your powers.

5. Ring the altar bell over the elemental bowls again three times, then tap each bowl three times with the spirit blade.

6. Place the spirit blade into the Spirit Flame and mentally draw out the blue flame into the blade.

7. Beginning at the North, tread the circle, laying out the blue power along the edge of the circle (visualize the blue flame pouring out through the blade into the circle's rim as you walk), and recite:

In the names of Diana and Dianus, and by the Old Ones, I conjure this circle of power: become a sphere of protection, a vessel to contain the power that shall be raised within,

wherefore do I charge you, and empower you.

8. Quarter candles are each touched to an elemental bowl (beginning North and moving clockwise), then each candle is placed and lighted at the proper quarter associated with the element. North = Earth, East = Air, South = Fire, and West = Water.

9. Calling the Grigori: Go to each quarter, beginning at the North and moving clockwise, and swing a censer of incense back and forth three times. Return to the altar and ring a bell three times, just before you recite the quarter invocations.

I call to You, O ancient Ones !
You who dwell beyond the Realms,
You who once reigned in the Time
*   before Time.*
Come! Hear the Call !
Assist me to open the Way, give me the
*   Power!*
Open wide the gates to the Realms of
*   the Gods*
and come forth by these names:

(Face North and ring bell three times)

TAGO!

(Face East and ring bell three times)

ALPENA!

(Face South and ring bell three times)

SETTRANO!

(Face West and ring bell three times)

MEANA!

10. Rap your wand three times on the altar and declare out loud that the circle is cast.

Banishing a Cast Circle

A circle must be dissolved when ritual is completed.

1. Beginning at the North quarter, ring the bell three times, salute, and recite:

   Hear me, Old Ones, I honor You for Your attendance and bid You now depart to your secret Realms. With peace I say now; Ave, Vale!

2. Repeat the above action at each of the quarters (moving West, South, East, and North again).

3. Point the spirit blade down toward the circle and walk counterclockwise from the North, mentally drawing the blue flame's power back up from the circle perimeter into the blade.

   After returning to the North quarter, stand before the altar and place the tip of the ritual blade into the Spirit Flame.

Visualize the power flowing back into the bowl. Recite the following invocation as you watch the spirit flame ebb away:

Sleep, Spirit of Flame, with your reaching blue arms, and red hair. Sleep soundly, soundly, very soundly, until I, your friend, come again to wake you. Sleep, Spirit of the Flame, sleep.

Once the flame has departed, dissolve the elements within each elemental bowl by snapping your fingers over them three times each. Beginning at the North, move counterclockwise.

4. Extinguish all quarter candles and all other ritual flames. Declare that the circle is dissolved.

FULL MOON RITUAL

1. Cast the circle in the usual manner.

2. Stand before the altar and look up at the moon, or a symbol of the moon, and say:

   I come on this sacred night of the Lady, beneath the full moon, to adore Her symbol, which She has placed among the stars. And to give due worship unto the Great Goddess, for this is the appointed time that the

Holy Strega bid me observe. As it was in the time of the beginning, so is it now, so shall it be.

3. Hold your palms out in front of you, facing away, and form a triangle with your hands by touching the index fingers and thumbs together (the gesture of manifestation). Enclose the moon or its symbol in the opening of the triangle you have formed with your hands, then recite:

Hail and adoration unto You, O Great Diana. Hail Goddess of the Moon, and of the Night. You have been since before the beginning, You who caused all things to appear, Giver and Sustainer of Life, Adoration unto You.

4. Perform the Rite of Union as you gaze upon the moon (see Figure 32, page 115):

Standing or kneeling before the *Light* (or symbol), raise your hands as in position 1, saying:

Hail and adoration unto Thee, O Source of All Enlightenment. I pray Thee impart to me Thy Illumination.

Lower arms to position #2, saying:

And enlighten my mind that I may perceive more clearly, all things in which I endeavor.

Lower your arms to position 3, saying:

And illuminate my soul, imparting Thy essence of Purity.

Lower your arms to positions 4 and 5, saying:

I reveal my Inner Self to Thee and ask that all be cleansed and purified within.

5. Place offerings to the Goddess at the West quarter.

6. Kneel before the offerings and recite:

O Great Diana, think yet even for a moment, upon this worshipper who kneels in Your name. Beneath the Sun do people toil, and go about, and attend to all worldly affairs. But beneath the Moon, Your children dream and awaken, and draw their power. Therefore, bless me O Great Diana, and impart to me Your mystic Light, in which I find my powers. Bless me, O Great Diana.

7. Look up at the full moon, and recite:

O Ancient Wanderer of the Dark Heavens, Mystery of the Mysteries, emanate Your sacred essence upon me as I wait below at this appointed time. Enlighten my inner mind and spirit, as do you lighten the darkness of night.

8. Sit quietly within the circle, and recite the Veglia:

Once, long ago, all Witches worshipped in the open fields and upon the ancient sites. And our chants were carried upon the winds. Our prayers were received upon the smoke of our incense by the Old Ones. But in time, we were enslaved by the worshippers of a jealous god, and our villages were given over to cruel Lords. The Old Ways were forbidden and we were forced to accept the ways of our oppressors.

Now it is a time of gathering in the shadows. We have suffered persecution for our beliefs, and many of us have died. Yet we have been reborn among our own again. Always has it been that the cycles of Life pass and return again. All things are remembered, and all things are restored.

I am one of the hidden children of the Goddess. From generation unto generation has the knowledge been passed and the Old Ways been kept by those who kindle the flame. In remembrance, I come this evening beneath the Full Moon, to honor the past, secure the future, and receive the essence of the Old Ones. As it was in the time of our beginning, so is it now, so shall it be.

9. Place something made from grain on a plate. Next to this set a chalice of wine. Bless them by tracing a crescent over them, and then recite:

Blessings upon this meal, which is as my own body. For without such sustenance, I would perish from this world. Blessings upon the grain, which as seed went into the earth where deep secrets hide. And there did dance with the elements, and spring forth as flowered plant, concealing secrets strange. When you were in the ear of grain, spirits of the field came to cast their light upon you, and aid you in your growth. Thus through you shall I be touched by that same Race, and the mysteries hidden within you, I shall obtain even unto the last of these grains.

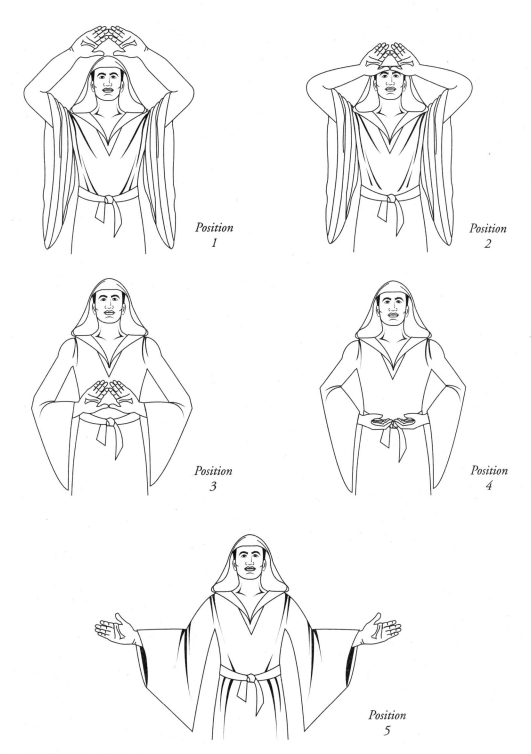

Figure 32. *The Rite of Union Postures*

10. Trace a crescent over the wine with your spirit blade and recite:

By virtue of this sacred blade, be this wine the vital essence of the Great Goddess.

Trace a crescent over the cakes, and recite:

By virtue of this sacred blade, be these cakes the vital substance of the Great God.

11. Lift up the plate and the chalice, look up at the moon, and recite:

Through these cakes and by this wine, Diana and Dianus bless me, and give me inner strength and vision. May I come to know that within me which is of the gods. May this blessing be so, in the names of Diana and Dianus.

Eat a portion of the meal and drink some of the wine. Leave some for libations at the close of the ritual.

12. Raise your chalice in a toast to Aradia, and in her memory recite the Charge:

Whenever you have need of anything, once in the month when the moon is full, then shall you come together at some deserted place, or where there are woods, and give worship to She who is Queen of all Witches. Come all together inside a circle, and secrets that are as yet unknown shall be revealed.

And your mind must be free and also your spirit, and as a sign that you are truly free, you shall be naked in your rites. And you shall rejoice, and sing; making music and love. For this is the essence of spirit, and the knowledge of joy.

Be true to your own beliefs, and keep to the Ways, beyond all obstacles. For ours is the key to the mysteries and the cycle of rebirth, which opens the way to the Womb of Enlightenment.

I am the spirit of Witches all, and this is joy and peace and harmony. In life does the Queen of all Witches reveal the knowledge of Spirit. And from death does the Queen deliver you to peace and renewal.

When I shall have departed from this world, in memory of me make cakes of grain, wine, and honey. These shall you shape like the moon, and then partake of wine and cakes, all in my memory. For I have been sent to you by the Spirits of Old, and I have come that you might be delivered from all slavery. I am the daughter of the sun and the moon, and even though I have been born into this world, my Race is of the stars.

Give offerings all to She who is our Mother. For She is the beauty of the Green Wood, and the light of the moon among the stars, and the mystery which gives life, and always calls us to come together in Her name. Let Her worship be the ways within your heart, for all acts of love and pleasure gain favor with the Goddess.

But to all who seek her, know that your seeking and desire will reward you not, until you realize the secret. Because if that which you seek is not found within your inner self, you will never find it from without. For she has been with you since you entered into the ways, and she is that which awaits at your journey's end.

13. Sit now before the altar, facing North. Look up and at the moon and visualize it as the goddess appearing to you in a sphere of light. Kiss the palm of your left hand and extend it up to her. Then recite:

O Great Diana, Queen of all Witches, hear my adoration. Hear my voice as I speak Your praises. Receive my words as they rise heavenward, when the Full Moon brightly shining fills the heavens with Your beauty. See me for I come before You, and reach my hand up to You. As the Full Moon shines upon me, give me all Your blessings.

O Great Goddess of the Moon, Goddess of the Mysteries of the Moon, teach me secrets yet revealed, ancient rites of invocation that the Holy Strega spoke of, for I believe the Strega's story; when she spoke of Your timeless glory, when she said to entreat You, and when seeking for knowledge to seek and find you above all others.

Give me power, O Most Secret Lady, to bind my enemies. Receive me as Your child, receive me though I am earthbound. When my body lies resting nightly, speak to my inner spirit, teach me all Your Holy Mysteries. I believe Your ancient promise that all who seek Your Holy Presence will receive of Your wisdom.

Behold, O Ancient Goddess, I have come beneath the Full Moon at this appointed time. Now the Full Moon shines upon me. Hear me and recall Your Ancient Promise. Let Your Glory

*shine about me. Bless me, O Gracious
Queen of Heaven. In your name, so be
it done.*

14. Three works of magic may be performed before the circle is closed, if
desired. Ritual tools may be blessed by
touching them to each of the four
elements represented upon the altar.
Close celebration and banish the
circle. Offer libations to the earth and
the moon. The celebration is
completed.

SHADOW FEST
(La Festa dell' Ombra)

Items required (in addition to standard altar
items):

    1 vial of essence Oil (god scent)
    2 red Candles for altar
    4 black Candles for quarter points
    1 Human Skull symbol placed at the
        West quarter
    Winter Treguenda incense
    root of Rue plant
    a small white Candle
    dried Leaves (Oak leaves or Pine needles)
    Personal Offering to the god
    Cauldron

The Rite:

1. Cast the circle in the usual manner.

2. Go before the altar and say:

*I come on this sacred night when the
veil between the worlds turns to mist.
I join now in spirit with those who
have gone before. As it was in the time
of the beginning, so is it now, so shall
it be.*

3. Place skull at the West quarter. Stand
before it in the Slain God Posture and
say:

*O ancient gods of my ancestors, bless
this sacred setting, that I who worship
in your ways may be protected from
the coming powers.*

4. Stand at the west quarter and read the
Myth of the Descent of the Goddess
aloud:

*Diana, my Lady and Goddess, would
solve all mysteries even the mystery of
Death. And so she journeyed to the
Underworld in her boat, upon the
Sacred River of Descent. Then it
came to pass that she entered before
the first of the seven gates to the
Underworld. And the Guardian
challenged her, demanding one of her
garments for passage, for nothing
may be received except that
something be given in return.*

And at each of the gates the goddess was required to pay the price of passage, for the guardians spoke to her: "Strip off your garments, and set aside your jewels, for nothing may you bring with you into this our realm."

So Diana surrendered her jewels and her clothing to the Guardians, and was bound as all living must be who seek to enter the realm of Death and the Mighty Ones. At the first gate she gave over her scepter, at the second her crown, at the third her necklace, at the fourth her ring, at the fifth her girdle, at the sixth her sandals, and at the seventh her gown.

Diana stood naked and was presented before Dis, and such was her beauty that he himself knelt as she entered. He laid his crown and his sword at her feet saying: "Blessed are your feet which have brought you upon this path." Then he arose and said to Diana: "Stay with me, I pray, and receive my touch upon your heart."

And Diana replied to Dis: "But I love you not, for why do you cause all the things that I love, and take delight in, to wither and die?"

"My Lady," replied Dis, "it is age and fate against which you speak. Thus I am helpless, for age causes all things to whither, but when all die at the end of their time, I give them rest, peace, and strength. For a time they dwell within the moon's light, and with the spirits of the moon; then may they return to the realm of the living. But you are so lovely, and I ask you to return not, but abide with me here."

But she answered: "No, for I do not love you." Then Dis said: "If you refuse to embrace me, then you must kneel to death's scourge." The goddess answered him: "If it is to be, then it is fate, and better served!" So Diana knelt in submission before the hand of death, and he scourged her with so tender a hand that she cried out "I know your pain, and the pain of love."

Dis raised her to her feet and said: "Blessed are you, my Queen and my Lady." Then he gave to her the five kisses of initiation, saying: "Only thus may you attain to knowledge and to joy." And he taught her all of his mysteries, and he gave her the necklace which is the circle of rebirth. And she taught him her mysteries of the sacred cup which is the cauldron of rebirth.

They loved and joined in union with each other, and for a time Diana dwelled in the realm of Dis. For there are three mysteries in the life of man which are: Birth, Life, and Death (and love controls them all). To fulfill love, you must return again at the same time and place as those whom you loved before. And you must meet, recognize, remember, and love them anew. But to be reborn you must die and be made ready for a new body. And to die you must be reborn, but without love you may not be born among your own.

But the Goddess is inclined to favor love, and joy and happiness. She guards and cherishes her hidden children in this life and the next. In death she reveals the way to her communion, and in life she teaches them the magic of the mystery of the Circle (which is set between the worlds of men and of the gods).

5. At the West quarter set a burning white candle. Pause for a moment and then extinguish it, saying:

Diana dwells now in the Realm of the Dread Lord of the Shadows. The world grows cold and lifeless. But I do not sorrow in this harsh season, for all is as it must be. Therefore, I draw close to the Dark Lord and embrace Him. I find comfort in the knowledge of His Essence. May my path be blessed in the name of the God.

6. At the North quarter lay down the spirit blade and wand. Then assume the God Posture, facing the tools (south). Recite the following:

The reign of the goddess surrenders in love to the reign of the god.

Then pick up the ritual tools, kiss them, and place them down at the North quarter again. Sit facing the skull and recite the Charge of the God:

These are the words of the God: "By the fallen temple stone or in a forgotten glen, there shall you gather, all who seek to know my secret mysteries. I am He who guards and He who reveals all of these things.

"I am the Lord of earth and sky, of rocky cliffs and forests deep and darkened. I was there when the world was new, and I taught you to hunt

and to gather plants for food. Look within yourselves, for I am there. I am that strength upon which you draw in times of need. I am that which conquers fear. I am the hero and the fool. I am your longing to be free, and your need to be bound.

"In my love for you, I give up my life. I die but rise up again. I prepare the path upon which you journey, going always on before you. For it is in becoming as you, that you may become as me.

"Hear the thunder, there am I. See the hawk and the raven soar, there am I. See the great wolf and the stag appear in the forest clearing, there am I. Close your eyes at the end of your days, and there am I, waiting by the temple stone."

7. Carry the goddess icon from the altar to the west quarter and place it there. Recite:

These are the words of the goddess: "The wheel of the year has turned, Cycle unto Cycle, Time unto Time. I have journeyed to the Hidden Realm of the Shadows; there to prepare a place for you. The harshness of the season I leave behind me; kindle for

yourselves a fire of love within, and I shall remember you, and return to you. For you are the Keepers of the Flame, and all who kindle the flame I shall never abandon.

"By the changing of the harsh season shall you know that I draw near you again. And I shall return then the greenness of plants and trees; then will you know that I have come."

8. Go to the altar and retrieve the chalice. Place the candle at the West quarter. Then set the chalice of wine in front of the goddess icon. Lift up the chalice, and dip the wand in it (tip down).

9. Move the candle in front of the chalice and light it. Go to the North quarter, pick up the skull, return to the West quarter and set the skull down in front of the candle.

10. Pick up the candle in one hand and the skull in the other. Then recite:

This is the light that was borne from the season before. I accept now the essence of the god.

10. Snuff out the candle with the skull.

11. Taste a small piece of rue root dipped in the wine.

12. Set the cauldron at the North quarter. Fill it with the dried leaves and ignite them. Place an offering in front of the cauldron. Look at the cauldron flames and recite:

Behold the womb of the Goddess of Night, that kindles the Child of the coming year. O symbol of the Mystery by which we return, I honor your Essence, and the magic that emanates from Union with you.

13. Perform gesture of manifestation to the cauldron and recite:

O bring forth the Child of Promise.

14. Retrieve the skull from the West quarter, and holding it, recite:

I shall be secure in the protective power of the god. Not shall I be in want, nor shall I suffer for I am in his care. Therefore I feast and celebrate all in his praise.

15. Celebrate with wine and cakes.

16. Close the ritual circle and snuff out all the candles.

Figure 33. *Venetian Festival Masks. These are modern replicas of traditional Medieval masks used in seasonal rites. From the Clan Umbrea collection.*

WINTER SOLSTICE
(La Festa dell' Inverno)

Items required (in addition to the usual ritual items):

Evergreen wreath
small log of Oak
small "newborn god" Candle for the
    god-flame
Cauldron
Offerings

1. Cast the ritual circle.

2. At the altar, recite:

I mark now at this sacred time, the rebirth of the Sun God. It is the Great Mother who gives him birth. It is the lord of life born again. From the Union of the Lord and Lady, hidden in the Realm of Shadows, comes forth now the Child of Promise!

3. Place the god icon at the North quarter. Perform the Rite of Union to the God image and recite:

I call forth now into the Portal of the Northern Power. I call to the Ancient God, He who brought forth the beasts of field and forest. I call upon the Ancient God, He who was beloved of the ancient tribes.

4. Assume the God Posture and recite:

My Lord, I greet You, O Horned One, horned with the rays of the Sun, by whose blessings and grace shall life always be born again. Behold, I have come before you at this appointed time. Bless me and the days before me. These gifts do I offer you.

5. Set a vessel at the North quarter and place an offering within it.

6. Sit in front of the cauldron and recite:

O most ancient provider, Lord of Light and Life, I pray You grow strong that I may pass the Winter in peace and fullness. Emanate Your warmth and Your Love that the cold and harshness of Winter not dwindle Your followers.

O most ancient One, hear me! Protect and provide in the harshness of these times. I give You adoration and place myself in Your care. Blessed be all in the God!

7. Anoint yourself with oil, and taste the prepared ruta (sprig of rue) saying:

Blessed be in His care.

8. Read the Myth of the Season aloud:

Now the time came, in the Hidden Realm of Shadows, that Diana would bear the Child of the Great Dark Lord. And the Lords of the four corners came and beheld the newborn God. So it came to pass that the Great Lords were brought before the throne of the Dark One. And they spoke, saying: "Do we find You here, O Dianus?" And the Great One replied: "Yes, it is I. Now you have truly seen my two faces." Then Diana spoke to the four Lords, saying: "Take my son who is born of Dianus, that he might bring Life to the World. For the World has grown cold and lifeless." So the Lords of the four corners departed to the world of men, bearing the new Lord of the Sun. And the People rejoiced, for the Lord had come that all upon the earth might be saved.

9. Place a candle in the cauldron and light it. Symbolically give it birth through the cauldron.

10. Once born, take the flame to the East quarter. Present it and proclaim:

Hail, to the newborn Sun. Hail Dianus, Hail Lupercus, Hail Lord of the Sun.

11. Repeat at each quarter.

12. Take the god-flame from the North and make one full pass around the circle again (holding up the god-flame). Upon returning to the North, raise the flame to this quarter. Then set it on the altar.

13. Recite at the altar:

Let the spirit be joyful and the heart to despair not. For on this sacred day is born He whose Light shall save the World. He has come forth from the Darkness and His Light has been seen in the east. He is Lord of Light and Life.

Gesture the horned god sign with your hand toward the god-flame.

Behold the Sacred One, the Child of Promise! He who is born into the World, is slain for the World, and ever rises again!

14. Now the sacred evergreen wreath is brought out and placed before the altar. The small oak log is set in the center of the wreath. The god-flame is then set on top of it (symbolic of the Lord of Light and the Lord of Vegetation, being as one and the same).

16. Extend palms out above the god-flame, and recite:

Behold the God whose life and light dwells within me. He is the Horned One; Lord of the forest, and the Hooded One; Lord of the Harvest, and The Old One; Lord of the Clans. Therefore do I honor Him.

17. The ritual is then concluded with the meal of cakes and wine. Close the circle when finished.

LUPERCUS
(Festa di Lupercus)

Items required (other than the usual ritual items):

   symbolic Wolf skin cloak
   symbolic Deer skin or goat skin strap
      (for scourge)
   small Fur or Skin piece for charging
      chalice (traditionally wolf, or goat)
   a small Candle for personal use
   a Lupercus Torch or Candle
      (for presentation)

1. The Circle is cast in usual manner.

2. Recite the opening for the rite:

I come at this sacred time to give due praise and worship to the Lord of Light. He who was Dianus has risen again, and enters into the World that all the People of the Earth might be saved. I mark now, at this appointed time, the waxing splendor of the young god. He who is Lupercus, Lord of Light, Banisher of Darkness, the Great Golden Wolf.

3. Light a candle from the altar and tread the circle from North, returning North again, as you recite:

Behold the Lord of Light, He who mastered the twelve labors of the Great Lords. He who causes the world to rejoice in his rising. He whose Light brings Salvation to the earth.

4. Go to the East quarter and begin the tonal invocation to the God as you assume the God posture:

Vorte tu apro Osa datae Lupercus! Orphae il athe daei aldus ayeo kae aeto. Nigla gai avato kiel nada omnae, arae il athe okri maedeta, doma akaes lae il ba!

5. Take an unlighted candle and move to the North, pause, then proceed to the South, saying:

O Ancient One, rayed in splendor and horned with power, embrace me for without You I shall surely perish. It is now the appointed time and I offer You this worship. Warm now the sleeping seeds that lie beneath the cool earth, within the womb of the Great Mother. Comfort me and renew my strength! Behold this circle I have prepared; I have lighted the ancient fires, and do faithfully serve you. I await Your emanation of warmth.

At the South quarter you light the candle and then move to the East and place an offering to Lupercus.

6. Move to the East and charge the chalice of wine (wrap it in a fur piece and twist it clockwise, while visualizing the newly kindled sun rise in the wine).

7. Hold up the chalice to the East and say:

   Behold the cool drink of Immortality. For herein is the Essence of Life, and the Giving of Life. Let my heart now be joyful as I drink of the Light of Rejuvenation, receiving this into my blood to be fulfilled.

8. Drink the wine.

9. Recite the closing prayer:

   I now give due praise and adoration unto the Lord of Light. For he is the symbol of the Mystery by which I am reborn again. May I always rejoice at His rising, for by this I am joined to the Essence of Rejuvenation, and Rebirth. Hail and adoration unto You, O Lord of Light

10. Cover yourself with the wolf cloak as you sit before the altar. Extinguish all candles except those on the altar, and open a gateway out of the circle.

11. Take the strap in your dominant hand and say:

    I awaken now to the lash of the God. Thus shall I be purified and rise anew from within.

    Flip the lash over the shoulder, striking the back at least three times. The force of the lash is meant to sting only. Traditionally the breasts, back, and buttocks are struck as well.

12. Conclude the celebration with cakes and wine.

SPRING EQUINOX

(Equinozio della Primavera)

Items required (other than usual):

Cauldron
Torch to represent the "God-Light"
Torch to represent the Goddess'
    returning light
Offerings for the Goddess
a small Cloth (hand size)
a length of red Cord to bind
    statues together
a small white Cloth with a red stain
    (originally a wolf pelt)
a Pouch to hold offerings
a Pouch of Soil
a Pouch of Seed
Seeds intended for blessing and
    planting (you can substitute
    symbols of your needs or desires)

1. Cast the circle in the usual manner,
   then place the god statue at the
   North quarter, along with the pouch
   of seeds. Also place the goddess statue
   at the East quarter, along with the
   pouch of soil.

2. Stand before the altar and say:

   *I mark now with this time of
   gathering, the beginning of the Ascent
   of our Lady from the Hidden Realm
   of Shadows. For this is the time of Her
   desire for the Light and Life of the*
   *World. I mark also the death of the
   wolf god, and the splendor of the new
   young god, rayed in power, Lord of
   the Sky.*

   Perform the Rite of Union to the altar
   (gazing upon the statues or symbolic
   torches). Then place the seeds upon
   the white cloth stained with a red
   mark, and bless the seeds for planting:

   *Blessed be these seeds in the names of
   Diana and Dianus. May they grow
   strong and abundant, providing a
   bountiful harvest for all. In the names
   of Diana and Dianus, so be it done.*

   Return the pouch of seeds to the
   North quarter.

3. Recite the Myth of the Ascent:

   *Now it came to pass that Diana
   longed for the Light of the World, and
   for Her many Children. And she
   departed from the Hidden Realm, in
   secret, leaving the Dark Lord in His
   solitude.*

   *In the Hidden Realm of Shadows
   Diana would bear the Child of the
   Great Dark Lord. And the Lords of
   the Four Corners came and beheld the
   newborn God. Then they spoke to
   Diana of the misery of the People who*

lived upon the World, and how they suffered in cold and in darkness. So Diana bid the Lords to carry Her son to the World, and so the People rejoiced for the Sun God had returned.

And it came to pass that Diana longed for the Light of the World, and for Her many Children. So She journeyed to the World and was welcomed in great celebration.

Then Diana saw the splendor of the new god as He crossed the heavens, and she desired Him. But each night He returned to the Hidden Realm and could not see the beauty of the goddess in the night sky.

So one morning the Goddess arose as the God came up from the Hidden Realm and She bathed nude in the sacred lake of Nemi. Then the Lords of the Four Corners appeared to Him and said: "Behold the sweet beauty of the Goddess of the Earth." And He looked upon Her and was struck with Her beauty so that He descended upon the earth in the form of a great stag.

"I have come to play beside your bath," He said, but Diana gazed upon the stag and said: "You are not a stag,

but a god!" Then He answered: "I am Faunus, god of the forest. Yet as a I stand upon the World I touch also the sky and I am Lupercus the sun, who banishes the Wolf Night. But beyond all of this I am Dianus, the firstborn of all the Gods!"

Diana smiled and stepped forth from the water in all Her beauty. "I am Fana, goddess of the forest, yet even as I stand before you I am Jana, goddess of the moon. But beyond all this I am Diana, first born of all Goddesses!"

And Dianus took Her by the hand and together they walked in the meadows and forests telling their tales of ancient mysteries. They loved and were One and together They ruled over the World. Yet even in love, Diana knew that the god would soon cross over to the Hidden realm and Death would come to the World. Then must She descend and embrace the Dark Lord, and bear the fruit of their Union.

4. At the North quarter, hold up the statue of the god, and say:

   Where is my Lady?

5. Set the statue down, and beginning at the North and bearing a lighted candle,

move to each quarter. Then, passing the North again, stop at the East quarter.

6. Hold out the candle to the North and say:

O Dark One, Your Lady comes to me and I welcome Her with great rejoicing. All living things do know that She is near and the world stirs with Life again. The Lady journeys now to return Her Essence to the forest, field, and glen.

7. Pick up the statue of the Goddess and say:

Hear me, for now I draw near! Hear me, all who sleep from Winter's embrace, awaken unto rebirth, come forth now. Receive now my essence and be full with Life, and the desire for Life.

8. Set the statue down, extend your palms over it, and say:

O Great Goddess of the earth, return in Your fair nature, lovely Maiden of Youth, and Joy and Love. Only You can break the spell of Winter, and enchant the Earth with Your Essence. Hail to the Great Goddess!

9. Take the pouch of soil and attach it to the goddess statue. Retrieve the god statue and seed pouch from the North quarter. Set it next to the goddess statue and attach the seed pouch to the god statue. Take a red cord and bind the statues together as a couple.

10. Open the pouch and pour a small amount of wine into it. Next open the pouch of seeds and push some seeds into the damp soil. Then take out the mixture and place it on a small cloth. Set the cloth into the cauldron (East quarter). Place the wand into the cauldron, gesture the triangle of manifestation over the cauldron, and say:

Blessed be the Plow, the Seed, and the Furrow.

11. Set the bound statues in front of the cauldron and say:

Behold the Beauty of the Goddess, She who is Fana, Lady of the Earth; She who is Jana, Mistress of the Moon; She who is Diana, Ruler of the Universe!

Behold the Power of the God. He who is Faunus, Lord of the earth; He who is Lupercus, Master of the Heavens; He who is Dianus, Ruler of the Universe!

12. Place your personal offering into the cauldron. Prayers, requests, or blessings may be offered now.

13. Take a lighted candle and, beginning at the North, tread the circle to all points three times.

14. Gesture the triangle of manifestation over the cauldron and statues, saying:

    You are truly the Power in all things.
    You are the earth, the sky, and beyond.

15. The celebration concludes with wine and cakes. Afterward, the items within the cauldron are collected and placed within a pouch or bag. To *charge* the area with fertile energy, bury the pouch in a planting field (for an increase of crops) or suspend it from a tree within the woods (for an abundant hunt). You can adapt this part of the ritual to your personal needs. For example, you may wish to carry the pouch hidden on your body when going for a job interview, seeking a home loan, or appearing in court.

DIANA'S DAY
(La Giornata di Diana)

Items required:

A small crown of Flowers
a small Candle
a fresh Flower
Ritual Sword

1. The circle is cast in the usual manner.

2. Give the address at the altar:

    At this joyous time I welcome the return of my Lady. That which began in the Time of Shadows has come to its fullness. Cycle unto Cycle, Time unto Time, Age unto Age.

    As it was in the time of the beginning, so is it now, so shall it be.

3. Move to the Southern quarter, and give the address:

    By and by all things pass, season unto season, year unto year. The Lady has come again to Her Hidden Children of Time. And the Goddess ever bestows love and peace, and guards and cherishes Her Hidden Children in Life.

    In Death She teaches the way to Her Communion, and in this world She teaches the mystery of the magic circle, which is placed between the worlds of men and of the gods. And for this the Lady descended, in times of old, into the Realm of Shadows.

And the Lord of the Shadows was bewitched by Her Beauty. And He taught Her the mysteries of Death and Rebirth. And in love He bowed before Her and gave Her all of His Power.

Place the crown of flowers on the head of the goddess statue. Perform the Rite of Union facing the Goddess statue.

4. Lay down the sword in front of the statue and say:

My lady, all power is given to You, for this is so ordained. And with love there is submission to Your ways, and reign is given over into Your hands.

5. Recite the Charge of Aradia:

"Whenever you have need of anything, once in the month when the moon is full, then shall you come together at some deserted place, or where there are woods, and give worship to She who is Queen of all Witches.

"Come all together inside a circle, and secrets that are as yet unknown shall be revealed. And your mind must be free and also your spirit, and as a sign that you are truly free, you shall be naked in your rites. And you shall rejoice and sing, making music and love. For this is the essence of spirit, and the knowledge of joy.

"Be true to your own beliefs, and keep to the Ways, beyond all obstacles. For ours is the key to the mysteries and the cycle of rebirth, which opens the way to the Womb of Enlightenment. I am the spirit of Witches all, and this is joy and peace and harmony.

"In life does the Queen of all Witches reveal the knowledge of spirit. And from death does the Queen deliver you to peace.

"When I shall have departed from this world, in memory of me make cakes of grain, wine and honey. These shall you shape like the moon, and then partake of wine and cakes all in my memory. For I have been sent to you by the Spirits of Old, and I have come that you might be delivered from all slavery. I am the daughter of the sun and moon, and even though I have been born into this world, my race is of the stars.

"Give offerings all to She who is our mother. For She is the beauty of the Green Wood, and the light of the moon among the stars, and the mystery which gives life, and always calls us to come together in Her name.

"Let Her worship be the ways within your heart, for all acts of love and pleasure are like rituals to the Goddess. But to all who seek her, know that your seeking and desire will reward you not, until you realize the secret. Because if that which you seek is not found within your inner self, you will never find it from without. For she has been with you since you entered into the ways, and she is that which awaits at your journey's end."

6. Move to the east quarter and recite:

Hail and adoration O Great Diana! You who are the Great Moon Goddess, Queen of Heaven, Lady of the earth, I welcome You, and rejoice in Your presence.

Place a fresh flower before the goddess statue, kiss the statue, and say:

Blessed be all in the Goddess.

7. Then take a chalice of wine, whisper the name of the goddess upon the surface of the wine, and then drink.

8. The ritual celebration continues with cakes and wine.

SUMMER FEST
(La Festa dell'Estate)

Items required (in addition to standard ritual setup):

Flowers for procession
Symbol for God and Goddess
Cauldron
Libation fluid (Nectar/ambrosia)
4 small bowls for Libation (at quarters)
offerings (one for Deities and another
    for Nature spirits)
Fennel stalk
Sorghum stalk

1. Cast the circle in the usual manner.

2. Open a threshold at the Northeast point.

3. Pass through the threshold, tossing flowers as you enter.

4. Seal the threshold.

5. At the altar recite:

I come on this sacred night of Summer's Eve, and join myself to the powers and forces of this mystical season. On this night the Folletti gather as do all those spirits of Nature to which I am kindred. For the Witch and the Fata are of a similar Race. So it was in the time of our beginning, so is it now, so shall it be.

6. Symbols of the God and Goddess are placed before the cauldron, which is set at the Southern quarter. Then recite:

Here is the Divine Couple, whose Union gives Life to the World. Blessed be all in the God and Goddess.

Perform the Rite of Union facing the symbols.

7. Place Deity offerings in the cauldron, at the South quarter.

8. Go to each of the four quarters and pour a libation of nectar into the bowls set there for libation.

9. Place Nature spirit offerings at the four quarters.

10. Recite from the altar:

O spirits of the Elemental forces, hear me, and receive these blessings. O spirits of the earth, O powers that be, hear me and receive these blessings.

Assist me on this sacred night to maintain the natural balance that keeps vital the essence of the earth. Let there always be clear, flowing water, freshness in the air, fertility in the soil, and abundant life within the world.

11. Perform the drama play of the struggle between the forces of Light and Darkness. (The fennel stalk represents the powers of Light and the sorghum stalk represents the powers of Darkness.) Hold the stalks in an "X" formation out in front of you. Beginning at the East quarter, walk around the circle, ending at the North. At the completion, the sorghum stalk is broken and the fennel stalk is raised in victory. Then present the fennel stalk at each quarter, saying:

Blessed be the power of Light. Blessed be the power of Life.

12. Place the cauldron at the east quarter. Snip off an inch or two of the fennel stalk and place it in the cauldron, along with some powdered incense. Light the incense and recite:

I release the power of light, the waxing force, whereby I charge You, O Sacred Ether of our world. Be free of all evil and negativity. I charge you for the good of all life within our world.

13. Visualize the power of light rising up on the smoke of the incense. Mentally direct the power up into the ether of the Community.

14. End the ritual with celebration of cakes and wine. Close the circle. Leave libation bowls out over night for the Nature spirits.

It is said that on the night of Summer's Eve, all the spirits of nature in celebration. Fairies, elves, and all the "little folk" gather in meadows, forests, and any secret or hidden place. If you see them or can find any evidence of their celebration the next day, then you will receive a special blessing. Should you come across any of their gathering sites, be sure not to disturb anything. Leave everything as you found it.

CORNUCOPIA

Items required (other than the usual ritual items):

1 Cornucopia icon
Offerings for the harvest
Cornucopia incense
Cauldron

1. The circle is cast in the usual manner.

2. At the altar recite:

I come on this appointed day in anticipation of plenty. I acknowledge the Grace of the Earth Mother and the Sky Father. From Him have I received the Sacred Emanation, which the Mother has nurtured, and delivers unto me.

Perform the Rite of Union to the altar torches/symbols of the God and Goddess.

3. Place offerings at the South, and recite:

It is good and right to give offerings to the Great God and Goddess. It is proper to give thanks of all that is good in my life. For the Great Ones provide for me, and I must always remember Them and give thanks.

4. Light the cauldron at the South quarter and place a token of your needs/requests in the flames. They may be written on parchment or cloth, and burned in the cauldron fire.

5. Place the cauldron before the altar and pour sweet incense into the cauldron flames, saying:

I call out to You, O Diana and Dianus, and pray that You receive my wishes and desires as they rise up to you on the smoke of this incense. I ask that You grant my requests and bring them to their fullness, even as You bring forth the fruit from the seed. In your names, so be it done.

6. Sit before the cauldron and recite:

I speak now the words of Aradia, the Holy Strega: "Know that every action brings forth another, and that these actions are linked together through their natures. Therefore, whatsoever you send forth, so shall you receive. A farmer can harvest for himself no more than he plants. Therefore, let us consider what is good in our lives, and what is full. Let us also consider what is bad and what is empty. And let us meditate upon the reasons for all of these things."

7. Bless the ritual cakes and wine. Lift up the wand, saying:

Blessed be the plow.

Then lift up the chalice, saying:

Blessed be the furrow.

Lower the wand into the wine, saying:

Herein is the Essence of the Union of Dianus and Diana, wherein all things are renewed and made vital.

Trace an "X" over the cakes, hold out palm of left hand over them and say:

Here is the substance of the Union of Dianus and Diana, wherein all things are established and renewed.

8. Place the cakes and wine on the altar, and say:

In the names of Diana and Dianus, blessed be these symbols. Blessed be the Plow, the Seed, and the Furrow. Blessed be your mysteries.

9. Conclude ritual with celebration of wine and cakes feast.

AUTUMN EQUINOX
(Equinozio di Autunno)

Required items:

A white Candle to represent
   the god-flame
Ruta (sprig of rue)
Receiving Vessel for grain "essence"
Cauldron for Offerings (west quarter)
Grain and Pouch
loaf of Bread
red Cord to tie around god candle
   on altar
Oak leaves and vessel to contain them
Slain God icon
Goddess icon

1. The circle is cast in the usual manner.

2. At the altar recite the following:

I come at this sacred time to rejoice for the abundance which has come into the world. Yet also to honor Dianus, the Lord who is sacrificed for my sake. The time has come when all things have grown into their fullness, and are gathered by hunter and fieldsman. As it was in the time of our beginning, so is it now, so shall it be.

3. Stand at the East quarter and then move to the West, bearing the god-flame candle and reciting:

Farewell, O Lord of Two Faces, who stands in the Light and within the Darkness. The Hidden God who ever remains, and ever departs to the Hidden Realm through the Gate of Shadows; Ruler of the Heights and of the Depths. Farewell O Lord of the Earth. Within You is the Union of humankind with the Gods. You dwell within the Sacred Seed, the seed of ripened grain and the seed of flesh. You are hidden in the Earth, and You rise up to touch the stars.

4. Tie the pouch of grain to your waist cord, positioning it to hang above the genital area. Take the god-flame candle and move around the circle three times, beginning at the North quarter.

5. Go to the West quarter carrying the god-flame. Remove the pouch suspended from your waist, and place it in the receiving vessel set within the Cauldron of Offering.

6. Extinguish the god-flame with a sprig of rue, and then recite:

The God has departed from His shining abode in the heavens, for the Season has come. And Death shall come to the world for the Winter draws near. The Lord of Light now becomes the Lord of the Shadows.

7. A vessel is brought out and placed in the West. Place some oak leaves within it and then taste some of the grain placed beside the vessel.

8. Recite:

In the earliest times, the Lord and Lady lived in the ancient forest of Nemi. The Lady seduced the Lord and there did She receive the Sacred Seed from which all things spring forth.

But the Lord knew not the secret which only the Goddess understood, for She had drawn the Life from Him. And the World was abundant with all manner of animal, and that which grows from the earth.

Now there came a time when all things grew to their fullness, and were to be gathered by hunter and fieldsman alike. And in that time was the God slain and drawn into the Harvest.

9. Place the Slain God icon at the North quarter, along with the Goddess icon. Here you will begin the sacred dialogue holding up the appropriate icon in both hands as you recite:

Goddess: *I have come in search of Thee, is this where I begin?*

God: *Begin to seek me out, and I shall become as small as a seed, so you may but pass me by.*

Goddess: *Then I shall split the rind, crack the grain, and break the pod.*

God: *But I shall hide beneath the earth, and lay so still, that you may but pass me by.*

Goddess: *Then I shall raise you up in praise, and place upon you a mantle of Green.*

God: *But I shall hide within the Green, and cover myself, and you may but pass me by.*

Goddess: *Then I shall tear the husk, and pull the root and thresh the chaff.*

God: *But I shall scatter, and divide, and be so many, that you may but pass me by.*

Goddess: *Then I shall gather you in, and bind you whole, and make you One again.*

11. Place the Sacred Bread Loaf on the altar.

12. Holding the ritual dagger pointed at the loaf, recite:

Behold the Harvest Lord. Blessed be the Lord of the Harvest.

13. Plunge the dagger into the loaf, and then cut the loaf into eight pieces. Then recite:

Behold the Lord, the Green Man, the Stag King, the Hooded Man. Now is he taken within, to be as One again.

14. Eat one piece of the loaf, and drink a portion of red wine. Recite:

With this I am now as One with Him. I am of the Sacred Blood. That which was, at the time of beginning, is now, and always shall be.

15. Place a piece of the loaf at each of the four quarters. The remaining three pieces represent the three aspects of the God: Hooded One, Horned One, and Old One. Bury these in the garden, in a fertile field, or in the woods.

The celebration concludes with cakes and wine.

The rue used in this ritual is taken from the whole plant, of which two pieces are used at the Autumn Equinox, and the rest dried and saved for Winter Solstice. It is the symbol of Death and Rebirth, Waxing and Waning, it is the God-Root Plant. This plant is grown from the seed planted at the Spring Equinox.

RUNIC RITES AND SYMBOLS

Almost every secret society possesses a secret alphabet or set of symbols. Generally speaking, the purpose of such symbols is to evoke a sense of mystery when employing them. This act helps to attune and align the mind, establishing the fact that the person has now entered into something no longer mundane. It marks the moment with an occult mentality, and the symbols draw upon ancient currents of energy waiting within our genetic memory.

Secret alphabets are also used to hide various writings from prying eyes. The well-known Theban Script, also known as the Witches' Alphabet, is one such example. During the sixteenth century the famous Italian Occultist Giovanni Porta employed a secret alphabet used by Italian Witches. In 1589 Porta published his famous classic text on astrology and natural magic titled *Magiae Naturalis Libri Viginti*. His writings were greatly influenced by the works of Plato, Empedocles, Pythagoras, and various Hermetic writings of the period. Porta later founded a magickal fraternity in Naples.

Most historians believe that runes originated in the Neolithic period where we find symbols carved upon rocks. The earliest and most abundant examples are found in northern Italy, Austria, and Germany. The so-called Manx runes originated in Sicily and were brought with the Normans when they invaded the Isle of Man. Some historians believe that Germanic and Celtic runes were simply crude attempts by these primitive people to copy Latin letters.

THE TUSCAN WITCHES' SCRIPT

The runic alphabet (Figure 34) pictured on the opposite page is an archaic form of the Etruscan alphabet used by many hereditary Italian Witches. It can be employed to preserve secret material from prying eyes, or to mark tools and other ritual objects. The runes can also be used to label bottles or jars containing potions or herbal mixtures. The main thing to remember is that this is a religious script. Therefore it should not be used for mundane non-Craft purposes.

THE TUSCAN WITCHES' RUNES

In Stregheria there exists a set of runic symbols employed for divination. The runes are cast upon a glyph or chart symbolizing the macrocosmic and microcosmic universe as reflected in Strega cosmology (see Figure 35, p. 142). The inner circle of the glyph relates to personal relationships and our place in the microcosmic universe. The outer circle corresponds to our interaction in the world, the macrocosmic universe of our greater life experience. The glyph might be reproduced on a large sheet of paper, or painted or drawn on a cloth or canvas; from 14 to 18 inches square is a convenient size.

Each circle is divided into four sections relating to the four cardinal points: North, East, South, West. The inner circle encloses *family,* intimate *relationships, opposing forces* in relationships, and the *inner self.* The outer circle encompasses the *foundation* or powers working in one's life, accumulated *spirituality,* forces working against one in his or her life, and *transformation.*

Thirty-three stones are used in this form of divination, twenty-seven of which are inscribed with ancient runic symbols. Each rune has a specific meaning attached to it (see Figure 36, p. 143). These symbols are called the Tuscan Runes. Three of the noninscribed stones are black and three more are white. One noninscribed stone is gray. The black and white stones represent negative and positive influences in one's life. The gray stone belongs to the weather magick group of four stones and represents draught. There are also two marker stones indicating gender, one is wand-shaped (masculine) and the other bowl-shaped (feminine).

To begin divination, the glyph is laid out on the ground. Incense is lighted and a prayer is spoken, asking for divine guidance.

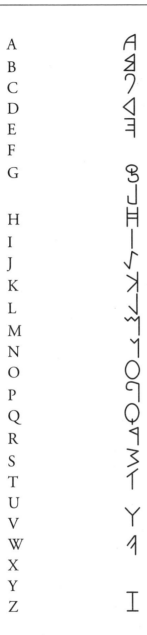

A	
B	
C	
D	
E	
F	
G	
H	
I	
J	
K	
L	
M	
N	
O	
P	
Q	
R	
S	
T	
U	
V	
W	
X	
Y	
Z	

Figure 34. *The Tuscan Script*

The appropriate gender stone is set on the intersecting lines of the "X" in the center of the inner circle. Then four black stones and four white stones are picked up, cupped between both hands, and mixed thoroughly by shaking them up and down. When the time feels right, the stones are lightly tossed up in the air, directly over the center of the glyph. The position in which they fall provides an overview of the forces of light and darkness operating in one's life.

Look closely at the pattern of black and white stones, noting in which circle they have landed. This will tell the diviner where negative and positive forces are most active. Any stones that fall outside of the glyph are disregarded. Note whether there are more of one color stone than another, as this will reveal the balance (or imbalance) of positive and negative. If two or more stones fall into one section of an outer or inner circle, this depicts a very strong influence at work in the associated section. Take special note if stones land in the inner circle and occupy the inner self section. This is an indication of the mindset of the individual for whom you are reading runes.

Once you have determined the balance of the forces of light and darkness, it is time to proceed with the divination of particular aspects. Set aside the weather rune stones, along with all of the black and white stones. Take the remaining twenty-seven stones and mix them thoroughly in a bag. Then reach

Figure 35. *Tuscan Runes would be cast on a Divination Glyph such as this, and the runes positions read as explained on pages 140–145.*

△ Earth; Unseen Forces	⊤ Sacrifice for Enlightenment	⊖ Good Weather
Sun; Mundane Forces	Power	3 Black Stones
Moon; Unseen Forces	Beginnings/Gains	3 White Stones
Star; Divine Activity	Severance/ Destruction	Transformation
Union	Passages	Fertility
Abundance	Serpent; Masculine	Death
→ Strife	Broom; Feminine	Dragon; Ability to Create or Destroy
Contentment	Storm	Occult Influences
Magical Portal; Magical Transformation	Rain	Cycles
Spiritual Portal; Religious Transformation	Draught (blank stone)	Pentagram; Protection, Harmony of the Elements

Figure 36. *The Tuscan Runes*

into the bag and draw out three stones. Cup these stones between your hands and toss them up over the center of the glyph, then observe where the stones have landed. Any stones that have fallen outside of the glyph are disregarded. Stones that have fallen together in the same section are interpreted both individually and together concerning their symbolism. The reading always begins from the circle into which the most colored stones first fell, then from the most occupied section in a clockwise manner.

As an example, consider the following stones and their placement. The original colored stones dominated the inner circle, and the majority of stones fell in the family section, so we begin reading there. Three randomly picked stones are now tossed: *magical portal, sacrifice for enlightenment,* and *transformation.* The *portal* stone and *sacrifice* stone fall together in the family section, inner circle. The *transformation* stone falls in spirituality, outer circle. If any white or black stones originally fell in any of these sections, then this would shift the interpretation to positive or negative influences.

For our example, two black stones fell in *family* and one white stone in *spirituality.* Therefore we read the *portal* stone as a negative event initiated by immediate family, leading to an existing or entering situation. The sacrifice stone is read as a selfish or negative sacrifice (because of the black stone). Since the two stones occupy the same section we read them again as a negative/selfish sacrifice leading to a negative ending or beginning. However, the stone of transformation laying in the spirituality section tells us (because of the original white stone) that this event leads to positive growth for the individual concerned.

To continue the reading, the stones are tossed four more times (three stones per casting). Each time the stones that were cast are mixed back into the bag of stones. After the fifth toss, a total of fifteen stones will have been cast. All that remains now is to cast the final outcome stone. In Tuscan cosmology there are sixteen spheres of occult influence, therefore the final stone completes the divinatory cycle. Mix the stones thoroughly inside the bag and draw out one that you have chosen using your intuition. Hold it out over the center of the glyph and flip it in the manner of flipping a coin. Read the position of the stone in context with the position of the other stones and the section in which it rests. If the stone lands outside of the glyph, you can try again one or two more times. If by the third toss the stone still lands outside of the glyph, then this is understood to mean that hidden forces are working against the outcome of the reading. The outcome is therefore undefined and delayed for the time being. Seven days (one lunar phase) must pass before reading again for the same purpose.

If no outcome can be read in the stones, then the person needs to perform personal purification before the stones can be tossed again. Offerings should be placed on the Lare shrine to ensure positive ancestral influences. It is wise also for the person to take magickal steps to charge an amulet or talisman for protection. Offerings to the Morae for good fortune, or to Bona Dea, are also a good idea. Wait at least seven days before performing the reading again. Seven is the period of astral flux. In other words, it takes seven days for energy forms to take shape or dissolve in the astral medium. After seven days the new astral formations can be discerned through continued divination.

SEA MAGICK RUNES

Since ancient times Witches have been associated with various bodies of water such as wells, springs, lakes, ponds, and even the ocean itself. Metaphysically speaking, water represents the subconscious mind and the emotions. The Witch is often the enchantress or guardian of the setting in which we find the water. The myths and legends from which we draw such tales retain the ancient memory of the powers of Witchcraft.

Italian Witches have long employed for magickal purposes the powers and forces inherent in the sea. The sea is deeply connected through ocean tides to the cycles of moon. In the coastal region of central Italy the Janarric Witches devised a set of symbols through which spells can be cast by drawing upon the power of the sea. Symbols are painted or etched on shells (see Figure 37, p. 146). The shells are then left on the sand to be carried out by the tide. In this manner the sea receives the spell and empowers it.

The phase of the moon is always considered when casting sea spells. Magick, for the gain of something, is performed during the waxing phase. Magick for the loss of something is employed when the moon is waning. When pure raw power is desired, the time of the full moon is best. Offerings to the god and goddess are also left on the sand when asking for their favors. Traditional offerings include white flowers, pearls, or silver objects. A traditional devotional offering is simply a large shell filled with nectar (a mixture of equal parts milk and wine, mixed with a little honey), which is set upon the shore.

Sea magick runes can be painted on shells for spell casting. You can use either food coloring or the juice of a dark berry (the rune has to dissolve in the sea water). Take a dry shell and paint the appropriate symbol on it corresponding to the desired outcome of the spell. Place the shell on the shore in a place where the tide will eventually pass the waves over it. Surround the shell with an offering of flowers to sea deities and then state your request. Note the phase of the moon and the zodiac sign it occupies; you will want to employ the occult correspondences of these associations.

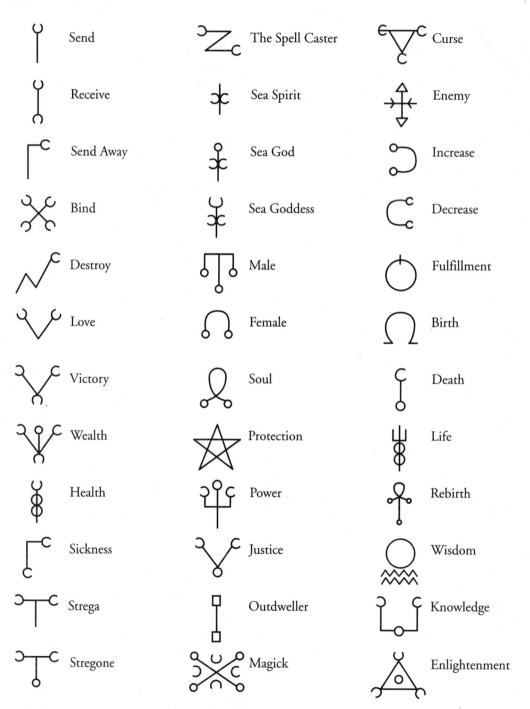

Send	The Spell Caster	Curse
Receive	Sea Spirit	Enemy
Send Away	Sea God	Increase
Bind	Sea Goddess	Decrease
Destroy	Male	Fulfillment
Love	Female	Birth
Victory	Soul	Death
Wealth	Protection	Life
Health	Power	Rebirth
Sickness	Justice	Wisdom
Strega	Outdweller	Knowledge
Stregone	Magick	Enlightenment

Figure 37. *Sea Magick Runes*

Employing magick for constructive purposes, or for the gain of something, is most effective when the moon is full or waxing. Spells designed for decline, dissolution, or cursing are best performed when the moon is waning. Zodiac signs imprint stellar energy on lunar energy as the moon enters a constellation's sphere of influence. Ancient occultists assigned specific effects to the moon as follows:

Moon in:

Taurus, Virgo, or Capricorn: all works involving the supernatural may be performed

Aries, Leo, Sagittarius: all works of love and friendship

Cancer, Scorpio, Pisces: all works involving binding/crossing

Gemini, Libra, Aquarius: all works of an unusual nature

When the shell is in place, draw a triangle around it in the sand (enclosing the shell completely.) The symbol on the shell must be face up. Now you are ready to speak the words of enchantment before you depart from the area:

> *Goddess of moon, earth, and the sea,*
> *each wish in thy name, must come to*
> *be.*
> *Powers and forces which tides do*
> *make,*

> *now summon thy waves, my spell*
> *to take.*

Besides the use of shells and runes, there are other ways to employ sea magick. To gain favor with the Goddess, form your name on the sand with white flower petals, and let the tide take the flowers. This is always recommended for new initiates of self-dedicants. Witches have long been associated with the sea, and ancient sailors even bought bags of wind from Witches before setting sail. The calm or storm of the sea has often been linked to Witchcraft in ancient legends. In all of this we see an intimate connection between Witches and the ocean.

Evil spells or bindings can be broken by sea magick. To do so, build a tower of sand near the water. Collect three dark shells and mark one with a rune indicating the nature of the spell you wish to break. Place this shell in between the other two shells. On the outer shells place the rune indicating either "send away" or "destroy" (see Figure 37, p. 146).

To help a soul return to physical life, find a white shell and mark upon it the name of the person who died. Above the name, place the symbol of their zodiac sign. Next set four smaller shells around the person's shell so that you have formed an elemental cross. On the North quarter shell, mark the symbol of the soul. On the East quarter shell place the symbol of rebirth. The South quarter shell is then marked with the symbol of fulfillment, and the West quarter shell is painted with the symbol of life. To conclude, lay a circle of nine red roses around the shells. This symbolizes the gestation period of the human fetus, and red is the color of blood connecting the spell to birth.

STAR MAGICK RUNES

Star magick, astrology, and astronomy are very old arts dating back to the cultures of ancient Mesopotamia. Occult manuscripts of the Middle Ages and Renaissance periods pictured many ancient symbols and designs related to the stars. Many of the old myths tell of the gods who came from the stars, particularly those of ancient Egypt. The famous occult text of the Renaissance period, known as *The Book of the Secrets of Enoch,* tells us that writing itself was first taught to humans by a race of gods who descended from Mt. Hennon. Remnants of this mythos are related to various Greek legends surrounding the Titans.

Among some Hereditary Italian Witches, a star alphabet commonly found in grimoires of the Renaissance period is often employed (see Figure 38). These Witches also use previously nonpublished magickal star runes (see Figure 39, p. 150). The Tanarric Witches of Italy, who call themselves "star Witches," are the clan that typically use these runes.

Star runes of the magickal variety are normally used to mark ritual tools, objects, or ritual settings in general. They can be drawn

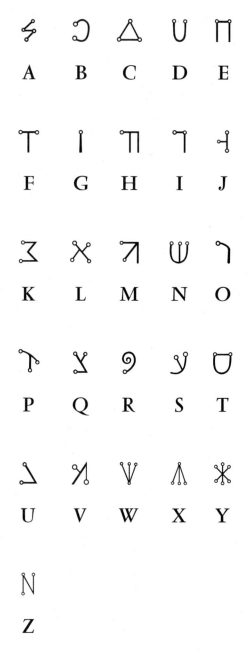

Figure 38. *Runic Star Alphabet*

upon paper and placed in the cauldron for spell casting. One of the oldest methods of using star runes involved tracing the lines in the sand or earth, and placing torches or candles in the circular areas of the symbol. This was designed to mimic the stars, and thereby draw down their magickal influence. Stones or pebbles were sometimes used to mark out the connective lines running from each circle. This made the entire design more visible at night, which was naturally the prescribed time for employing star magick.

Constellations are considered powerful zones of occult energy. In the Craft, talismanic symbols are linked to a table of correspondences through mystical symbols (see Figure 40, p. 151). The following correlations are traditionally applied in works of magick related to the stars.

Cauda Ursae

Metal: Silver or Copper
Stone: Lodestone
Herb: Mugwort, Chicory, Periwinkle
Charm: Wolf tooth
Image: Bull

Cauda Ursa is of the nature of Venus and the moon. When bound to a ring it is said to generate love and friendship. It is also said to protect the traveler and to draw like-minded persons.

Ala Corvi

(Gienah in the wings of the crow)
Metal: Silver or Lead
Stone: Black onyx
Herbs: Comfrey, Henbane
Charm: Frog
Image: Raven

Ala Corvi is of the nature of Mars and Saturn. When bound to a ring it is said to restrict or bind another person's magick. It is also said to give power over spirits.

Spica

(First magnitude star in Virgo)
Metal: Copper
Stone: Emerald
Herb: Sage, Mandrake
Charm: A shaft of wheat
Image: A bird clasping a jewel

Spica is of the nature of Venus and Mercury. Its influence is similar to Cauda Ursa, but also binds enemies and enhances telepathy.

Pleiades

Metal: Quicksilver
Stone: Crystal, Diodocus
Herbs: Fennel, Diacedon
Charm: Pentacle
Image: A torch

Pleiades is of the nature of the Moon and Mars. Its influence is similar to Ala Corvi except that its powers are manifest within the earth and sea. Its major influence is upon Nature through the forces behind Nature.

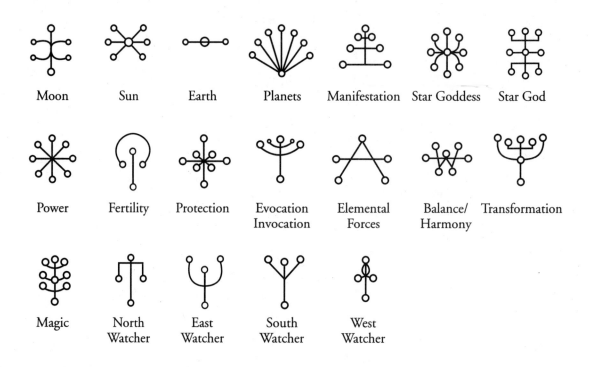

Figure 39. *Magickal Star Runes*

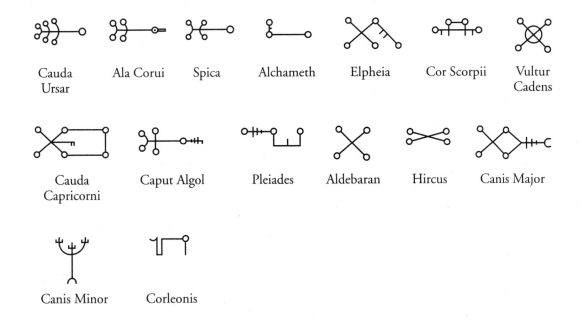

Figure 40. *Talismanic Star Symbols*

Canis Major

Metal: Silver
Stone: Beryl
Herbs: Mugwort, Dragonswort
Image: Hunting dog

Canis Major is of the nature of Cancer and Venus. Its influence is upon the subconscious mind, and the emotions. It is said to aid in the development of psychic powers.

Canis Minor

Metal: Quicksilver
Stone: Agate
Herb: Pennyroyal
Image: A cock

Canis Minor is of the nature of Mercury and Mars. When bound to a ring it is said to bind another's Witchcraft, and to bring the aid of the gods and spirits.

Hircus

(Capella in Auriga)
Metal: Tin
Stone: Sapphire
Herb: Horehound, Mandrake
Image: A minstrel

Hircus is of the nature of Jupiter and Saturn. It is said to draw the favor of authorities, and to aid in the healing of bones and teeth.

Aldebaran

Metal: Iron
Stone: Ruby
Herb: Milky thistle
Image: An ascending god

Aldebaran is of the nature of Venus and Mars. It is said to be destructive and binding, yet it protects and defends magickally.

Caput Algol

Metal: Lead
Stone: Diamond
Herb: Mugwort
Image: A severed head

Caput Algol is of the nature of Saturn and Jupiter. When bound to a ring it is said to protect against another's Witchcraft. It can turn spells back upon their senders. It also vitalizes the physical body.

Elpheia

Metal: Copper
Stone: Topaz
Herb: Rosemary
Image: A crowned person

Elpheia is of the nature of Venus and Mars. It can bind one's sexuality, causing them to be chaste. It can also generate love and goodwill.

Alchameth

Metal: Iron
Stone: Jasper
Herb: Plantain
Image: A leaping wolf

Alchameth is of the nature of Mars and Jupiter. Its influence is upon the blood system. It is also said to be effective against fevers.

Cor Leonis

(Regulus in Leo)
Metal: Iron
Stone: Garnet or Granite
Herb: Mastic, Mugwort
Image: A cat sitting on a throne

Cor Leonis is of the nature of Jupiter and Mars. It is said to influence temperaments in a positive manner.

Cor Scorpii

(Antares in Scorpio)
Metal: Iron
Stone: Amethyst
Herb: Saffron
Image: A scorpion

Cor Scorpii is of the nature of Jupiter and Mars. When bound to a ring it is said to bind or drive away evil spirits.

Vultur Cadens

(Vega in Lyra)
Metal: Tin
Stone: Chrysolite
Herb: Succory
Image: Descending vulture

Vultur Cadens is of the nature of Venus and Mercury. Its influence is over beasts and evil spirits.

Cauda Capricorni

Metal: Lead
Stone: Chalcedony
Herb: Catnip, Marjoram
Image: A goat

Cauda Capricorni is of the nature of Saturn and Mercury. Its influence is upon physical or material wealth.

MOON SPIRIT SYMBOLS

In Italian Witchcraft we employ the spirits of the moon to aid in our magickal workings. The ceremonial sigils appearing in this system were most likely derived from such occult texts as *The Key of Solomon* and other manuscripts dating from the Middle Ages through the Renaissance periods. As we saw in chapter one, the records of the Inquisition reveal that Italian Witches in Venice were copying from *The Key of Solomon* circa 1654.

The first step in securing the aid of these spirits is to evoke the assistance of Ofanius, a moon spirit who turns the *wheel of the moon*. What this refers to is the occult mechanism operating within the etheric substance of lunar emanations. The wheel thus brings into play the influences of the moon spirits. Then we may call upon any of the twenty-eight spirits of the Moon Mansions (see symbols, Figure 41, p. 156).

Ofanius can be evoked by drawing his symbol upon a piece of paper with dark food coloring. Then drop the paper into a steaming cup of herbal tea, so that his symbol dissolves and rises up into the steam. Traditionally you will say something like:

> *Hear me Ofanius, by all the names*
> *that you obey, I call upon you now to*

aid me in my work of magick. Turn now your wheel and grant me entrance to the portals that open up into the realm of the twenty-eight spirits of the moon.

To evoke the other spirits, simply draw their symbol inside a triangle placed at the west quarter of your ritual circle. The symbol must be drawn on the outside of a glass bottle filled with purified water. Burn an incense containing camphor, and recite an evocation of this nature, stating what it is you wish the spirit to do on your behalf:

Hear me _____, spirit of the moon, come now to my aid by the names Ofanius, Phius, Lucinus, and Mensus, and by the name Diana at whose utterance do we all give bended knee. I call upon you now to

_____.

Once this is completed, place an offering of white flowers into the bottle of water. When evoking moon spirits you will naturally want to call upon the appropriate spirit who has power over the outcome you desire. The associations that follow this section are the most common in the old grimoires.

THE LUNAR MANSIONS

The Lunar Mansions are marked by the constellations through which the moon seemingly passes over the course of twenty-eight days (the twenty-eight Mansions of the Moon). The North and South nodes of the Moon, known as the Dragons of the Moon, are also of noted importance in magick. The old order of Moon Mansions begins with the star called Alcyone, which is the Pleiades. The current order now begins in Aries. The problem with using the Moon Mansion System is that it differs, with regard to stellar correspondence, from cultural system to cultural system. The most commonly used system today is the Chaldean, which also appeared in grimoires of the Middle Ages and Renaissance periods.

THE CHALDEAN MANSIONS

1. Al Thurayya   (Taurus)
2. Al Dabaran   (Taurus)
3. Al Hak' ah   (Orion)
4. Al Han' ah   (Gemini)
5. Al Dhira   (Gemini)
6. Al Nathrah   (Cancer)
7. Al Tarf   (Leo)
8. Al Jabhah   (Leo)
9. Al Zubrah   (Leo)
10. Al Sarfah   (Leo)
11. Al Awwa   (Virgo)
12. Al Simak   (Virgo)
13. Al Ghafr   (Virgo)

14.	Al Jubana	(Libra)
15.	Iklil Al Jabhah	(Scorpio)
16.	Al Kalb	(Scorpio)
17.	Al Shaulah	(Scorpio)
18.	Al Na' am	(Sagittarius)
19.	Al Baldah	(Sagittarius)
20.	Al Sa'd Al Dhabih	(Capricorn)
21.	Al Sa'd Al Bula	(Aquarius)
22.	Al Sa'd Al Su'ud	(Aquarius)
23.	Al Sa'd Al Ahbiyah	(Aquarius)
24.	Al Farch Al Mukdim	(Pegasus)
25.	Al Fargh Al Thani	(Pegasus and Andromeda)
26.	Al Batn Al Hut	(Andromeda)
27.	Al Sharatain	(Aries)
28.	Al Butain	(Aries)

LUNAR INFLUENCE OF THE MANSIONS

When the moon occupies one of the Chaldean Mansion constellations, various occult influences are generated. These are the traditional correspondences of those influences:

1. Good fortune
2. Ill will, separation, revenge
3. Secures favor with authority
4. Secures love
5. Secures material desires
6. Aids in battle
7. Causes illness
8. Aids in childbirth and healing
9. Causes fear or reverence
10. Causes disharmony between lovers
11. Creates harmony between lovers
12. Influences divorce and separation
13. Influences friendship and good will
14. Secures material increase
15. Inhibits thieves
16. Aids against poisons
17. Aids childbirth
18. Aids the hunter
19. Causes misfortune for enemies
20. Aids the fugitive
21. Influences destruction and decline
22. Aids fertility in animals
23. Aids the harvest, and plants in general
24. Influences love and favor
25. Fouls liquids
26. Aids the fisher
27. Aids in the destruction of enemies
28. Aids in reconciliation

THE TWENTY-EIGHT SPIRITS OF THE MOON MANSIONS

The symbols of the twenty-eight spirits of the moon mansion shown in this book (see page 156) may well have been influenced by a nineteenth-century Hermetic group in Naples called *Fratellanza Terapeutico-Magica di Myriam*. Many of the symbols are similar to those used by Guilian Kremmerz, its founder. A few symbols even resemble some used by the German occultist Franz Bardon. The actual origins are unknown.

The pagan names of the Tuscan Lunar Spirits who rule over the Moon Mansions are shown on page 156, along with their symbols.

1. Arisham
2. Estanacohn
3. Evonacus
4. Miracohn
5. Sendomahr
6. Therassus
7. Viracus

15. Trutus
16. Tiniah
17. Satur
18. Venu
19. Totorum
20. Arogus
21. Diona

8. Lucinus
9. Selahna
10. Mensus
11. Kirahm
12. Morgronus
13. Thera
14. Atava

22. Pahnus
23. Niah
24. Silvus
25. Aquosus
26. Undia
27. Cosus
28. Poscinia

Figure 41. *Moon Mansion Spirit Symbols.*

Part Four

Legacy and Legend

10

HEREDITARY WITCHCRAFT

This chapter is a collection of Witch lore, drawn in part from the nineteenth-century field studies of Charles Leland on Italian Witchcraft. I have added hereditary material he did not address, and have also corrected and completed various elements of his research. I present the old Witch tales here mainly to preserve the concepts as well as the lore, as Leland's books are extremely hard to find since they have been out-of-print for almost a century. Even the few reprints of the past two decades have quickly disappeared, and this is truly a loss for those who cherish folklore related to Witchcraft. The hereditary material I have added to Leland's field studies on Italian Witchcraft should provide the reader with a practical and more accurate overview of the Old Craft.

I feel it is important to preserve these quaint beliefs because these things are the ways of a people almost extinct now. The beauty of their seemingly outdated concepts and customs is slipping silently into the shadow of things forgotten. I recall a cyberconversation on Compuserve's *Wicca Forum,* where I passed along some tooth fairy magick material. I later added that if anyone wanted the Old Ways recipe for fairy dust they could ask me for it and I would pass it along. In response I received a lot of requests for additional tooth fairy magick techniques, but not one person ever asked for the old recipe. I sat in front of my computer, and felt for the first time in my life that the Old Ways were truly lost.

When I feel this way now, I sit quietly and I think about the words of my teachers. I think about the old beliefs that without the Strega, the sun and moon will no longer rise. I remember the teaching that unless the old rites are performed, season to season, that Nature will withdraw from humankind. In all of this I embrace the metaphor, and I know that there must always be one who will tell the Strega's story. There must always be one who will tend the ancient campfire. For it is the Witch and the kindred fairy who gives the life essence to the mundane world of men and women. We are the possibilities and the unshattered dream, we are what give life magick. So, I will recount the old tales here and try to preserve them for yet another generation. It is my hope that after I am gone, another will come and blow upon the embers, and tend the old campfire for yet another who may someday come. Let us turn then and hear of things once whispered only in the night, before the glowing hearths of family Witches.

THE CIMARUTA

The cimaruta, sometimes called the Witches' talisman, is perhaps the oldest surviving symbol of hereditary Witchcraft (see Figure 42, p. 161). It is likely descended from the ancient bronze Etruscan rue amulet now housed in the Bologna museum. As late as the nineteenth century, antique cimaruta amulets were made of silver, still the common practice today. The cimaruta symbol itself is a sprig of the herb known as rue, worn as a sign of membership in the Society of Diana, the Old Religion of the Witches. The rue sprig symbol divides into three branches, representing Diana Triformis, the three-fold goddess (the Italian equivalent of the Greek Hecate). Each branch ends in bud-like formations from which sprout various occult symbols.

Among hereditary Witches the cimaruta bears the symbols of the fish, the cock, the moon, the serpent, the key, the dagger, and the blossom. The fish is sacred to Diana-Proserpine, who was a sea goddess, and as such is an Underworld creature.

The fish is symbolic of the occult life force, or procreative fertile power, submerged and only slightly visible beneath the surface when it is active.

The cock is sacred to the sun and is nicknamed the "watchful guardian." It is the herald of the sunrise, but cocks also are very aggressive and will chase off even large animal intruders within their territory. Legend says that cocks also chase off unwelcome spirits, and in this we see their association with sunrise dispelling the darkness. Therefore the cock appears as a symbol of vigilance and protection.

The moon appears on the cimaruta as a sign of following the moon goddess, for in ancient times the moon itself was believed to be the living goddess herself. Therefore to bear the sign of the moon was to proclaim allegiance to what it represented.

The serpent is a sign of health, as reflected in the ancient Caduceus symbolism. The gateway to the Underworld was guarded by snakes, sometimes represented by ropes, and in this we are reminded that health blocks the way to death. The snake is associated also with the Underworld because it disappears into holes and crevices. From ancient times it has also been connected to themes of sensuality and sexuality (the vital essence of the life force). In this theme we see both natures of the snake: the fertile essence, and the phallus moving in and out of the crevice to the Underworld of rebirth. In ancient art we often find the snake forming a circle, with its tail in its mouth, thus symbolizing perpetual union. The venomous snake is a symbol of the transformative powers of the sexual aspects of magickal fluids produced in the body through stimulation of the endocrine system.

Figure 42. *The Cimaruta Witch Charm*

The key is a symbol of the gatekeeper. Keys allow access into forbidden or restricted places. The key appearing on the cimaruta indicates that the bearer possesses the key to the Mysteries.

The dagger is the dart of Diana Venatrix, which has the power to slay and transform (much like the venomous snake). It is the symbol of the magician's power. The blossom on the cimaruta is the vervain flower, its five petals symbolizing the pentagram of protection and the sign of the Witch. It is interesting to note that Hecate Triformis, from whom Diana is descended, in ancient iconography holds the symbols of the key, serpent, and dagger.

HERBS OF THE OLD RELIGION

Vervain

Vervain is one of the sacred herbs of Italian Witchcraft. The Italian witch charm known as the cimaruta features a vervain blossom, symbolizing protection. The herb is also used as an offering to the Goddess, and can be planted around shrines dedicated to her. When casting a circle for magical workings, vervain can be sprinkled along the perimeter of the circle for extra protection.

Vervain is also an herb that brings good fortune. If you purchase some you should say:

> *I do not buy the vervain because of*
> *the herb*
> *but because of the fortune it carries.*

In ancient times, vervain was regarded as a potent magical herb, especially when used to evoke spirits or for divination. In the latter attribute we find the connection to fate or fortune associated with the little spell spoken when buying some of the herb. Hereditary Witches say that if someone offers to sell you vervain you should not decline or haggle over the price. This is connected to the belief that a fairy dwells within the vervain plant. This fairy bestows good fortune on anyone who invokes her, which is accomplished by touching the herb to your heart, lips, and then to your nose (at which point you deeply inhale the scent of the herb, thus invoking the fairy).

Vervain is also known as the *Herb of Grace, Herba Sacra,* and *Herba Veneris.* Ancients called this herb "Herba Veneris" because of the aphrodisiac qualities they attributed to it. Priests used it for sacrifices, hence the name "Herba sacra." The name "verbena" was the classical Roman name for altar-plants in general, and for this species in particular. Bruised, it was worn around the neck as a charm against headaches, and also against snake and other venomous bites, as well as for general good luck. In context of the snake, the appearance of the vervain blossom on the cimaruta indicates that the Witch has power over controlling transformation.

Old folklore says that vervain will open locks, and unshoe any horse that treads upon it. This lore stems from the fact that horses were forbidden in the Arician grove at Nemi where vervain was grown, in memory of one of Diana's lovers (Virbius) who was slain by horses. Among Witches, vervain is sometimes called "frog's foot," and the accounts of Italian Witch trials often mention the use of vervain, along with rue. Wreaths of vervain flowers have sometimes been worn around the neck as an amulet or charm, just as little bags of camphor are still worn by peasant folks to guard against or ward off illness.

Rue

The name of this herb is derived from the Greek *reuo*, meaning "to set free." Aradia taught that Witches must be free, as we see in Leland's *Gospel of the Witches:*

> . . . and you shall be freed from slavery, and so shall you be free in everything; and as a sign that you are truly free, you shall be naked in your rites . . .

Here we have the connection back to Diana—Aradia being her daughter—and thus the rue connection to Diana through the cimaruta. The rue plant is also the symbol of the ever-dying and returning god, found in the etymology of the word "rue," derived from the Greek word meaning "to set free."

Curiously, rue was also used to sprinkle Holy Water at High Catholic Masses during the Medieval period. In Italian Witchcraft rue is associated with the Harvest Lord and is called *the bitter essence of the God.* Magickally it is an herb of protection from the powers of Darkness and is associated with the forces of Light. Through this connection it is linked to the east, the quarter of rising light. Rue is a fragrant woody plant and is associat-

ed with the wand. It is placed at the east quarter to empower sacred space.

Ivy

Although not truly an herb, ivy is a plant used in Italian Witchcraft. It can be used for binding because of its rope-like nature and its ability to climb and wrap around things. It is also associated with the needle and with weaving and sewing. Through the needle association it is connected to the ritual dagger, the dart of Diana Venatrix, and the fangs of the serpent (ivy being serpent-like). This is why needles are used in puppet magick (similar to the voodoo doll). Ivy is placed at the south quarter of a ritual circle to empower sacred space.

Fennel

This is a protection herb and a counter to black magick. Mixed with St. John's wort on Midsummer's Eve it was used to banish evil. Giant stalks of fennel were fitted with sprigs of rue by Italian Witches, who fought ritual battles for an abundant harvest during the ember days as late as the sixteenth and seventeenth centuries. It is interesting to note that these Witches also wore sprigs of rue tied to a cord on their waist. Fennel seeds may be burned in incense for protection as well.

The Walnut Tree

During the Middle Ages, and from earlier times, the walnut tree was regarded as sacred to night spirits and Witches. Many legends of southern Europe identify the site of a walnut tree as a gathering place for magick and ritual celebration. To the ancient Romans, the walnut tree was a symbol of night and darkness. The walnut was also associated with fertility and eroticism in general, and in Italian folklore women could become pregnant by simply spending time next to the walnut tree. Perhaps this stems from the fact that walnuts are similar in appearance to human testicles. In southern Europe it was, and in some areas still is, the custom to scatter walnuts around the wedding site.

During the Middle Ages in Italy, it was the custom to plant a walnut tree to mark the birth of a daughter. When the daughter grew up and was married, the walnut tree was cut down and her bridal bed was made from the wood. A liqueur known as *nocello* or *nocino* was made from the walnuts, and was the traditional drink in the marriage toast. It is interesting to note that nocello was also the traditional drink of Witches at the time of the Summer Solstice, as it still is today.

In northern Europe the legendary meeting place of Witches was known as the *Brocken* or *Blocksberg*. In Italy, Witches gathered at the site of an ancient walnut tree in Benevento. Peter Pipernus wrote in his *De Nuce Maga Beneventana* and *De Effectibus Magicis* of the magickal and curative powers of the walnut, and stated that it was "of the highest degree supernatural." Walnuts were said to protect against accidents and earthquakes, which is not surprising since the walnut tree was equally sacred to Underworld gods and deities of Fate. Pipernus writes that the walnut tree was sacred to Proserpine, Night, and the Infernal Gods.

The Italian Inquisition records from various Witch trials mention the walnut tree of Benevento. From these transcripts emerges a legend in which a specific walnut tree stood in Benevento, and was "in leaf all the year." The nuts of this walnut tree were of a pyramidal or triangular shape, *qua tragularibus lineis emittebat.* High prices were paid to the Witches of Benevento who sold the curious walnuts as amulets. Leland says that triangular nuts were made into rosaries and sold in Florence as late as the nineteenth century.

Pipernus tells us that the great walnut tree of Benevento was cut down by St. Barbatus, who converted Romualdus (the ruler of Benevento) to Christianity. Pipernus goes on to say that another walnut tree grew in its place, and in his time he found evidence of Witches' banquets still taking place beneath the tree. Leland reports in *Etruscan Roman Remains in Popular Tradition* that the Benevento Witches "do not seem to have been by any means a bad lot." Legends of the Witches of Benevento tell of them healing hunchbacks and bringing star-crossed lovers together. Often the Witches of Benevento were called the "Walnut Witches."

ITALIAN WITCHES

In *Aradia: Gospel of the Witches* (1899), Leland mentions the popular Christian image of the evil witch, and discounting it due to his investigations into Italian Witchcraft, he writes:

> But the Italian Strega or sorceress is in certain respects a different character from these. In most cases she comes of a family in which her calling or art has been practiced for many generations. . . .

In chapter 8 of Leland's *Etruscan Magic and Occult Remedies* we find a section titled "Diana and Herodias," containing these words:

> It is remarkable that while witchcraft was regarded in later times among Northern races as a creation of Satan, it never lost in Italy a classic character. In this country the witch is only a sorceress, and she is often a beneficent fairy. Her ruler is not the devil, but Diana . . . it is true enough that the monks imported and forced into popular Italian superstition strong infusions of the devil. Yet with all this, in the main, the real Italian witch has nothing to do with Satan or a Christian hell, and remains as of yore a daughter of Diana. There is

something almost reviving or refreshing in the thought that there is one place in the world—and that in papal Italy itself—where the poison of diabolism did not utterly prevail.

The connection between Witches and Fairies, mentioned by Leland, is preserved in an old Italian fairy tale recounted in *Etruscan Magic and Occult Remedies*. In this legend a young man is befriended by fairies dwelling in the great walnut tree of Benevento, who emerge from each nut he opens. He is then given three magical walnuts, one of which makes him rich, the other handsome, and with the third he wins the heart of the princess and eventually marries her. After a few months she gives birth to a beautiful babe whom they call, in gratitude to the fairy ladies, the "Walnut of Benevento."

The fairies in this tale are reminiscent of Benevento's Witches, and it is safe to state that they are actually one and the same. This is implied by the setting at Benevento, the uniting of unlikely lovers, and magickal talismans designed to attract a lover. Even today, the famous Strega liqueur brewed in Benevento recalls the connection between love magick and Witches. One company enclosure in a holiday issue of *Strega liqueur* noted that it all began when the "good witches of Benevento" brewed a love potion that had the power to bind together for eternity a man and woman who truly loved one another.

Leland tells us (*Etruscan Magic & Occult Remedies*) that Italian Witchcraft is:

> . . . like an endowment and may be assumed by keeping company with Witches, studying their lore, and taking part in their enchantments.

As we have seen earlier in this book, hereditary Witches believe that an occult property is passed in the blood down through the generations. This may be passed on to others outside the bloodline through various body fluids employed in a prescribed magickal rite. Family Witches often refer to this occult property as *the legacy* or *the gift*. Leland, in *Etruscan Magic & Occult Remedies,* writes of this:

> As for families in which stregheria, or a knowledge of charms, old traditions and songs is preserved . . . as the children grow older, if any aptitude is observed in them for sorcery, some old grandmother or aunt takes them in hand, and initiates them into the ancient faith.

It is an old legend that before a hereditary Witch can die, he or she must pass on the art to at least one other individual. Leland mentions this in *Etruscan Magic & Occult Remedies.* Here he tells the story of a Christian priest who became a Witch through no desire of his own. He was called in one day to take the confession of a dying woman. After hearing her confession, the Witch said there was something she wanted to leave him, and asked if he would accept it. He replied that he would, and she quickly said: "Then I leave you my Witchcraft," and immediately passed away before he could protest.

Old Craft legends say that when Witches die they become great spirits who sweep over the country in clouds or vapors or storms, or wander again on earth as mortals. It is also believed in the Romagna that when those who are especially *of the Strega Faith* die, they reappear again in human form among their former family bloodline. Leland says this is a rather obscure esoteric doctrine, known in the Witch families but not much talked about. When a child is born, after due family consultation, some very old and wise Strega looks to detect in it a departed family member by his or her smile, features, or expression. Through this process of death and rebirth, the Witch becomes more powerful and passes to the higher stage of a spirit. As Leland notes "the belief that men could become gods is very Etruscan."

THE OLD ONES

The Old Ones (*i spiriti di vecchio*) is a title referring to the first spirits to dwell upon the earth—those spirits we now call the Grigori. It can also mean all of the preexisting spirits in general, such as the elementals and the spirits of Nature—in other words, all spirits that existed before humankind. Leland notes the existence of the Old Ones in *Aradia; Gospel of the Witches* where we read:

> Then Diana went to the fathers of the Beginning, to the mothers, the spirits who were before the first spirit. . . .

Among many of the Old Witch bloodlines, the Tuscan names of the old spirits have been preserved: Tago, Bellaria, Settrano, and Meana. Some Traditions use the old Roman names of the four winds when they speak of the elemental spirits: Boreas, Eurus, Notus, and Zephyrus. Generally speaking, however, their association with the sky indicates a higher level than elemental beings, and they are more accurately perceived as belonging among the Grigori race.

The elemental races associated with hereditary Italian Witchcraft are called the Pala, Bellarie, Settiano, and Manii. The Pala are creatures of earth, the Bellarie of air, Settiano of fire, and the Manii of water. North is the quarter associated with earth, East to air, South to fire, and West to water. These associations most likely arose from the fact that northern Italy is mountainous, the trade winds blow from the East, the desert areas of Africa lie to the South, and the Mediterranean opens into the Atlantic Ocean to the West.

Each elemental kingdom has its ruler. The Pala are ruled by Tago, who in some traditions is also known as Taga. The Bellarie are ruled by Bellaria. The Settiano are ruled by Settrano, and the Manii are ruled by Meana. In my book *Ways of the Strega*, I modified these actual assignments because I was not prepared at the time to divulge the inner hereditary material. I replaced the Manii with the Lasa, who are very much related. Even though this current book is not a "tell all" on the Old Religion, I do wish to assure the reader that nothing has been intentionally altered in this present volume.

SPIRITS OF THE DEAD

In Latin the word *anima* can mean several things: wind, breeze, breath, breath of life. Anima can also mean the soul as the principle of life (as opposed to animus as the principle of thought and feelings, the ghost or spirit). In ancient times breath was the life. It was the first act of the newborn and the last act of the dying. Primitive thought held that the soul was exhaled at the moment of death. The soul then rose up into the air like a bird. In ancient Rome it was the custom to "give the last kiss" to a loved one when they died by blowing a kiss upward into the air.

The association of the bird with the soul is found among hereditary Italian Witches. Not only does the soul begin its journey in the form of a bird, the enemies of the soul circle above in bird form, in an attempt to snare it before the soul can free itself from the physical plane. It is likely that this concept evolved from Neolithic times when primitive humans noted the gathering of birds around a dead carcass. In the metaphysical concept of "as above, so below" they attempted to also feed upon the escaping soul. It is interesting to note that in Old Europe some of the earliest depictions of deity found by archaeologists are humanoid-like birds.

To prevent the soul catcher birds from snaring the departed spirit, the body of the dead is marked with certain occult signs known as the lineage symbols. The bird clan symbol of the family bloodline is painted on the left forearm. Below this are drawn four parallel lines denoting the four worlds through which the soul must pass: physical, lunar, solar, and stellar. The sign of joining is drawn on the wrist, symbolizing the bond between this world and the spirit world. On the right forearm is drawn the totem bird-of-prey (an important sign of power) and below this are the four world lines again. The protective symbol of the Old Ones, the Grigori, is drawn on the right wrist.

Immediately after the funeral ceremony, a basket is set for the dead containing eggs, bread, lentils, salt, flour, and wine. This is repeated again exactly nine days later, and is referred to as the moon feast. All of this stems from the ancient belief that the departed soul requires nourishment during the transitional stage from physical to spiritual existence. In the hereditary death ritual observances, we find an overlapping of concepts, which is not surprising, considering the antiquity of the sect.

The concept of the soul departing in bird-like form immediately following death is mixed with the concept of the dead in a transitional period when they remain earth-bound for a time. Additionally we also find the ritual memorial rite known as *Shadowfest*, when food is again prepared for the dead who return on November's eve. This is all resolved in the old hereditary belief that a Witch can transform into a powerful spirit shortly after death, employing the lineage symbols painted upon its former body, thereby avoiding further danger from non-material enemies.

In the Fall season, a special nectar is prepared of wine, milk, and honey, mixed with three drops of blood. The blood must come from a relative of the dead person or the former mate. In addition a special meal of fava bean soup is prepared for the returning dead. These observances conclude on the third of November. It is traditional to decorate the Lare shrine with roses on the first day of May in remembrance of departed family members. In ancient Rome it was the custom to adorn the tomb with roses on the festival day of Rosalia, in May. It was also an ancient belief that the dead took their final earthly merriment through the drunkenness of those who celebrated during the wake (a sort of Bacchic ritual possession of the body).

Once eventually released from the physical world, the soul passes into the lunar world, the realm of Luna. It is an old belief, connected to the moon's phases, that as the moon collects departed souls it grows full with light, and as it releases them its light diminishes. Luna is something like the Summerland of the Wiccans, a Pagan paradise of mythical beings where the soul rests and prepares for the next stage of its development. From Luna, the soul either reincarnates in the physical dimension or passes into the solar realm. From the solar realm it eventually passes into the stellar realm, returning to Aster where it is reunited with the Source of its origin.

Because of the power a Witch accumulates over the course of many lives, he or she has more control over what becomes of the soul following release from the physical dimension. This is where the hereditary belief emerges, stating that a Witch may become a powerful spirit choosing to continue interaction with the world of the living, rather than departing the physical realm. In this belief we find ourselves in the midst of an even more ancient connection wherein the spirit of the dead and the fairy are actually one and the same creature. This association was covered at length in my previous book *The Wiccan Mysteries* (1997).

THE SPIRIT NUMEN

According to the ancient teachings, there dwells within all objects a *conscious power* known as the *numen*. In some non-Italian traditions this is referred to as *mana,* although in actuality mana is not quite the same thing as numen. The two are similar except with regard to consciousness. Mana is traditionally viewed as a type of raw energy or force which may be collected and employed for magical purposes. Numen is an indwelling force which is both energy and consciousness together. Numen has an *awareness* of both itself and its surroundings. It is numen that gives a place that certain *feel,* and it is numen that responds within an object when it *feels right* to the touch (such as a person experiences when choosing a crystal, or some other tool).

When ancient occultists established the magical correspondences commonly associated today with such things as herbs and crystals, it was the emanation of specific indwelling numen that caused them to make those connections. This is why herbs and crystals can possess certain magical properties; it is the power of their numen spirit. The numen must be communicated with, usually through visual imagery and/or tonal sounds (vibration), in order to establish the link necessary to employ its power. Otherwise all you end up with is a pretty lump of mineral formation or a fragrant pile of dead plant material.

In essence the numen can be thought of as the divine spark within all matter. It is not, however, a living soul or spirit itself, but simply a reflection of Divine consciousness. In some respects it may be thought of as a divine imprint, or a contagious energy-form left by the hand of the Source of All Things.

Mana, on the other hand, is more like radiation or heat emanating from an object—void of independent action and limited to its effect upon other objects by proximity.

It is one of the arts of Witchcraft to pass mental images (thought-forms) into the numen. Through this a magical rapport is established between the Witch and the crystal or herb, etc. Once this is done, then the object may be employed according to the desire or need of the Witch, as is customary with spell casting and the like. For herbs it is best to start with the seed and continue with the mental imagery as the sprout appears and the plant grows to fullness. In this way the numen of the herb can form and condense the necessary magical effect desired of it.

For crystal magick, one must first awaken the crystal before passing mental images to it, or the effect is weakened and the charge is diminished in length. Traditionally the crystal is tapped with a stone (or another crystal) three times while gazing upon the full moon, in order to awaken it. The term "awaken" in this context means to align it to the person who possesses the crystal. During an initiation ceremony the initiator can tap the initiate's crystal with their own crystal three times and thus pass the power to the initiate. There is a certain beauty in possessing a crystal that has received the charge from an initiator's crystal (whose own crystal received it from another, and so on).

THE OLD RELIGION

Witchcraft is known to its followers as *The Old Religion* (*La Vecchia Religione*). It is also simply referred to as "the ways" (*di modi*). In essence, the Old Religion is an ancient view of the Earth as a living creature, the Mother of Life. Living under Her care are various physical and spiritual beings. The physical beings are the caretakers of Nature as expressed in material form. The spiritual beings vitalize and animate the etheric counterparts of the material forms. In other words, they impart vitality and the *life essence* into plants and animals. This is why offerings are made to various spirits in an attempt to get them to make specific crops yield more fully, and to make one's flocks or herds flourish.

Among Italian hereditary Witches, a specific offering is always carried when seeking the favor of a spirit or a deity. The following items are placed in a red pouch: salt, ivy, and rue. Red wine is carried along with the pouch and the offering is traditionally made at midnight during the full moon. Some Witches prefer to perform this at a crossroads, an ancient Italic custom that endured even up into Roman times. Other Witches prefer to place the time-honored offerings on the shore of a lake, by a stream, or in an open meadow.

The ritual circle for both religious and magickal ceremonies was traditionally set before a large tree, near a running stream.

The running water served two purposes. First it created an energy flow in the bound ether of the setting, simply by the movement of its own current. The subconscious mind was stimulated by the sound of the water, thereby connecting the raised magickal energy of the ritual to the emotional level. The correspondence of water to emotions and emotions to the subconscious created, by extension, a pathway into the astral. The presence of a running stream also allowed for the placing of libations directly into the living spirit of the setting, the flowing water.

Trees are magickal beings, rooted in the earth and extending upward into the sky. The trunk of the tree is a bridge between the worlds. This is why the stump was often used as an altar. It is also why slain gods were hung/sacrificed upon a tree (Lupus, Odin, Quetzalcoatl, Jesus, etc.). Here they become the bridge themselves between humankind and the gods. To perform a ritual in front of a tree is to connect with the Underworld (through the roots) and with the heavens (through the branches). The old legends say that the tree must not be gnarled. This is because evil spirits used to be magickally bound or imprisoned in trees, and the tree became disfigured by the indwelling spirit. Therefore it was a bad omen to perform a ritual by a gnarled tree.

The focus of the Witches' celebrations is upon deity personified as a goddess and a god. The Witches' goddess is the ancient Neolithic Great Goddess, She who gives life and receives it back into Herself. The god is Her Neolithic animal consort, the Horned God of Nature. Together the God and Goddess empower Nature and all living things. In Leland's *Aradia,* he tells us that Italian Witches worshipped Diana and Lucifer, both Roman deities of light. Both lights, of the night and day, were vital to the cycles of growth for plants, animals, and humans. Modern science is just now catching up with the ancient knowledge concerning light and its effects upon the cycles of reproduction. Unique to Italian Witchcraft is the request made by the Witch, beneath the light of the full moon, to be taught the ancient mysteries in his or her sleep. In this we see the metaphysical reflection of the light principle (enlightenment) and the sleeping seed of reproduction.

The ritual celebrations of the Witches' year serve not only as devotional acts, but also function to empower the environment. Circular dancing, sensual dancing, or other acts of raising energy impregnates the setting with what is now called odic energy. Heat acts to release the odic energy concentrated within the ritual circle. This is why bonfires are lit, and candles/torches are always present, so that the raised energy can be released into the atmosphere. The magnetic quality of odic energy absorbs the mental images directed into it by the ritual participants, and condenses it into a vital force. This energy is contained within the candle wax, wine, bonfire wood, and anything else inside the ritual circle. Once properly released it merges with the atmosphere and influences the collective energy field or "aura" of the surrounding community as well as the astral material of the connecting dimension.

Various plants and animals were seen as allies of the Witches. From this perception arose the concept of the familiar and the indwelling spirit within a variety of herbs. The popular concept of a familiar as a cat, bird, or other physical creature is relatively modern. Originally the familiar was a spirit evoked by the Witch to aid in spell casting, astral work, or other occult acts. Because an otherworld spirit can only exist for a very brief time within the physical dimension, it requires a physical vehicle in order to extend its existence here. Therefore it became a very common practice to bind the spirit to a physical creature such as a cat. This resulted in a consciousness sharing between the pet and the spirit. The natural rapport with the cat had a controlling influence upon the new indwelling spirit. The otherworld spirit empowered the cat and elevated its own consciousness. This allowed the Witch to work with the familiar in both the physical and spiritual worlds.

Whether a person is in contact with an animal spirit or an otherworld spirit dwelling in the nonphysical world, we say that person has a Spirit Guide. The purpose of a Spirit Guide is to assist an individual in this physical life to experience those things that will lead to the evolution of his or her soul. Such spirits speak to us in our thoughts, through our feelings, and are present to us in the situations to which they direct us. Spirit Guides walk with us upon our Path, and we are never truly alone when we embrace the Old Ways, for we are part of the community of spirits.

This is the Group Soul Consciousness, that aspect of the "Great Spirit" that teaches birds to make nests and to migrate, wolves to hunt, whales to return to spawning waters, and so forth. When we speak of the Raven Spirit or Wolf Spirit, for example, we are talking about the Collective Consciousness of the Animal Kingdom empowered by the

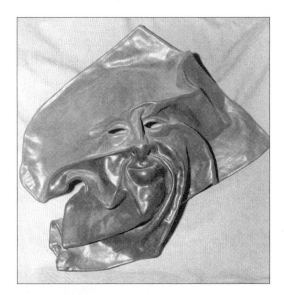

Figure 43. *Nineteenth-century ritual mask representing the Spirit of the Old Ways. From the Clan Umbrea collection.*

presence of Divine Consciousness residing within it (much like a seed within a grape). This is not some mere principle, but rather a conscious entity (an aspect of the Source of All Things, the Spirit of the Old Ways).

Uniting all of us in a web of energy is a spiritual force inherent within Nature. It is the essence of all things, the empowering principle. To walk in the Old Ways is to learn how to access the inner mechanism of Nature. From this we can draw the inner knowledge to perform healings and other acts of power. Knowing the Old Ways imparts the ability to discern energy patterns and vibratory rates, understanding how to interpret them. Such knowledge manifests in the understanding of action and reaction within the natural order as well as the supernatural order. In understanding this inner mechanism is the ability to manifest one's desire by drawing, condensing, and directing etheric energy toward a personal goal. Some people call this magick.

Magick is, however, a secondary aspect of the Old Religion. It is the benefit of practicing the Craft, and not the reason for it. The Old Religion teaches alignment to the ways of Nature. When we speak of the Old Ways we are talking about pre-Christian concepts originating among the early people who lived in harmony with Nature. Every land had an Old Ways People, whether they were the shamans of Europe or the American Indians of North America. These were a people whose lives and spirits were intimately connected to the Cycles of Nature, and so we call such People—Old Ways People.

The Old Ways are the collected teachings containing knowledge of the Path leading to union with the Great Spirit. Spiritual evolution is the basis for the practices found among Old Ways People and Traditions. There are as many Paths to the Great Spirit as there are people on the Earth. The Great Deities created all that is. Within creation itself we can discern something of the Creator. Just as an artist leaves something of his or her own nature in a painting or carving (which we can look at and then discern the artist), so too can we discover something of Divinity within the workings of Nature. In a way, Nature is a diminished reflection of the higher nature from which it issued forth. Old Ways People look to the principles and the inner workings of Nature in order to better understand the Consciousness that brought it into manifestation.

There is an old saying: "that which is below is as that which is above." We have shortened this to "As above, so below." Our own inner natures are diminished reflections of that which created us as well. By discerning our own spirits and looking into the reflection of Nature, we can come to a closer understanding of Divinity, the Universe, and our relationship therein. Perhaps above all, this is the true gift of practicing the Old Ways.

OLD WAYS MAGICK

The magickal knowledge of hereditary Witches is an old faith. It is based in the belief that spirits inhabit all physical objects and every setting within Nature. Magick is, in part, the knowledge of the inner mechanisms that animate and empower Nature. Beyond this, magick is the understanding of the ways of spirit; how to communicate beyond the veil separating the world of the living from the world of spirits. Such knowledge is the Witches' Craft, and has drawn people throughout the ages to seek out Witches for spells or divination, or to hunt them down and kill them for fear of that power.

The Witches' Craft is comprised of the following arts: herbal, divinatory, magickal, pharmaceutical, talismanic, and invocational/evocational. Everything that one may attribute to Witchcraft can be delegated to one of these ancient arts. There are essentially two primary ways of raising the Witch's power. Power is either raised within the Witch, or is drawn to him or her. Raised power arises within the mind or is generated by emotional or sexual energy. Drawn power is either the invocation or evocation of a deity or a spirit of some type (see glossary).

A great deal of folk magick is present in modern Witchcraft. In folk magick we often encounter the belief that a certain herb can produce specified results when employed as a charm. This type of magick is self-enchantment, wherein the powers of the mind are tapped. Self-enchantment relies upon personal belief, empowered by the catalyst of a symbol, charm, herb, chant, or ritual tool.

In Old Ways Witchcraft, we find the power of the mind directing the heartbeat, breathing, and discharge of endocrine secretions into the bloodstream. The mind becomes inflamed with the emotional investment and the body becomes empowered by the chemical changes within it. Sometimes this is assisted through the use of various herbal potions. The mind then directs the accumulated energy into the aura—either through the breath or through extension of the bioelectromagnetic energy that is generated. To the hereditary Witch, magick is a matter of blood, breath, and spirit. The mind is the directing and controlling mechanism. It oversees the creation of energy and then directs the launching of it.

Another aspect of Old Ways magick is related to a belief in the spirit world. The hereditary Witch carried a red pouch, signifying the blood connection. He or she bore in this pouch the sacred herbs of the Old Religion: ivy and rue. Ivy is the symbol of the weaver, for Witches are weavers of magick. Rue is the symbol of the Old Ways; as the rue plant divides into three branches, so

too were the old Witch clans divided into three, the keepers of the mysteries of the earth, moon, and the stars.

The Witch set out bearing these items as he or she searched for power objects such as a stone with a hole through it. It was believed that a fairy could be bound to the stone and thus be a magickal helper to the Witch. The Fata, or fairy beings, recognized the Witch by these symbols and willingly aided the Witch in his or her spells or rituals. The Witch shared the power of the blood with the Fata by anointing the stone with three drops. This is the origin of the legend wherein Witches feed or suckle their familiars. In the sharing of blood we see the ancient connection between fairies and ancestral spirits.

In the Witches' pantheon of spirits there is a race known as the Grigori. The Grigori are guardians of the portals connecting the material world to the spirit worlds. Long ago gestures and postures were created in order to communicate with these powerful spirits. When a person is initiated into the Old Religion, they are presented to the four quarters within the ritual circle. At each quarter a Grigori keeps watch. By displaying a ritual gesture or assuming a posture, the Witch announces that he or she is heir to keys that open the portals.

The Grigori recognize the ritual signs that only an initiate can possess. This is a statement to them that the person standing before them is trained in the Craft, and will

Figure 44. *Nineteenth-century Grigori, or Watcher, Masks. Traditionally the masks are hung on quarter torches during rituals (Clan Umbrea collection).*

act responsibly because of their oaths. In this respect the ritual postures and gestures become the *signs of passage* allowing the Witch to access the spirit worlds through the portals, unobstructed by the Grigori. The Grigori have the power to allow or deny a spell or work of magick from passing into the astral dimension where magick takes root. Therefore, the power of a Witch is often linked to his or her rapport with the Watchers.

In addition to the Grigori, each elemental quarter is influenced by an elemental ruler. The Witch can evoke these entities and request their aid in ritual and magickal endeavors. The elemental spirits can impart the vital essence of the elemental power into the fabric of the spell. The advantage of this is that the elemental essence is pure. Power simply raised by the Witch alone carries his or her own inner qualities, and being human we are something less than perfect. By merging elemental energy with our own, the quality of energy is raised to a higher level, more in harmony with the nonphysical dimensions.

In an occult sense, like attracts like. Energy sent out into the other worlds tends to move toward harmonious realms that resonate with its own vibration. This is not always a good thing, especially where greed, manipulation, anger, or evil is the seed of the spell to begin with. The advantage of evoking elemental energy into the spell is that it helps to align the spell to Nature instead of human nature. Nature has no agenda other than harmony, and cause and effect. In addition, the Grigori are present to sense the intent of the spell, and to serve as a reminder that watchers are near by. Yes, there are ways to get around this, but in the end we all have our karmic debts to pay.

Hereditary Witches have a saying that there are only two reasons why your magick can fail. You either performed it incorrectly or a greater force opposes it. Performing it incorrectly can mean that you were working against the natural tides of energy, or that you were using the wrong associations or alignments. Everything in Nature has its season and its alignments. Planting a seed in the snow of winter is not going to result in a growing plant in that season. Pulling up a sprout in the spring is not going to get you a carrot in the summer. For most people, the power of the mind or personal belief is not going to change this reality.

The same is true of the lunar energies associated with the phases of the moon, as well as the tides of energy flowing during the solstices and equinoxes (and their cross quarters). Some of these tides and energies are naturally conducive to gain and growth, others to loss and decline. Witchcraft is a Nature religion, and Witches work with Nature, not against her. Working with the formula of Nature will give you consistent and successful works of magick. Working against the natural formula will give you hit and miss results. The best rule of thumb is to consider that Nature is the blueprint by which we formulate magick and upon which our religion is built.

THE MYSTIC WILL

There is a mysterious power of the mind that seemingly works on its own. We catch a glimpse of it when a successful self-suggestion at bedtime to awaken at a specific time becomes a reality in the morning. This quiet, behind-the-scenes type of consciousness is also the *mind* that accepts occult symbols as tangible concepts and merges with the astral level in order to manifest the desired effect within the physical dimension. For the purposes of this chapter we can say that there are two types of will. One type is the concentrated, forceful power of the mind—the personal focus that gets the job done. The second type, of which I write here, is what can be called the mystic will.

If we can say that the forceful will is a creature of the conscious mind, we can equally state that the mystic will is one of the subconscious. The subconscious mind is linked to the astral level, just as the conscious mind is linked to the material level. Stimulation of the physical senses within the material dimension causes the conscious mind to react in some manner. The same is true of the subconscious mind when stimulation of the astral senses occurs. Stimulation may occur within the brain, telling it that the body needs food or drink. The conscious mind then surveys the options and initiates an action that will create a result. Likewise, stimulation may occur within the brain, suggesting that the spirit needs nourishment, and the subconscious mind will then draw upon the astral material to establish an image that will create the desired result.

Together with the conscious mind, the subconscious mind has connected all of our experiences into a web of memory pathways. Everything is linked and associated, categorized, and charted. Because of this, we actually possess more knowledge than we realize. We are not consciously aware of the total integration of all our memories and stored facts. It is the mystic will that oversees the stored data and retrieves it when the correlations are required. Conscious knowledge of the mystic will is a powerful thing.

The following five precepts on the mystic will are taken unabridged from Charles Leland's book *Gypsy Sorcery and Fortune Telling* (T. Fischer Unwin: London, 1891). It wasn't until I read these words aloud that I truly understood their meaning, and I would suggest the reader do the same:

1. We have a conscious will which, whether it be an independent incomprehensible spirit, or simply the correlative result or action of all our other brain powers, exists, and during our waking hours directs our thoughts and acts. While it is at work in the world with social influences, its general tendency is towards average common sense.

2. This conscious will sleeps when we sleep. But the collective images which form memory, each being indeed a separate memory, as an aggregate of bees' cells form a comb, are always ready to come forth, just as honey is always sweet, limpid, and fluid. There is between them all an associative faculty, or a strange and singular power, which begins to act when the will sleeps. Whether it be also an independent Self which plays capriciously while conscious will sleeps, or a result of correlated forces, it is not as yet possible to determine. What we know is that it calls forth the images by association, and in a fantastic, capricious manner, imitates and combines what we have experienced, or read, or thought, during our waking hours.

3. Our waking will can only realize or act on such images as it has kept familiarly before it, or such as have been so often recalled that they recur spontaneously. But all the treasures of memory seem to be available to the dream ruler, and with them a loose facile power of grouping them into kaleidoscopic combinations. Thus, if one could imagine a kaleidoscope which at every turn made varied groups of human or other figures in different attitudes, with changing scenery; and then suppose this to be turned round by some simple vital or mechanical action, he would have an idea of the action of dreams. It is probable that the radical function of the dream-power is to prevent images from becoming utterly forgotten or rusty; and by exercising the faculty of facile or chance combination to keep awake in man originality and creativeness. For it is almost certain that, but for the intrusion of this faculty into our waking thoughts, man would become a mere animal, without an idea beyond the joint common appetites, instincts, and emotions of the lowest of his kind.

4. The dream-power intrudes, more or less, into all waking life. Then it acts, though irregularly, yet in harmony, with conscious will. When it is powerful and has great skill in forming associations of images—and by images I mean "ideas"—and can also submit these to waking wisdom, the result is poetry or art. In recalling strange, beautiful images, and in imagining scenes, we partly lapse into dreaming; in fact, we do dream, though conscious will sits by us all the time and even aids our work. And most poets and artists, and many inventors, will testify that, while imagining or inventing, they abstract the "mind" from the world and common-place events, seek calm and quiet, and try to get into a "brown study," which is a waking dream. That is to say, a condition which is in some respects analogous to sleep is necessary to stimulate the flow and combination of images. This brown study is a state of mind in which images flow and blend and form new shapes far more easily than when Will and Reason have the upper hand. For they act only in a conventional beaten track, and deal only with the known and familiar.

5. Magic is the production of that which is not measured by the capacity of the conscious working will. The dream spirit, or that which knows all our memories, and which combines, blends, sepa-rates, scatters, unites, confuses, intensifies, beautifies, or makes terrible all the persons, by instantaneous reasoning or intuition, perceive what waking common sense does not. We visit a sick man, and the dream spirit, out of inexhaustible hoards of memory aided by association, which results in subtle, occult reasoning, perceives that the patient will die in a certain time, and this result is served up in a dramatic dream. The amount of miracles, mysteries, apparitions, omens, and theurgia which the action of these latent faculties cause, or seem to cause, is simply illimitable, for no man knows how much he knows.

Few, indeed, are the ordinary well-educated Europeans of average experience of life, whose memories are not inexhaustible encyclopedias, and whose intellects are not infinite; if all that is really in them could be wakened from slumber, "know thyself" would mean "know the universe." Now, there are people who, without being able to say why, are often inspired by this power which intuitively divines or guesses without revealing the process and tones, gestures, mien, and address, suggests at once an assertion or a prediction which proves to be true.

Considering that the dream-power has millions of experiences or images at its command, that it flits over them all like lightning, that it can combine, abstract, compare, and deduct, that it being, so to speak, more of a thaumaturgical artist than anything else, excels waking wisdom in subtle trickery, the wonder is, not that we so often hear of marvelous, magical, inexplicable wonders, but that they are not of daily or hourly occurrence. When we think of what we might be if we could master ourselves, and call on the vast sea of knowledge which is in the brain of every one who reads these lines, to give strict reckoning of its every wave and every drop of water, and every shell, pebble, wreck, weed, or grain of sand over which it rolls, and withal master the forces which make its tides and storms, then we may comprehend that all the wonder-working power attributed to all the sorcerers of olden time was nothing compared to what we really have within us.

FULL MOON CEREMONY

An aspect of the Mystic Will plays an important part in the Full Moon ceremony. This ritual ends with a prayer requesting that the Goddess speak to us in our dreams, teaching us while we sleep. Since the mystic will, in effect, keeps vigil even while we sleep, then it is the conscious receiver of the teachings sent to us in slumber. The prayer requests:

Goddess of the Mysteries of the Moon, teach me secrets yet revealed, ancient rites of invocation that the Holy Strega spoke of, for I believe the Strega's story; when she spoke of Your timeless glory, when she said to entreat You, and when seeking for knowledge to seek and find you above all others.

Give me power, O Most Secret Lady, to bind my enemies. Receive me as Your child, receive me though I am earthbound. When my body lies resting nightly, speak to my inner spirit, teach me all Your Holy Mysteries. I believe Your ancient promise that all who seek Your Holy Presence will receive of Your wisdom.

This concept is one of the keys to hereditary Italian Witchcraft. While it is important for our teachers to pass on the ancient wisdom, we are also passed teachings directly on the astral level. This is the act of balance, the body and the soul, the material, and the spiritual, all connected together. Sometimes the conscious mind (the so-called rational mind) can become the dreaded guardian, keeping us from embracing metaphysical or supernatural concepts or realizing the validity of the occult experiences/encounters. The guardian cannot be conquered by direct assault. One must slip unnoticed past the guardian in the night, for the guardian is quick to dismiss magick as a trick, manifestation as illusion, and supernatural phenomena as hallucination. Therefore we call upon the Goddess to teach us while the guardian is unaware.

OCCULT MAGNETIC MAGICK

When we speak of magnetic energies or forces in an occult context, we are speaking of the metaphysical counterpart as it manifests in the physical dimension.

Among initiates, the magnetic force is perceived as an extremely refined substance that can be controlled and directed by the mind. It can be condensed and *stored* within inanimate objects. These objects then become *charged* objects. Liquids of any kind, and all metals, readily accept and store an occult magnetic charge. Wood or wood products will accept a charge but will not store it for long periods of time. Silk is the only known material that will not accept or store this type of charge. This is why silk has been used since ancient times as an insulation against occult magnetic charges and magnetic contamination. Thus it is useful to wrap charged objects in silk so that the magnetic charge does not leak away from the object, or become mixed with the energy of other charged objects.

The power to employ occult magnetism can also be termed *fascination* or *enchantment.* Basically there are two methods of using personal magnetism. One is to impregnate the aura of another person with a thought-form generated by your own mind. The other is to persuade the individual so that their own personal will shapes the thought-form. This may be accomplished by accumulating energy within your own aura for projection, by physically touching the other person, by projecting the magickal vapor through your eyes, or by the tonal quality of your voice.

The vibrational tones of the voice carry personal magnetism, stimulating the etheric substance of astral light. There is a direct link to the spoken word and to the breath. From an occult perspective the element of air is the mediating element between electrical and magnetic energy. Through slow deep breathing and emotional arousal, the blood accumulates odic energy from the pranic atmosphere around us. This charged blood passes through the lungs imparting magnetic energy into the breath. When merged with the personal desire of the individual, a powerful thought-form can be created within this magnetic field. It can be projected out through the eyes by focusing upon a person or an object, holding in the breath, and visualizing a stream of vapor passing out through the eyes as though you out through them. The key to employing elemental energy is strongly linked to controlled breathing, because the breath can be strongly charged with odic energy.

Warming the breath (from a deep inhale) carries an electrical charge, and a cool breath (blown from a shallow puff of air) carries a magnetic charge. This is apparent when the breath is applied to another person just at the base of their cerebellum. A puff will send a magnetic current into the person's aura, resulting in an electrical response. Usually this is annoying to the person and so you get a startled reaction, an electrical snap. A slow exhale from deep within the lungs sends an electrical current resulting in a magnetic response. This is usually an erotic response, the receptive magnetic energy associated with sexual submission.

When employing odic breath in connection with any life-form, an opposite polarity will result: magnetic breath evokes an electrical response and an electrical breath evokes a magnetic response. When using breath charges on inanimate objects, the active charge is delivered without a polarity response. An exception to this rule is any inanimate object already bearing a magickal charge, or any magnetized object. Essentially you will want to bear in mind that magnetic energies draw, and electrical energies vitalize. With experimentation you will also find that magnetic energies can sometimes deflect directed charges, just as electrical energies can sometimes cause inertia.

For healing purposes you will generally want to use a magnetic breath so that the electrical response will accelerate the healing process. This is particularly effective with wounds, burns, and other short-term injuries. An electrical breath is best used in the healing of long-term illnesses only in conjunction with other magickal techniques. The magnetic response is useful in allowing the illness to be receptive to other types of magickal energy directed toward the patient. Electrical breath will also enhance the effects of medication.

THE MAGICK MIRROR

The magick mirror is an old hereditary tool for both divination and spell casting. It involves a dark concave surface of reflective material. One can easily be constructed by using the curved glass face of a clock and painting the convex side with glossy black paint. To prepare a magick mirror, begin on the night of the full moon. It is particularly effective to do this when the moon is in the sign of Pisces, Cancer, or Scorpio.

Once the paint has thoroughly dried, bathe the mirror in an herbal brew of rosemary, fennel, rue, vervain, ivy, and walnut leaves or bark. If you want to be truly traditional, pour some sea foam into the mixture. While the glass is sitting in the potion, hold both your hands out over it, palms down, and say:

I awaken the sleeping spirits of old,
whose eyes reveal all that is told,
give to me visions within this dark
well,

and make this a portal of magickal spell.

Envision in your mind a mist forming around the mirror. Take a deep breath and then slowly exhale outward upon the potion. Repeat this three times. Remove the mirror from the potion and dry it off thoroughly. Prop the mirror up vertically, sandwiched between two sturdy books or book ends to hold it in place. The supports should not obscure more than half of the mirror. Hold your right hand out in front of you so that your palm is facing the convex side of the mirror. Then place the left palm facing the concave side, about three inches away from the glass surface. You are now ready to magnetize the mirror to your aura. With the left hand, begin making a circular clockwise motion, staying within the dimensions of the mirror. Do this for a few minutes and then perform the same motion on the convex side of the mirror with the right hand. The opposite hand is always held still while the moving hand circulates.

Once completed, take the mirror out beneath the full moon and allow the moonlight to fall upon the concave side. Slowly fill the glass to the brim with the herbal potion. Hold it up toward the moon, almost level with your eyes. Don't worry about spilling. While looking at the moon allow your eyes to unfocus slightly. If you are doing this correctly, you will see three lines of light seemingly emanating from the moon. Continue

to squint until the vertical line coming from the bottom of the moon seems to touch upon the mirror.

Once the moonbeam is touching the mirror, speak these words:

> *Three are the lights seen*
> *and one not between,*
> *for the Enchantress at last*
> *dwells within the dark glass.*

Quickly close your eyes so that you break eye contact. Open them again, looking down toward the glass. Kneel and pour out the potion on the earth in the manner of libation. Then rinse the mirror off with fresh clear water. Finally, wrap the mirror in a silk cloth to protect its lunar magnetism. Never allow sunlight to fall directly on the mirror. The mirror is now ready to be used for divination or spell casting.

The technique is a very ancient one common among Shamanistic Traditions. Divination is the ability to see what patterns are forming toward manifestation. What you see is actually what is likely to occur if nothing changes the pattern being woven in the astral material. The following technique will provide you with the basic foundation for performing the art of divination known as scrying. Place two candles (as your source of light) so that the light does not reflect directly upon the mirror (off a foot or two, in front of you, flanking the mirror should do it).

Next, perform a series of slow and deliberate hand passes over the mirror. Magically speaking, the right hand has an electrical nature/active charge, and the left hand has a magnetic/receptive charge. A left-handed pass will attract an image toward formation and right-handed passes will strengthen or focus the image. Begin by making left-handed passes over the mirror, in a clockwise circle, just a few inches above it, with palms open and facing down. Stop and gaze into the dark reflection—not at it but into it. You will need to repeat these passes as you await the vision. Alternate between the left hand and the right hand. This requires patience and time. Use your intuition as you sit before the mirror. Make sure the setting is quiet without distractions. Drinking a cup of rosemary tea prior to divination can aid in the work. Bear in mind that rosemary can be toxic when ingested in large amounts, so limit yourself to no more than one or two cups.

The magick mirror can also be used for spell casting. This is a simple technique involving reflections or sigils. Light two candles and set them off to each side of the mirror—about three inches away. Place a photograph, image, or sigil of the target of your spell so that it reflects in the mirror. Gaze into the mirror and imagine the desired effect. Make up a short rhyme if you like, so you can state your desire without breaking your concentration. If you desire to

be rid of an influence or situation, you can sigilize it and then burn the sigil while gazing into the reflected flames in the mirror.

Another effective method is to gently blow incense smoke onto the mirror as you gaze at the reflection. Allow yourself to stir your emotions, then deeply inhale, and slowly exhale across a stick of incense. Imagine the smoke to be a magickal vapor carrying your will. As it touches the mirror, imagine the target responding as you wish it to. Do this a total of three times. Creating a short rhyme for your spell can be helpful in this technique as well.

Once you are finished, combine the melted wax, ashes from the incense, and the photo or image you used. Dispose of this in a manner in keeping with the elemental nature of your spell. Matters of love and feelings generally belong to water. Creative or artistic ventures belong to air. Situations of loss, separation, or destruction can be associated with fire. Endurance, strength, fertility, and stability are typically linked to earth.

To toss something into moving water will merge it with the water element, thus connecting it on a macrocosmic level with the higher nature of the spell. This helps to empower your act of magick. For earth-related spells you would bury the object in an area connected to your target. Spells related to the element of fire involve burning the links. Finally, for an air-related spell you would use steam or smoke.

THE VAPOROUS MAGICK

The term "vaporous magick" refers to an etheric substance generated from the circulatory system into the lungs. One aspect of vaporous magick is related to occult magnetism and is known as fascination or enchantment. As with occult magnetic energy in general, vaporous magick is raised by the odic breath and launched through the eyes, the renowned magickal gaze.In many cultures this power was feared and came to be known as "the evil eye." People who fell under the influence of vaporous magick were said to be bewitched.

The ancients believed that mysterious forces darted from the eyes of envious or angry persons. This energy, often seen as malevolent, contaminated the atmosphere around the person to whom it was directed. The ability of a glance to transmit power is a widespread belief throughout Europe. In Italy it is often referred to as the *jettarore*. People particularly feared the power of sorcerers to enchant livestock by their magickal glance. For this reason, ornamental charms were hung on horses, cattle, and other livestock. Such charms, traditionally made with shiny reflective surfaces, were thought to dispel the evil eye.

The ancients believed that the power to enchant through the eyes was more pronounced in women. In modern Italy, however, folklore belief now attributes this power to be stronger in men. Italian folklore prescribes, as a protection, the carrying of the herb rue, a wolf's tail, a piece of onion, or the root of an herb known as Lady's Glove. Italian folklore also holds that to avert the magickal glance, one need only quickly dart two extended fingers toward the perpetrator.

In ancient Rome, charms known as *fascinum* were devised as protections against the magickal glance. The most popular was a small hand which is closed, the thumb protruding between the fore and middle fingers. It is one of the oldest forms still in use today, and relates to phallic symbolism. The god Fascinus was worshiped under the form of a phallus, and he was associated with the sea. For this reason, the hand charm is traditionally made from coral, particularly red coral. Red is the color of life and vitality, an energy that protects against misfortune or decline.

The fact that the magickal glance can be used for healing and other positive forms of magick has become lost in folklore following the rise of Christianity. Magick was, and still is, discouraged by the Church, and therefore all acts of magick have come to be viewed as malevolent in common European folklore. Modern Italian Witches typically employ vaporous magick for healing illness and for charging items with personal power. It is particularly effective when combined with the magical emanation of moonlight.

DRAWING THE MOON'S LIGHT

To draw the moon's light is, in effect, to capture power emanating from its light. In Old Ways magick there are two basic methods of drawing the moon's light. The first is to snare it using the gesture known as the *talons*. Here is the technique: hold your hand out in front of you, palm facing away from you. Bend the little finger down, leaving the other three fingers and thumb up. Next bend the three fingers and thumb halfway down, forming a "bird's claw." Then turn your hand sideways with your thumb in front of you at about eye level. Turn your hand away from you, outward in a sweeping semicircle as though brushing something away. As you do this, quickly close the talons together as though you are a bird of prey catching something in midflight.

The talons are used to catch moonlight at specific times. The times of power are at rising, immediately as the full moon clears the horizon (hills, buildings, or whatever), and when the moon is directly overhead. Once snared, the power is placed within an object, which serves to charge the object with astral energy. To do this, simply snare the light and then press the three fingers and thumbs together tightly. Place the fingertips directly upon the object, press firmly, and then quickly open and withdraw your fingers upward. This action will release the energy and the charge is completed. This is a good method for recharging ritual blades, penta-grams, crystals, divinatory runes, and magickal/ritual items.

The second technique is a modern one and employs the use of a crystal. The crystal is held between the thumb and forefinger, with the pointed end of the crystal toward the palm, but the sweeping motion is the same. The main difference is that once you sweep outward, quickly fold your other three fingers over the crystal, enclosing it in your hand. Then squeeze the crystal firmly in your hand. Next place your opposite hand over the closed hand, and again squeeze firmly. The charge is now set within the crystal.

The talons technique can be used to capture the essence of the moon's influence as it occupies a specific zodiac sign. It can also be used to capture the essence of a rainbow, a comet, or any phenomena that you wish to align with. To release a charge, simply pass the crystal through a candle flame several times, and then place the crystal in salt water for about an hour. Take the crystal out, rinse it in clear water, and then set in out in the sun for fifteen minutes or more, but no longer than one hour.

THE WITCHES' TOOLS

The oldest Witches' tool is the staff or wand. This tool originates from the early days of tree worship. Tree roots went deep into the ground and their branches reached upward into the sky. The trunk of the tree thus formed a bridge between the Underworld and the Heavens. For this reason tree stumps were often used as altars by the Witches of old. This sacred connection is why the Slain God or Divine King was hung on the tree; in this manner he himself became the bridge between the land of his tribe and the realm of the gods.

Certain trees, especially the oak and the walnut, were considered to be gods themselves. For a Witch to bear a branch formed into a staff or wand meant that he or she was an emissary from the gods. This was his or her authority to act as a priest or priestess of the God or Goddess. The second oldest Witches' tool is the ritual cup, which evolved from a simple gourd or wooden bowl. It was used to contain wine and other ritual liquids.

Following the cup was the pentacle, which was also made of wood—evolving as a type of portable altar. On it was engraved the five-pointed star, symbolizing the power of the four elements of Nature held in harmony by the presence of a fifth element known as spirit. Objects were placed on the pentacle, focusing creative elements there in order to cast spells. Last in line was the dagger, which evolved from the sickle used to harvest crops or slay animals for sacrifice. This tool did not appear in the Old Religion until around the Agrarian period. In what is known today as the Cary-Yale Visconti tarot, dating from the fifteenth century, the images of the traditional tools of Western Occultism (wand, cup, pentacle, and blade) have been preserved in the Magician card.

During the Middle Ages, and into the Renaissance period, many family witches preferred to use the mortar and pestle as ritual tools, in order to avoid accusations of Witchcraft. This provided the Witch with a wand and chalice. A simple platter and a common knife completed the set of tools. The tools were marked with a washable dye that could be quickly removed in case of intruders. By the nineteenth century, secure in the facade of Masonry, many family Witches went back to using the formal traditional tools crafted in the Old Ways with permanent designs and symbols.

The cauldron is featured prominently in Italian Witchcraft, most likely due to the Italic Pagan associations of the hearth with family, ancestral spirits, and household spirits known as the Lare or Lasa. The gift-bearing Witch known as Befana who fills the stockings of children during the holiday season in Italy is strongly connected to the hearth. Her basket or sack of presents is a remnant of the magickal cauldron. In modern times she also carries a broom, but in ancient times Befana would have flown on the back of a goat, for she is the goddess Fana whose consort was Faunus, the goat-horned god. In early Italian lore, Witches did not fly on broomsticks but on the backs of magickal goats that carried them to the Treguenda.

As a ritual tool the broom is used to cleanse the ritual setting. It is also laid, as a protective barrier, across the portal opening in a ritual circle when it is left open. Symbolically the broom represents purification, and since "thoughts are things" to an astral entity, the broom becomes a very real deterrent. On a magickal level, a Witch's broomstick was comprised of three different plant materials. The handle was made of ash, the sweep of birch twigs, and the handle binding was made of willow strips. Ash gave Witches power over the elements, birch protected them from evil spirits, and willow declared their allegiance to the goddess Hecate Triformis. The broomstick was comprised of three materials, a triad symbol announcing to all spirits that the Witch was given authority in the name of Hecate. Therefore the broom can become a tool of banishment by sweeping toward the portal, or thrashing the air to chase off unwanted spirits.

Figure 45. *The Witch Befana in traditional folk costume. Family Witches place a statue of Befana on the mantle, and the children's stockings are hung there to be filled with treats on the night of January 6. Befana is the gift-giver, an ancestral spirit who binds together both past and present generations.*

THE WITCHES' GOSPEL

The idea, much less the existence, of a Witches' *gospel* is something very controversial in the Craft today. Yet, it is really not so unreasonable to consider that sacred writings exist within the Witches' sect. Most religions possess a sacred text of some nature, whether written by their founders or created by disciples. In those Italian traditions arising from the teachings of Aradia, we do indeed find a collection of texts commonly referred to as the Book of the Holy Strega. The so-called *Gospel of the Witches* is part of these sacred writings.

Following the publication of *Ways of the Strega,* some readers questioned the validity of concepts attributed therein to the time of Aradia. Primarily in doubt were such elements as a female "messiah" figure, along with the prophecy of a coming age that she would usher in. To avoid further misunderstandings, in this chapter we will examine the religious influences and the historical setting in Italy during the fourteenth century, the time of Aradia.

In the late twelfth century, Joachim de Flora (also called Joachim de Fieore), the Abbot of Corazzo, wrote a prophetic text on the Age of Reason.

191

His writings had a major influence on religious thought throughout the remainder of the Middle Ages. In 1200 Joachim passed his writings on to the Holy See for approval. Concerning the Age of Reason to come, Joachim wrote:

> The Old Testament period was under the direct influence of God the Father. With the advent of Christ, came the age of God the Son. The time was now ripe for the reign of God the Holy Ghost. A new era was being introduced, a culmination; in the new day man would not have to rely on faith for everything would be founded on knowledge and reason.

The year 1300 was declared a Jubilee Year by Boniface VIII. It was also the year that Dante had his "vision: of Inferno Panderers." A sect known as the Guglielmites believed that a certain woman named Guglielma of Milan was the incarnation of the Holy Spirit and wished to establish a church with a female pope and female cardinals. Millennialism has frequently provided a basis for social progress for women. Women have historically taken very active and creative roles in millennial groups, even in societies where their voices would normally have been repressed, as was the case concerning Guglielma of Milan.

Manfreda Visconti was elected by the Guglielmites to be their Papess. The year 1300 was to usher in a new era of female popes, with Manfreda officiating at a mass at Ste. Maria Maggiore. She was later burned at the stake as a heretic. Guglielma was, in reality, Princess Blazena Vilemina, daughter of the King of Bohemia. She was born in 1210, arrived in Milan around 1260, and reportedly died on August 12, 1281. Guglielma appeared in Milan dressed as a "common woman," but because of her noble background, she attracted followers from both the Visconti family and the Torriani family (noble rivals of the time) and was seen as a "peacemaker" between the families. There is some conjecture that she might have been influenced by the sisters of the "Free Spirit," a very prominent heretical group of the time, which preached the teachings of Joachim.

Guglielma's chief disciple, Andrea Saramita, said that he heard her make claims to "divinity." He was a rather wealthy layman, well versed in the teachings of Joachim concerning the Age of the Spirit. He wrote most of the documents and was the chief theologian of the sect.

Maifreda da Pirovano, cousin of Matteo Visconti, was appointed chief of the Guglielmite sect. Maifreda was actually granted the title of Pope by the sect, vicar of the Holy Spirit upon earth. According to legend, it is her portrait on the Papessa card of the Visconti tarot deck. Of the approximately thirty members of the sect from about seven Milanese families, women outnumbered men, but ten of the most fervent members were male. The sect had an interesting social life, practicing equality of the genders in all regards. There was no emphasis on virginity or chastity in the sect, although a number of the female members were widowed or unmarried.

What is interesting is that, unheard of in their time, the members of the sect crossed social boundaries. Both wealthy and poor people, including servants, were involved— membership ranged from the ruler's son, Galeazzo Visconti, to a poor seamstress named Taria, and Bianca, a serving maid. On the grounds that Guglielma had wanted her devotees to remain together as a family, they held frequent commemorative meals in her honor. Reportedly there were attempts throughout the 1300s to continue the remembrance of Guglielma by hiding her image in paintings and calling her by various names.

The theme of a female messiah, a commemorative meal, and a coming Age of Reason may well have laid the foundation for the legends surrounding Aradia. At the very least it demonstrates that such a theme was known in Italy during the early fourteenth century. The preexistence of these themes later appearing in the Aradia material lends credence to the Streghe legends, thus providing some historical foundation for the theme's logical appearance in Old Italy.

According to legend, Aradia was born in 1313 in the town of Volterra in northern Italy. She gathered a small band of followers and went about the countryside, teaching and preaching the Old Religion of Italy. Aradia spoke of an Age of Reason to come that would replace the Age of the Son. When she departed, Aradia requested that a meal be held in her honor, and that she be remembered by future generations.

In this chapter the Witches' Gospel is presented as it was passed to me, but in a modified form. I have tried to preserve the quaint quality of the old style for the sake of tradition and the feel of antiquity. What you are about to read is my own rendering, drawn from both written and oral tradition. In 1981 I produced a version of the Witches' Gospel through private publication. The Gospel as depicted in this current book is based upon the former work, but is rooted in old traditional teachings.

Whether the Gospel of the Witches has come down to us from the fourteenth century, or whether Aradia ever existed as a historical person is of secondary importance, if important at all. What is worthwhile are the spiritual teachings and the message of the gospel itself. For here is the tale of the struggle of the human spirit for release from bondage. Here also is the strength of the human spirit in adversity, the power to endure, and the tenacity of a belief system surviving against all the odds.

Personally, I believe in the actual existence of Aradia, and I believe in her teachings. But I believe in many impossible things; I believe that someday the lives of people will be more important than the thriving of corporations, and that the health of our planet will be held in greater value than quarterly profit margins. I believe that someday we shall all be united by our similarities instead of divided by our differences. Yes, I'm a dreamer, but dreams give beauty to the world. So when I look up at the dirty skyline of the city, gaze out over polluted lakes and rivers, and absorb the cancer-causing rays of the sun streaming through holes in the Earth's ozone layer, I believe in the Old Ways, in Aradia, and in the impossible.

GOSPEL OF THE HOLY STREGA

Aradia was a child of the spirit, and even in her youth she heard the voices that only the ancients once knew. In the early hours of the dawn she walked among the Alban hills near lake Nemi. One day, after having journeyed far into the hills, she grew tired and took her rest beneath the shade of a large tree. As she centered her thoughts within her mind, a voice spoke to her, saying:

"Look well into the skies, and know that you are chosen."

Aradia gazed upward, the skies darkened, and the voice whispered to her the words *"Moon shadow."* Something within her awoke, and she understood the path that lay ahead of her. Looking about from the hillside, she saw the beauty of Creation and the equality of all things. An understanding of

the inner workings of Nature awoke within her, and with this enlightenment she opened up her heart and mind to the vastness of all she perceived. Then Aradia beheld the oppression of the peasant people, knew their sorrows, and was greatly moved with compassion.

In the time of Aradia, many peasant slaves had escaped into the hills and forests. These people gathered into bands of outlaws in order to survive. Aradia sought them out, living with them for a period of time in the woodland camps near lake Nemi. There she listened to the plight of her people. Many suffered persecution from the Church because they worshiped in the Old Ways. Others were made slaves by evil Lords who held power in the land. Among these outlaws Aradia came to know many Witches who were also in hiding.

In time Aradia went down into the villages and towns in order to give hope to the people. She taught them, saying:

"Blessed be the free. Blessed be they who rejoice in truth and love, and seek not to maintain evil and misguided teachings. Know that the spirit is upon you all, and that spirit is love. Love punishes not, neither a day nor an eternity. Do not lend yourselves to teachings of fear and restriction. Blessed be the free in spirit for their kingdom is of both worlds. They are the Children of the Earth who neither hate nor teach hate, fear nor teach fear, restrict nor teach restriction. These same are the Children of Spirit."

Aradia gathered disciples and taught them the inner mysteries of the Old Ways that their ancestors once embraced. She revealed the true nature of the name Aradia, taken in honor of the ancient mythological daughter of Diana. Many people knew Aradia in her home town of Volterra, and in Benevento, before she took this name. Her fame soon spread to all regions of Italy; people came to listen to the words of Aradia and to join her as followers. She taught them the doctrine of reincarnation, and about the old gods. Aradia revealed the secrets of the earth and the knowledge of ancient teachings. Because of her fame, she fell into disfavor with the Church, and the priests plotted against her. Soldiers were sent to arrest her for heresy, and she was placed inside a prison. There Aradia suffered humiliation and torture. The officials feared her popularity among the peasants and desired to sentence her to death.

When morning arrived on the day the priests were to meet, they ordered Aradia brought before them, but she was not found in her cell. A search began for her, but she could not be located anywhere in the region. Later, in the south of Rome, Aradia appeared again and continued to teach. The people were amazed because they believed she had been killed or imprisoned for life. Hearing the news of her appearance in Rome the soldiers came to retrieve her. But none questioned by the soldiers claimed to know anything about Aradia. After the soldiers departed, the priests sent spies to dwell among the peasants in hopes of discovering her whereabouts.

In that same month some people discovered Aradia sitting with her disciples and instructing them. Aradia saw that they were joyful to encounter her, and she stood to teach them, saying:

"Blessed be the free in spirit and they who love without profit. For love is the greatest attainment. It is the gift of the spirit's blessing. Therefore never betray a love, nor deceive one. Love each other and care for each other, and for each thing, with the heart and soul of a poet.

"Strive to see the world as does the artist. Go, seek, and capture the beauty which is there. And take care that you hurt not even one that is among you. But love, and live, to the fullest, in awareness and compassion to the minds and hearts and souls of everyone around you. Live in peace."

Many people began to question one another concerning Aradia. Her disciples came to her and said, "My Lady, some say you are a prophetess, and some say you are a Magus. What shall we tell them?" Aradia picked up a handful of earth, and looking at the crowd, she said:

"I am the Daughter of the Sun and the Moon. I am the Earth. I am the love of freedom which is the love of the gods. And whosoever shall believe in me, the same shall be a child of the Mother and Father who dwell in all things."

A spy from the Church approached and asked: "Lady, we know that you are a holy one: tell us of the God from which your power comes."

Aradia replied: "Though men shall call upon many gods, there is but One, which is the many. A man in his life is called by many names. Some may know him as Father, or a friend. To some he may be an enemy or a brother, and to another a cousin. Yet is he still not the one man?"

Another spy asked her: "The priests tell us that God is male, and that women must submit to men. What do you say?"

Aradia answered: "Does not even Nature show you, in all ways, that all is equal? In all flora and fauna, there is male and female. Who among you can truly say which is more important? One cannot be without the other."

After this a disciple asked: "Lady, if all you speak is so, why then do the priests not tell us?"

Aradia replied: "These priests tell what they have been told. It is with they who are above the priests that the truth is known, and hidden. There are many greedy and power-hungry men who profit from the Church. It is better for them to control with false teachings, that restrict and threaten independence from the priesthood."

The spies returned to the priests and reported what they had heard. The priests were angry and spread lies concerning Aradia's teachings, claiming they were evil. After Aradia and her disciples had left the area the soldiers returned again, seeking to arrest her. On the road they surrounded Aradia and her followers, taking her into custody. As they traveled back to Rome a band of outlaws approached them. The leader was a slave whom Aradia had converted to moon worship in the cult of Diana. A fight resulted in which Aradia was freed and taken by the outlaws into a hiding place.

The outlaws escorted Aradia and her followers to their camp in the forest. There she chose twelve of her disciples, six male and six female, and took them into a clearing in order to instruct them.

Aradia spoke to them: "With you I now reestablish the Old Religion. Know that there are others who still worship in the ways of their ancestors. Seek them out and tell them the Mother is with Child, and they will understand my meaning. Seek out also they who will come to follow us."

The disciples asked her: "Who is this Child? Tell us of her."

Aradia answered: "The infant is the Child of the Mother of the Earth. She shall be known as that which is reason and wisdom. She shall come to the world and deliver all people of all nations from the rule of kings, and of authorities. In this Age of the Daughter, great changes shall occur such as the world has never known. This shall be a time of renewal."

Her disciples asked her: "When shall this occur?"

She told them: "The dawning of the Age will be signaled by the Will of the Daughter. Her words will be heard among the words of men. Then women shall walk in the ways of men, and the law shall know no difference. When this occurs the Age has begun. And my prophet shall then restore my teachings, making ready the dawn of the Age for she who will come. And in the year of this prophet's birth there shall be a sign for which all witches may rejoice. For this year shall be the rebirth of the Old Religion."

Aradia spoke further: "Yet before this time there shall be death among our people. The time is near when my followers shall be taken before the courts. And they shall persecute you and deliver you to the dungeons. And my people shall be tortured and killed by order of the Church. Even as they were once persecuted, so shall the Christians persecute you. But the Age of the Son shall draw to an end, giving way to the Age of the Daughter.

"You have heard the priests tell you of hell, and of damnation. But I say to you, believe not in such things. For the spirit of the Great One is love, and love damns not, but blesses. For a Father's and Mother's love does not forget the child, nor does it put one child away and keep the other."

All that day Aradia instructed her disciples and answered their questions. She taught them the secrets of magick and the knowledge of ritual. Aradia and her disciples went again out into the villages and towns in order for her to heal the sick and teach the Old Religion, even though they feared for their safety.

Soldiers, accompanied by several priests, came to arrest her. Realizing she was trapped, Aradia looked upon them sternly, saying: "I rebuke you, and I cast you out from the people because you teach punishment and shame to those who would free themselves from the slavery of the Church. These symbols and apparel of authority which you bear serve only to hide the nakedness in which we are all equal. You say that you serve your God, but you serve only your own fears and restrictions."

The soldiers seized her, even though many people tried to protect her. Her disciples fled to avoid being captured themselves. In the town of Benevento they took refuge among the followers of Aradia already living there. Aradia was put into prison and was condemned for heresy and treason. While in prison a certain guard was very moved by her beauty and charm. Aradia allowed him to come to her as a lover. On the eve of her execution, Aradia persuaded him to take her into the courtyard, so she could pray out in the open.

Two other guards overlooked the courtyard as she prayed. After she had finished, a storm gathered and the guard told Aradia to return to her cell. As she complied, the storm crashed over them with great fury. An earthquake shook the ground and the buildings fell, stone by stone. When calm returned at last, only a few people were found alive. Word spread far and wide that Aradia had perished.

Seven days later, Aradia appeared in the camp of the forest outlaws; everyone was amazed to see her because it was reported that she had died. Aradia would not speak to them concerning this, and she gathered together those disciples who still followed her and left the forest. They journeyed into the hills near Nemi. When they had settled for the night, Aradia came to them and said: "The time is now marked, and I shall remain with you for but a short while longer."

Aradia marked a circle upon the ground, spanning nine paces from the center. She gathered her disciples into the circle and formally instructed them. Following this, Aradia addressed them: "When you have need of anything, gather then in secret when the moon is full, and worship the spirit of the Queen of all Witches. Gather yourself within the circle of the arts, and secrets that are as yet unknown shall be revealed. And you shall be free of mind and spirit, and as a sign that you are truly free, you shall be naked in your rites. For such is the essence of spirit and joy upon the earth. And your law shall be love unto all. Be true to your own beliefs. Keep to your ways beyond all obstacles. For

ours is the key to the mysteries, and the cycle of rebirth, which opens the door unto the womb of enlightenment. I am the Spirit of all Witches, which is joy and peace, and harmony. In life does the Queen of all Witches reveal the knowledge of Spirit. And from Death does the Queen deliver you unto peace and renew your life again."

Aradia next taught her disciples about the secrets of the circle. She spoke of the gods and the Old Ones, known as the Grigori (Watchers). She taught them all types of enchantments, signs in the sky, and of the seasons.

When Aradia had revealed these things to her disciples, she told them: "In memory of me you shall eat cakes of grain, wine, salt, and honey. These shall you shape like the crescent of the moon. Then shall you bless them in my name and partake of them upon your sacred gatherings. As of old, you shall hold sacred the first day of May, and of August, and also the eve of November, which is the time of Shadows. Of February shall you observe its second day. Also shall you observe the Solstices of midsummer and midwinter, and the Equinoxes of Spring and Autumn. To all who observe these sacred times will the Queen of Heaven give the power. And you shall enjoy success in love. And you shall have power to bless and to consecrate. And you shall know the tongue of the spirits, obtain knowledge of hidden things, and raise forth the spirits from beyond the void. You shall understand the Voice of the Wind, and the knowledge of the changing of forms. To you shall the future be known and secret signs revealed. And you shall have power to cure disease and to bring forth beauty. Wild beasts shall know you and cause you no harm. Know that the power is gained through knowledge, and the knowledge is gained through understanding. Know therefore that you must obtain the balance. Everything which lives is of male and female essence. Do not exalt the one without the other. Come to know both as to be complete. Blessed be the free in spirit. When you hate, or despair, or do not understand, it is because you are not in balance with yourself or your surroundings. I do not speak alone of masculine and feminine, but of elements and causes and forces. Seek first the balance, then you will understand, and understanding you will overcome what you must."

Aradia stood in the midst of her disciples and spoke: "My purpose is firmly set forth, and to you I now give the Power. In my name shall you go forth and teach the ways of freedom and magic."

Aradia let her garments fall, fully revealing herself to her disciples. She took one of them by the hand and brought him beside her upon the ground. There upon the sacred earth, beneath the star-filled night, they were joined in love. After this, each disciple was joined to the other. In this way the power passed in love among the followers of Aradia.

It was early morning when the disciples gathered again to hear Aradia speak. She said to them: "With you I now establish a covenant, between you and me and likewise to all who shall come to follow in the ways."

Aradia then placed a scroll into the hands of the disciples upon which were written thirteen laws. She also gave them the nine sacred scrolls that she had written. This was the foundation of all the teachings that she had come into this life to teach.

Aradia spoke again to her disciples: "Soon you shall go forth among they who dwell outside of the Ways. And you shall meet ignorance, fear, and misunderstanding. Therefore, protect yourselves in all ways. And you shall come upon many who truly seek to be one with the nature of things. Teach all whom you find sincere and truly worthy. Yet take care that you do not become judgmental. Keep your own manner of being separate, and do not expect everyone to be a likeness of yourself. Show love and warmth to all persons, for if you do not then many shall turn away from you. How then shall you serve the ways? Know that your first allegiance is to the God and Goddess, your second allegiance is to the Old Ways, and the third is to Witches all. If you serve yourself then you do not serve. When you serve your own self-importance you are out of balance with Nature. For in Nature all things are equal. Nothing is more important than any other thing. And yet all living things have the right to do what they must to survive. This is to the disadvantage of other living things, which becomes the essence for survival. Who can speak against the order of things? Therefore, live your life as you must, according to the laws which I have given you. Enjoy each day and long not for the next. The only certainty is now. Do not become bitter or cold at the seeming harshness and unfairness of life, for love has the power to overcome all things. Nothing lasts forever and nothing remains the same, for everything is even now moving toward that which it will become. Therefore I tell you to observe the cycles of everything, within you and outside you."

It was her practice to teach her disciples in this manner. As the time for instruction was almost completed one of the disciples asked Aradia to speak again of the coming Age.

Aradia told them: "The Age of the Daughter is the final Age to dawn upon the earth. The first Age was that of the Mother, when all people worshiped the Great Goddess. The second Age was that of the Father and the third Age is the Son. Under the Mother there arose all goddesses and their cults. With the Age of the Father arose the gods which came to then dominate the female cults. It was then that the warrior cults began to rule the world. The dawning of the Son brought love and compassion to the world. From this Age arose the Christ spirit, but men clung to their stern Father God. Now when the Age of the Daughter shall come, then shall reason be restored and the world shall be in balance. To herald the coming of the Daughter, and to keep it remembered upon the earth, every two hundred years there shall arise a prophet. This prophet shall be a great teacher, and shall give life to the Old Religion. When the Age of the Daughter draws near, there shall be an awakening in the awareness of women, and their will shall be asserted. Laws will then change and women shall walk in the ways of men. And there shall be a time when the last of the laws which persecute and suppress us shall be removed. In that year all of Stregeria shall rejoice. When the Age of the Daughter begins to replace that of the Son, then shall my prophet appear. And many shall call this one the Silent Prophet. At this time there shall come many changes. Changes shall occur in the earth which the people of that time have never seen before. And there will be great renewal and upheaval. When the Age of the Daughter replaces that of the Son, then shall she appear who is to establish reason. And she will be thirty-six at this time. And she will come in Power, for the Silent Prophet will have established the way. As this Age progresses great trial and tribulation shall befall the people of all nations. And out of the ashes shall arise the new world of reason. People shall no longer be ruled by governments. Nor shall one people oppress another. There shall be no rulers, but only teachers and counselors. No one shall possess power over another, nor shall anyone restrict or control any other person. The earth shall be of one people, and they will all live under the emanating rays of love, peace, and reason."

All that day and into the evening Aradia spoke of future events. The next day Her disciples departed as instructed, in pairs of male and female to teach others the Gospel of Aradia. She had bid them farewell and directed them to go out into all the towns and villages.

In the days that followed, the fame of Aradia and her wisdom and beauty went forth over all the land. People began to worship her, calling her *The Beautiful Pilgrim.* There were those who said she was the Goddess in human form. Her disciples traveled with a heavy heart because Aradia had spoken of the darkness of the times to come. They carried with them the thought of the many centuries that were to pass before the promised Age would dawn.

After traveling from village to village, the disciples returned to the town of Benevento. There they gathered the covens of Aradia which she had favored. The disciples taught them each the final words that Aradia had spoken, and they shared the knowledge of the sacred scrolls with them. The followers of Aradia formed into Clans, and a covenant was established to secure the teachings of Aradia for the future. The Laws of the Covenant of Aradia were established at this time in order to unite the Clans in the Old Ways.

These groups then departed to distant places, fearing further persecution by the enemies of Aradia. However, there remained those followers who would not depart. Aradia was not seen again by the people of that region. But her followers remembered her teachings, and gathered and celebrated as the Holy One had bid them, even as they do to this very day.

Here ends the Gospel of the Holy Strega.

THE COVENANT OF ARADIA

I. Observe the times of the sacred gatherings, for therein is the foundation of the powers.

II. When good is done for you, you are bound to return it threefold. And if you shall help another you will not accept payment but shall bind the one served to likewise help yet another three (people).

III. Use not your power or knowledge of the Craft, neither call forth your aids, for your own glory or as proof of your standing. Work instead for the good of your coven or for those who are outside (should they prove worthy). For your own need you may work if no harm is done through your gain.

IV. Take not the life of any living thing except it be to preserve another life. If you take a life to provide food, then all of its being must be used in respect to its life force. That which cannot be used must be returned to the Earth with blessings made.

V. Give not your word lightly, for you are bound by your words, and by your oaths.

VI. You shall not bow before any authority over you except it be that of the Creators, or their emissaries. All others are worldly ego.

VII. You are bound to teach and initiate all who appear worthy, and to aid in the continuance of the Old Religion.

VIII. Belittle not another's beliefs nor degrade another for their ways. But offer your own truth without argument and strive to dwell in peace with those who differ.

IX. As there be no harm to another, then let your actions be as you will. Love and freedom are the essence of the Law.

X. Strive to live your life in compassion and awareness to the minds and hearts of all who share in your presence.

XI. Be true to your own understanding and strive to turn away from that which is opposed within you.

XII. Destroy not, neither scar, the beauty of Nature around you. Hold reverence for all things in Nature, second only to the Creators. Waste nothing.

XIII. Remain open in your heart and in your mind to the Great Ones, the Creators, and to your brothers and sisters alike.

THE WANDERINGS

In this chapter I present the tale referred to as "the Wanderings," which is an account of the followers of Aradia and their deeds after the disappearance of Aradia. Like the Gospel of the Holy Strega in chapter 12, I have tried to maintain the flavor of the material by leaving it as close as possible to the quaint form in which it was told at the turn of the century. However, in order to provide ease of reading for the modern reader, I have modified the style in which I first presented the material through private publication in 1981. The reader will notice that this chapter repeats portions of the Gospel theme presented in chapter 12. This is because the text known as the "Wanderings" is an extension of the Gospel story as it relates to Aradia's followers. Although we do encounter the same basic underlying theme found in the Witches' Gospel, the Wanderings provides further insights and completes the tale.

The text comprising the Wanderings here is my own rendering, based on oral legends passed down through the centuries. I do not claim to possess the original writings, nor do I know how old they may be, or even if they still exist. My intent in presenting the material here is simply to preserve a heroic tale. No mythos would be complete without representation of the hero path; as Joseph Campbell calls it "the one deed done by many." Whether we speak of the legend of Hercules, Ulysses, or some other hero, we are telling the tale of that which is noble and enduring in human nature. Obviously not all legends are historical accounts, though indeed many are based on actual events. In a spiritual tradition, legends present important information in the form of metaphors. The meaning is all important; what it says to the heart rather than to the mind. So with this understanding, let us turn now and hear the tale of a band of vagabonds on a sacred quest.

THE WANDERINGS

This is the account of the followers of Aradia in the days subsequent to her disappearance. Aradia presented the nine sacred scrolls of the Teachings to her followers who were called the Keepers of the Covenant of Aradia. The Holy Strega requested that all the Clan should know of the final Teachings and of the Covenant. So the followers of Aradia assembled in the city of Benevento, and to them was made known all that Aradia had spoken. There was sorrow among the Clan because of Aradia's absence, and no one could say where she had gone.

All of the twelve, favored of Aradia, formed a group and separated themselves from those who had gathered in Benevento. Then it was decided who was to depart and to what places. Teresa and Alono left for Rome with Martea and Leo. To Naples went Maria and Niccolo with Sophia and Marcello. To the towns within the Kingdom went Andrea and Giovanni with Laura and Owen (the Celt). In the days that followed, the Teachings of Aradia were brought to the people wherever the disciples journeyed, and all were amazed at what they heard.

Not everyone welcomed the words of Aradia, and some went before the authorities to report all they had heard. The men in power remembered Aradia and, wishing to suppress support for her followers, they sent soldiers out among the people to threaten and cause fear. The soldiers then went out on the roads under orders to capture fleeing heretics and pagans.

Many of the people turned against the disciples of Aradia for their own safety, and the disciples were forced to flee from Naples and Rome. Martea and Leo were ambushed as they fled. Leo was slain and Martea was never seen or heard from again. Teresa and Alono fled to the old camp of the outlaws and were given shelter. When word reached the other disciples concerning the death of Leo, they too journeyed from Naples to the camp of the outlaws.

On the third day the disciples arrived in the camp and spoke of the path ahead. The sacred scrolls were given to Andrea, and the

Covenant of Aradia was placed in the hands of Alono. The disciples pledged their loyalty, renewed their love, and decided to travel to the north of Italy. Owen swore to guard the scrolls and Andrea with his life, and accompanied her to Volterra. He had been one of the *Condottiere* and was skilled with the sword. He was a large and powerful man.

The disciples journeyed to the North and began to teach in that region. They went forth as priests and priestesses of the Goddess, and established the Old Ways among the people. In the second year following the departure of Aradia, the disciples returned to the city of Benevento. With them were many followers who had come from the north, for there was danger from the mercenaries of powerful families (for Christian and Pagan alike).

Therefore, in the region of Benevento, the disciples went in secret and taught the people, establishing many Groves (covens). They divided the Kingdom into separate Clans, so that within the Kingdom of Naples there were three Clans. Andrea departed toward Rome with Owen, Laura, and Giovanni. They journeyed to the sacred hills of Nemi, and established yet another three Clans in the region of the Alban hills. All that winter the disciples were given shelter by outlaws. In the spring the other disciples joined them from the south. In the summer the people of the region came and joined in the teachings and the feasts.

One day there came to the camp a woman who was called Madrona. She was a Strega, well known for her powers in that region. At great length did the disciples speak with her, and together they shared much concerning the Old Ways. Madrona decided to travel with the disciples, and in her company was a man called Olar (some say he was a Gypsy). Often he would entertain the disciples with strange songs and stories of distant places, and from Olar the disciples learned many things. Olar was a man of many powers, and his ways were not unlike those of the Old Religion. The disciples were pleased to number twelve again. Olar and Madrona swore to the Covenant of Aradia, becoming true followers of Aradia.

In time word came to the outlaws that the people of Rome were summoned for an official proclamation. So the disciples went into Rome to obtain knowledge of this occasion. There they found a man who spoke out against the nobles of Rome, claiming power for himself. This man began to call himself by the ancient title of Tribune, and the disciples were divided by their hopes for the future of the Old Religion.

In a short time the nobles rose up against the Tribune and a battle occurred. They were not successful and many were killed. The disciples left Rome and returned to the hills. The outlaws were joyful at the news that the disciples brought because there was no love for the nobles among any who dwelled in the camp, but word came to the disciples, as winter approached, that the nobles had again taken control of Rome.

The disciples returned to Rome for awhile, but it was discovered that they came and went in the company of outlaws dwelling in the hills of Nemi. So the nobles decided to send fighting men out against them, claiming that all were threats to the peace and safety of honest men. With them were priests who began to question the people of the region about the sacred scrolls of Aradia. When word of this reached the disciples they were angry and saddened that someone had betrayed them. Then they began to regret that they had stayed so long in Rome.

The soldiers of the nobles set out and arrived at the place known by the outlaws as Diana's Embrace. The outlaws ambushed them with bows and swords. Some of the soldiers slipped through the passage during the battle and came upon the camp where the disciples were hiding.

They stormed the camp and set fire to the shelters. The disciples and all others in the camp, tried to flee, but many died that day. Owen was the first, as he took up his sword to protect Andrea, who was escaping with the scrolls. The soldiers rushed him but he fought with such fury that even the soldiers were moved by his courage. There were many soldiers who never lived to see him fall.

Andrea fell to the arrows of the enemy, and they took her bag containing the scrolls, killing Giovanni who had rushed to her side in an attempt to rescue the scrolls. Then the soldiers killed Marcello, and with him Laura and Sophia. Olar was captured as the other disciples escaped into the hills. The soldiers returned to Rome, and the priests were given the sacred scrolls of Aradia, which they sent to the Pope in Avignon. Fearing the end had come for the followers of Aradia, Alono took the other four disciples and departed to the north once again.

The disciples of Aradia went to the city (known now as Florence), bringing with them a small band of followers they had gathered during their journey. In that city many people were dying, for the Black Death had come upon them. The disciples began to despair and to regret their lot. They said among themselves: "How can it be that we find so much sorrow, for are we not true to the ancient ways?"

Alono and Madrona comforted them and reminded them of the teachings of Aradia, saying: "Did not our mistress bid us not to strive against the order of things, and has she not spoken of the dark times through which we must pass?" So the disciples stayed in Florence, helping the ill and giving comfort to the souls of both the living and the departed. Within the region of Florence the followers began to establish another three Clans.

In the second year of the plague, several of the followers of Aradia perished, and the disciples decided to separate to ensure that the Teachings would survive. Maria and Niccolo continued north and left Italy, eventually arriving in France at their journey's end. Madrona remained in the region of Florence and continued to teach the people there. Teresa and Alono traveled to the southern region and settled for a time. They did not teach in that region, neither did they establish any clan.

A year later, Teresa and Alono returned to Benevento and remained in secret. They wrote an account of the days which they had spent with Aradia, and of the times which followed (Teresa had been educated in the home of a noble family some years before). These writings they called the *Gospel,* in order to speak openly about the Teachings in safety. In Benevento they continued to teach the followers of Aradia, and the clans still met beneath the sacred walnut tree.

The disciples of Aradia gathered all the teachings that could be remembered, which Aradia had recorded in the Sacred Scrolls. They wrote these teachings down so that some portion of the scrolls might survive, and the disciples called this the *Words of Aradia.* In peace the followers of Aradia lived within the region, awaiting the prophecy that would mark the beginning of all that Aradia had spoken would come to pass:

"Now there shall shortly come the time when the Pope shall return to Rome. And he shall establish the ancient city again as his capital. This is the beginning of the sorrows which shall come upon our people. For this is the sign that the Church shall move against us in full power. But before the time of death, which we shall suffer at their hands, they shall pervert all knowledge of us and our ways. And they shall interpret scriptures against us and pass laws against us. All this shall come among the first sorrows. Yet this is not new to their ways. And for a time they shall prevail against us, and we shall seemingly vanish from the world. Yet we shall always remain. For we shall be reborn, and we shall remember, though they kill us a thousand times. And my words shall be spoken again and again. And my Teachings shall be restored. For there are none upon the earth who have power to slay the Spirit."

In the last days before Aradia departed, her disciples gathered before her one evening. To each of those gathered were the final instructions made known. Varro, who was greatly loved by Aradia, was called before her and was given charge over the favored disciples. Aradia spoke to Varro, in front of the twelve disciples, and she said:

"Swear now before me and my followers, and join yourself to solemn covenant, for all things such as I have told you. For you have agreed, and given your sworn oath, to fulfill my words now and at the appointed times."

Then when he had so sworn and sealed this covenant, Varro began to question Aradia concerning those who would not receive him or accept him. Aradia answered him, saying:

"Truly there shall be those who cannot, and those who will not, receive you. Such has it always been with those who speak of Spirit and of Truth. And among those who know you and love you, shall your greatest adversaries be.

"Say to all who do not receive your words, that which I now say to you: I speak of that which I know, beyond mere belief. And I tell you of things which I have seen, and of ways. If you cannot believe me when I speak of Nature, and of common ways, how then can I speak to you of higher things and different ways?

"If you say to me prove this or prove that, and shall put to the test all which I tell you, how shall I make you understand that which you are not prepared to receive?"

Aradia rose up and began to pace within the clearing. After a short time she turned to the disciples and said:

"Those who put you to the test and who ask for things beyond their own understanding, are like little children who ask questions which cannot be answered. And so you must make up stories for them and give simple replies, lest they become frustrated and confused.

"Therefore, speak not of the heavens to children, neither speak of the mysteries to fools. You have seen the light of the campfire, how insects are drawn into its flame. And you have seen the wild beasts flee before it, for they dare not to approach it. Yet do we not gather around it ourselves, and draw from it comfort? So is it with your own light unto all who behold it."

After Aradia had spoken to them concerning these things, she went with Varro into the woods that they might speak alone. Half the day was spent in this manner. When Varro returned, the disciples began to question him concerning what Aradia had spoken to him. Varro told them many things that disturbed them; he was chosen to bear her words in the time to come and many of the disciples were jealous.

When Aradia heard the disciples arguing, she was angered and rebuked them, saying:

"Have you not understood as I have taught you? Tell me what thing is greater than another, or what person?

"Who among you knows the course of things which are to be, and who among you has power and vision to secure the future?

"I am no greater than any one of you, yet I stand upon a hill and can see that which you cannot. I stand where I stand because I have journeyed there. This place belongs to me, yet only for an instant. Then I am no longer at the end of my journey, but once again at the beginning of another. You have called me your teacher, and you have followed me. I ask now that you trust me. You have seen my light, you have heard my words. Receive me."

Upon hearing her speak, the disciples were ashamed and they went to Aradia and pledged their love and their loyalty anew. Aradia welcomed them into her arms. Then Aradia departed from the camp and Varro remained with the disciples, answering their questions and speaking of prophesies.

The next morning Aradia gathered all of her disciples together and with great sadness she spoke to them: "The time is near now when you shall go forth and teach the people, but not for me alone. This you do for She who is greater than all things. This you do for freedom, and for liberation.

"But take care that you be not like the Christians; speak instead of your own truths and respect another's. Do not force the teachings upon anyone, not by sword nor clever tongue, nor threats of everlasting torment. This is not our way.

"Do not fill your heart and mind with pride, nor be self-righteous. Do not place our ways above another's. Speak only of the words which I have given you, lending not your own. If you must add to what I have spoken, then better it be that this shall serve to clarify or aid in understanding.

"Be not discouraged at what shall come upon you as you wander. Remember that you plant the seeds of a harvest that shall ever spring forth. Even though our enemies shall cut it down and burn it, it shall return even as the Spring. And what I have spoken will not be forgotten, neither will you be forgotten.

"We are of the Old Religion. Our ways are the roots of all races. We are the foundation of all things upon this world. And we are the key to the gates of the next world. But do not think that we are the only way.

"There is much work to be done, within both worlds, to undo the injuries which the Church has inflicted, and will inflict. There is much work to be done to restore our ways and to teach the truth. But this we shall not see in our lifetime, nor in an age of lifetimes. But we shall be reborn in the time to come. Then shall the world see our return, and know that we have come again into power, as it was in the days of old.

"And know that all of you who now stand before me shall see this time of power arise. And my messenger, who stands now beside me, shall draw you to himself. And you shall know and remember. Remember then also she who loved you.

"Soon I shall leave you, though stay I would if it could be allowed. But I am to be called away now, for my time is almost gone. Go forth in peace and despair not. I am with you in spirit even as I have been with you in these days so quickly passed.

"If it could be that the world would forget what I have spoken, and I should be remembered but for one thing, then I would will that it be recalled that I was loved by such as you, my disciples."

Aradia soon departed from the region and was not seen again by those who dwelled there. Varro journeyed from the Alban hills, taking with him the twelve disciples to the city of Benevento. In the city of Benevento the disciples went about and gathered the followers of Aradia who still remained in the city. Once they came together, the disciples passed on the words of the Holy Strega, so that her final words would be remembered.

When all had gathered at the meeting place (now called the *Stretto di Barba*) the disciples spoke with them concerning Aradia and the Covenant. They shared with Aradia's followers the nine sacred scrolls that Aradia had written. After they had spoken long into the night, the disciples departed with Varro and slept outside of the city, taking with them the scrolls of Aradia for safekeeping.

When morning came, Varro woke the disciples and spoke with them. Then it was decided who was to depart, and to what places.

The disciples journeyed to Naples and to Rome, and to many of the towns and villages of these regions. In their wanderings, many followers were drawn to the Old Ways. The disciples established the Triads (three clans to a region) wherever they were welcomed. As the number of clans and followers grew, the men in power became concerned and they struck out against the disciples.

Soldiers were sent out to the villages and they found the outlaw camp. The followers of Aradia engaged the soldiers in battle at the place known as Diana's Embrace. Here many of the disciples were slain along with the followers of Aradia. The survivors fled with the outlaws. The soldiers seized the sacred scrolls that Aradia placed with the twelve disciples, and these were sent to the Pope in Avignon. Thus were the disciples once again scattered.

Maria and Niccolo (of the house of Landulphus) journeyed to Cologne and came to dwell in France after a time. Madrona, the new disciple, went to Florence. Alono and Teresa returned to Benevento. Varro passed through to the other world in the fifty-first year, having lived his last days in Benevento. With his passing Teresa was made Guardian of the clans (and Keeper of the Knowledge).

Here ends the account of they who wandered.

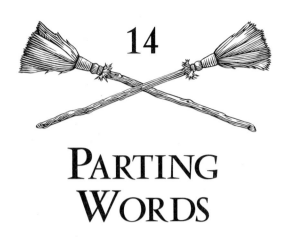

14

PARTING WORDS

With this chapter we come to the close of our Witches' tale. Once again I have told the Strega's story as it was recounted around the old campfires long ago. In looking at the Craft today I reflect upon recent camping experiences. The campsite is tended by the older folks while the young people go off exploring. When they are hungry enough they return for food and warmth by the fireside. At the campsite there is always one person who will tend the fire, knowing that as day slips into night others will gather.

When the young people first approach the fire, they speak of their explorations, their discoveries, and of the world seen through youthful eyes. As the night grows more quiet, one of the older folks begins to recount the tales of days long past. The stories speak of lessons learned and provide the young people with the knowledge of things they have yet to experience. Sharing ebbs and flows between both young and old, silences filled with only the gentle crackling of wood in the fire. It is here that the modern ways meet with the old ways, in the cycle of things that are ever ancient and ever new.

Family Witches have a word they use when speaking of the Old Ways. The word is *veglia* (pronounced vay-yah) and translates as "to stay awake." The word veglia has its etymology in the Latin *vigilia,* meaning to keep vigil. In Italy the veglia has always been the social occasion whereby social rules and values were transmitted to close family members. The veglia is the time when oral traditions are passed on, and the ancient tales are retold, connecting one generation to the next. The earliest references to the veglia in literature date from the fifteenth century, although this practice was certainly much older.

In *Ways of the Strega* I wrote of Italian peasants returning from the fields at sunset and gathering in front of the fireplace. Here they told fairy tales to the youngest children—tales containing various cultural messages and morals intended to merge the child with his or her community. Once the youngest children were put to bed, the older children were told stories of their family members and ancestors, establishing their sense of identity and their place in the world. Before the veglia was concluded the Elders spoke of their religious beliefs and customs in order to preserve their traditions.

The fireplace provided all the comforts for a family: light, heat, and the means to prepare food. Around the hearth were the items common to domestic family life such as the cauldron, the broom, the fire poker, and tongs. Here before the broom and the cauldron the family gathered to hear the old stories recounted yet once more. The fire flickered as the narrator told the old stories, by all appearances magickally transformed by the cascade of light and shadow playing across the room. Here, in this world between the worlds, family values and world views were shared among those of the same blood. It was through such family tales of bloodline, mixed with folklore and legend, that hereditary Witches were bound together from one generation to the next.

Traditionally only members of the family could attend a veglia, those considered to be "of the blood." However, relatives of the same bloodline or persons married into the family could also attend. The fireside hearth was the center of the Italian pagan's home and family life, maintaining its vital place over the passing centuries. The family and the fireplace belonged to the mother of the home, for it was she who tended the fire. Fire became the symbol of teaching, gathering, and of family bonds.

The ritual focal point of the veglia fire is a log taken from the tree closest to the roots. This is the connection of the log to family roots. The Italian word for a log is *ceppo,* which can also mean a group of homes or a family. A pregnant woman is sometimes called *ceppa inceppita,* which means "a budding branch." In ancient Rome the log was the symbol of marriage and the woman symbolized the tree of life itself. These are all very ancient concepts demonstrating the great antiquity of the veglia concepts.

The fire of the veglia is still kindled today by family Witches in the form of the spirit flame, a ritual fire burning upon the altar. Placed directly in the center of the altar is a bowl which holds the blue flame symbolizing the presence of the ancient spirit of the Old Ways. In a real sense however this is more than a symbol, as the Strega invoke the ancient ones directly within the flame and draw their power from divine fire. Fire is one of the most ancient forms of divinity.

In an old hereditary rite we read these words of the goddess: ". . . and of those who kindle still the ancient fire, I will always remember, and to those will I always return, for they are my secret children, they who are the keepers of the flame."

To this day the Strega still kindle the blue flame. To the followers of Aradia, fire was the symbol of her teachings. Today the image of triple flames parting from the fire is the symbol of the Old Ways. This is the symbol of the Keepers of the Flame, they who preserve the Old Ways.

Over the past two or three decades I have noted that less and less of the material published in the past has been passed on by new writers on the Craft. In my travels as an author, doing book signings and workshops, I have encountered many new Craft people, for example, who know nothing of the runes, symbols, and chants common to the Craft in the late 1960s to early 1970s. Many have had a vague understanding of the astral plane and of the metaphysical principles of magick. All of this concerns me greatly, for what is it that modern Craft people will pass on to future generations? The main focus of the Craft today is upon gathering and creating techniques that are useful for the unique needs of the individual. But how does a person pass on to others what works uniquely for him or her? Yes, we can pass on the knowledge of how to design our own spirituality, but what about our religion? Sometimes I fear that future generations will know nothing of the Old Religion.

In *Etruscan Roman Remains in Popular Tradition*, Leland noted the survival of an intact tradition of Witchcraft in Tuscany, circa 1886:

> For it is really not a mere chance survival of superstitions here and there, as in England or France, but a complete system . . .

It was in northern Italy in the mountain district of Romagna Toscana that Leland encountered a people of whom he wrote:

> . . . a very ancient race (who) appear to have preserved traditions and observances little changed from an incredibly early time . . . among these people, stregeria, or witchcraft—or as I have heard it called: "la vecchia religione" (or "the old religion") exists to a degree

which would even astonish many Italians.

Leland goes on to say that these Witches believe in old deities and in "spirits of every element or thing created." They believed that every plant and mineral had a guardian spirit, one good and one evil. It was held by these people that sorcerers and Witches could be born again in their descendants. Common also was a belief in familiar spirits and in the folletti or fairy race. Leland says of this:

> Connected in turn with these beliefs in folletti, or minor spirits, and their attendant observances and traditions, are vast numbers of magical cures with appropriate incantations, spells, and ceremonies, to attract love, to remove all evil influences or bring certain things to pass; to win in gaming, to evoke spirits, to insure good crops or a traveler's happy return, and to effect divination or deviltry in many curious ways—all being ancient, as shown by allusions in classical writers to whom these spirits were well known. And I believe that in some cases what I have gathered and given will possibly be found to supply much that is missing in earlier authors—*sit verbo venia.*

During his era, Leland was criticized for his claims that a surviving tradition of Witchcraft actually existed. If it did, the critics pressed, then why was it not known by the Italians living in the region in and around these Witches. Leland replied that it was not unlike the white people of his native Philadelphia who knew nothing of the voodoo of the black servants in their own homes. The same was true of the Americans on the east coast who knew little if anything of the local Indian lore that Leland collected among the tribes still residing there.

The lore of Italian Witches did not remain only in Italy, which I believe is a testimony to its endurance and its widespread roots. For example, the *red cap* spirit of Ireland known as a Leprechaun is depicted on Etruscan vases and Roman murals dating centuries before the Celtic invasion of northern Italy. In Roman art he is depicted with a scanty shirt and a red cap. Italian folklorists claim that this spirit was derived from the redheaded woodpecker; in ancient Italic lore the woodpecker was believed to guard treasure hidden within the hollows of trees.

The intertwining of knots is an old magickal art originating in Italy, but in modern times commonly attributed to Celtic Witches. In Rome knots were tied in cords to protect virginity, and it was traditional for the groom to untie his bride's knot on the wedding night. Leland says that the interlace itself guards against evil magick. The cord has a curious connection to holy stones (stones with a hole through them). In old lore it was believed that earthworms made these holes. The earthworm is a creature of the underworld who has intimate knowledge of the deep mysteries of the earth, drawing from it an occult force as it rises up from beneath the surface of the soil (as does the grain). Thus the cord is the earthworm, and the hole in the stone is a portal into the Otherworld, created by the worm.

It has for generations been the custom among Italian peasants to prune a mulberry tree (for silk worms) so that the branches are interlaced. This protects the silk from evil influences. Silk was often used in magick to protect against occult contamination. Ritual tools were wrapped in silk and crystal balls were covered with a silk cloth to protect them against sunlight which dispels astral energy. Here again we see the connection between the worm and the darkness. The worm, like the snake, is a symbol of transformation and hidden occult power.

So complete is the old tradition of the Strega, that such connections appear in every thing and in every place. Leland, who lived among the English Gypsies for quite some time, and was an acknowledged expert on the Romany Gypsies at the turn of the century, says that Strega lore far exceeded what had been preserved among the Gypsies. In *Etruscan Roman Remains in Popular Tradition,* Leland writes:

> Such familiarity with folk lore and sorcery as I possess . . . the end being that I succeeded in penetrating this obscure and strange forest inhabited by witches and shadows, faded gods and forgotten goblins of the olden time, where folk lore abounded to such excess that. . . . I in time had more thereof than I could publish...to do this I went to strange places and made strange acquaintances . . . to collect volumes of folk lore among very reticent Red Indians, and reserved Romanys is not unknown to me, but the extracting of witchcraft from Italian strege far surpasses it.

All of which I have spoken of in this book is the legacy I now pass on to you through its pages. Gladly, there will always be new ways, but will there always be the Old Ways? That is something that only you have the power to decide, for the fate of the Old Religion is now equally in your hands. What could it hurt to "keep a candle burning in the window," should the goddess return in search of her secret children? So I close now with the well-considered words Leland wrote in the appendix of his book *Aradia; Gospel of the Witches*.

Yet a few years, reader, and all of this will have vanished . . . old traditions are, in fact, disappearing with such incredible rapidity that I am assured on best authority—and can indeed see for myself—that what I collected or had recorded for me ten years ago in the Romagna Toscana, with exceptional skillful aid, could not now be gathered at all by anybody, since it no longer exists, save in the memories of a few old sorcerers who are daily disappearing, leaving no trace behind . . . the women or witches, having more vitality, will last a little longer . . . .

Appendix 1

CHARLES GODFREY LELAND: FATHER OF MODERN WITCHCRAFT

Many people today think of Gerald Gardner as the founder of modern Wicca/Witchcraft. Gardner's books on Witchcraft, published in the mid-twentieth century, brought about a growing interest in the Old Religion of pre-Christian Europe. However, over half a century earlier Charles Godfrey Leland wrote on many of the same topics later popularized by Gerald Gardner. For example, the theme of witches meeting at the time of the full moon, being nude, calling their ways *The Old Religion*, celebrating with ritual cakes and wine, and worshipping a god and goddess all appear in Leland's writings on Italian Witchcraft, circa 1896.

Charles Leland was a famous folklorist who wrote several classic texts on English Gypsies and Italian Witches. He was born in Philadelphia, August 15, 1824, and died in Florence, Italy, March 20, 1903. Leland was fascinated by folklore and folk magic, even as a child, and went on to write such important works as *Etruscan Roman Remains, Legends of Florence, The Gypsies, Gypsy Sorcery*, and *Aradia: Gospel of the Witches*.

In 1906, a two-volume biography of Charles Godfrey Leland was written by his niece, Elizabeth Robins Pennell.[1] In chapter one, recounting his personal memoirs, Pennell writes of Leland's infancy:

> In both the "Memoirs" and the "Memoranda" he tells how he was carried up to the garret by his old Dutch nurse, who was said to be a sorceress, and left there with a Bible, a key, and a knife on his breast, lighted candles, money, and a plate of salt at his head: rites that were to make luck doubly certain by helping him to rise in life, and become a scholar and a wizard.

Pennell goes on to tell us that Leland's mother claimed an ancestress who married into "sorcery." Leland writes in his memoirs: "my mother's opinion was that this was a very strong case of atavism, and that the mysterious ancestor had through the ages cropped out in me." The biography of Charles Leland is filled with accounts of his early interest in the supernatural, and interest that turned into a life-long passion. Of this passion, Pennell writes:

> It is what might be expected . . . of the man who was called Master by the witches and Gypsies, whose pockets were always full of charms and amulets, who owned the Black Stone of the Voodoos, who could not see a bit of red string at his feet and not pick it up, or find a pebble with a hole in it and not add it to his store—who, in a word, not only studied witchcraft with the impersonal curiosity of the scholar, but practised it with the zest of the initiated.

As a young boy, Leland grew up in a household that employed servants. According to Pennell, Leland learned of fairies from Irish immigrant women working in his home, and from the black servant women in the kitchen he learned about Voodoo. Leland writes of his boyhood: "I was always given to loneliness in gardens and woods when I could get into them, and to hearing words in bird's songs and running or falling water." Pennell notes that throughout Leland's life, he could never get away from the fascination of the supernatural, nor did he ever show any desire to.

Fluent in several foreign languages, at age eighteen Leland wrote an unpublished English translation of *Pymander of Trismegistus,* a hermetic text now commonly known as *Hermes Trismegistus; His Divine Pymander. The Pymander,* as it was often called for short, was the foundation for much of the hermetic writings that inspired many Western Occultists during the later part of the nineteenth century and early part of the twentieth century.

In 1870, Leland moved to England, where he eventually studied Gypsy society

---

1   Elizabeth Pennell, *Charles Godfrey Leland: A Biography* (New York: Houghton, Mifflin and Company, 1906).

and lore. Over the course of time he won the confidence of Matty Cooper, the king of the Gypsies in England. Cooper personally taught Leland to speak Romany, the language of the Gypsies. It took many years before Leland was totally accepted by the Gypsies. In a letter dated November 16, 1886, Leland wrote to Pennell: "I have been by moonlight amid Gypsy ruins with a whole camp of Gypsies, who danced and sang. . . . " Having penetrated their mysteries to such a degree, Leland went on to write two classic texts on Gypsies, establishing himself as an authority on the subject among the scholars of his time.

In 1888, Leland found himself in Florence, Italy, where he lived out the remainder of his life. It was here that Leland met the woman whom he always referred to as Maddalena. Her real name was Maddalena Alenti, although some people have mistaken her for another woman Leland knew named Margherita Taleni. Maddelena worked as a "card reader," telling fortunes in the back streets of Florence, and later married Lorenzo Bruciatelli, with whom she moved to America. Leland soon discovered that Maddalena was a Witch, and employed her to help gather material for his research on Italian Witchcraft. In Leland's biography, Pennell mentions running across the manuscript notes where he writes of Maddalena:

> A young woman who would have been taken for a Gypsy in England, but in whose face, in Italy, I soon learned to know the antique Etruscan, with its strange mysteries, to which was added the indefinable glance of the Witch. She was from the Romagna Toscana, born in the heart of its unsurpassingly wild and romantic scenery, amid cliffs, headlong torrents, forests, and old legendary castles. I did not gather all the facts for a long time, but gradually found that she was of a Witch family, or one whose members had, from time immemorial, told fortunes, repeated ancient legends, gathered incantations, and learned how to intone them, prepared enchanted medicines, philtres, or spells. As a girl, her Witch grandmother, aunt and especially her stepmother brought her up to believe in her destiny as a sorceress, and taught her in the forests, afar from human ear, to chant in strange prescribed tones, incantations or evocations to the ancient gods of Italy, under names but little changed, who are now known as Folletti, spiriti, fate, or lari—the Lares or household goblins of the ancient Etruscans.

Maddelena introduced Leland to another woman named Marietta, who assisted her in providing him with research materials. Pennell, who inherited the bulk of Leland's notes, letters, and unpublished materials, refers to Marietta as a sorceress, but Leland's own description of her in his published works is less clear. At one point Leland mused, in a letter to Pennell dated June 28, 1889, that Maddalena and Marietta might be inventing various verses and passing them off as something of antiquity. However, Leland seems to have had a change of heart, as reflected in another letter to Pennell written in January 1891. Here Leland writes:

> It turns out that Maddalena was regularly trained as a witch. She said the other day, you can never get to the end of all this Stregheria—witchcraft. Her memory seems to be inexhaustible, and when anything is wanting she consults some other witch and always gets it. It is part of the education of a witch to learn endless incantations, and these I am sure were originally Etruscan. I can't prove it, but I believe I have more Etruscan poetry than is to be found in all the remains. Maddalena has written me herself about 200 pages of this folklore—incantations and stories.

In another letter dated April 8, 1891 (written to Mr. Macritchie), Leland indicates still other Witches who assisted him in his research:

> . . . But ten times more remarkable is my manuscript on the Tuscan Traditions and Florentine Folk Lore. I have actually not only found all of the old Etruscan gods still known to the peasantry of the Tuscan Romagna, but what is more, have succeeded in proving thoroughly that they are still known. A clever young contadino and his father (of a witch family), having a list of all the Etruscan gods, went on market days to all the old people from different parts of the country, and not only took their testimony, but made them write certificates that the Etruscan Jupiter, Bacchus, etc. were known to them. With these I have a number of Roman minor rural deities, etc.

In Florence, Leland spent all of his spare time collecting Witch lore, and purchasing items of antiquity as he chanced upon them. In a letter written to Mary Owen, Leland says: "I have been living in an atmosphere of witchcraft and sorcery, engaged in collecting songs, spells, and stories of sorcery, so that I was amused to hear the other day that an eminent scholar said that I could do well at folklore, but that I had too many irons in the fire." Leland describes the Italian Witches he met as "living in a bygone age." It was an age that Leland apparently longed for himself.

Leland apparently did more than interview Italian Witches, or simply keep in their company. A passage from his book *Etruscan Roman Remains* strongly suggests that Leland was himself initiated into Stregheria, as indicated in the last sentence of the following passage:

But, in fact, as I became familiar with the real, deeply seated belief in a religion of Witchcraft in Tuscany, I found that there is no such great anomaly after all in a priest's being a wizard, for witchcraft is a business, like any other. Or it may come upon you like love, or a cold, or a profession, and you must bear it till you can give it or your practice to somebody else. What is pleasant to reflect on is that there is no devil in it. If you lose it you at once become good, and you cannot die till you get rid of it. It is not considered by any means a Christianly, pious possession, but in some strange way the strega works clear of Theology. True, there are witches good and bad, but all whom I ever met belonged entirely to the buone. It was their rivals and enemies who were maladette streghe, et cetera, but the latter I never met. We were all good.

There is another passage given in the same book. In the chapter titled "Witches and Witchcraft," Leland is interviewing a strega, and asks her how a certain priest became a Stregone. In doing so, he asks her how he (the priest) "came to practise our noble profession." Leland seems to be referring to the Strega and himself as being part of something which the priest had also joined.

One of the most puzzling aspects of Leland's writings on Italian Witchcraft is the fact that he goes back and forth between speaking of Witchcraft in common Christian stereotypes of the period, and portraying Witchcraft practictioners as "good" and "noble" followers of the goddess Diana instead of the devil. His book *Aradia: Gospel of the Witches* is certainly a shocking turn from his general theme of the good witches of Benevento. Was he trying to please both sides? Or was he laying the foundation for a greater revelation to come? Perhaps we may never know, as Leland died without completing his work on Italian Witchcraft. One of his last wishes was to ask that someone compile all of the material he had written on the subject into one single volume. I am currently working on such a compilation drawn from *Etruscan Roman Remains, Aradia: Gospel of the Witches, Legends of Florence,* and *Legends of Virgil.*

Appendix 2

HISTORICAL REFERENCES TO ARADIA

In the oral traditions surrounding Aradia, residing in the Old Religion of Italy, it is said that she lived and taught during the latter half of the fourteenth century. The Italian Inquisitor Bernardo Rategno documented in his *Tractatus de Strigibus* (written in A.D. 1508) that a "rapid expansion" of the "witches sect" had begun 150 years prior to his time. Rategno studied many transcripts concerning Witchcraft from the trials of the Inquisition. Tracing back over the years, he pinpointed the beginnings of the Witch trials, and noted their sharp increase over a period of years. Following a thorough study of these records (kept in the Archives of the Inquisition at Como, Italy), Rategno fixed the time of this Witches' revival somewhere around 1358, the latter half of the fourteenth century.

If Aradia had been born in 1313, as the legends claim, this would certainly have made her old enough to have taught and influenced others, and for groups to have formed that carried on her teachings. Thus, Rategno's dates lend support to the oral tradition concerning Aradia's influence on the growth of the Old Religion. In 1890, author and folklorist Charles Leland published a book on Italian Witchcraft titled *Aradia: Gospel of the Witches*. Leland's account of Aradia includes a legend about the "beautiful

Pilgrim" preserved among Tuscan peasants for generations. In part this legend says:

> Then having obtained a pilgrim's dress, she traveled far and wide, teaching and preaching the religion of old times, the religion of Diana, the Queen of the Fairies and of the Moon, the goddess of the poor and the oppressed. And the fame of her wisdom and beauty went forth over all the land, and people worshipped her, calling her *La Bella Pellegrina* (the beautiful pilgrim).[1]

In 1962, T. C. Lethbridge (former Director for Cambridge University Museum of Archaeology and Ethnology) published a book called *Witches* that refers to Aradia in several chapters. In chapter 2, he writes:

> We can then, I think, assume that Leland's Vangelo and Dr. Murray's trial evidence are more or less contemporary and that it is reasonable to use the two together to form a picture of the witch cult at about A.D. 1400. . . . Aradia was sent to earth to teach this art to Mankind. That is, she was, in the opinion of her devotees, a personage, known in Hindu Religion as an Avatar, who taught them how to harness magic power. Aradia, at some far-off time, may have been as much an historical person as Christ, Krishna or Buddha . . . [2]

I found it also interesting to note that *Ecstasies—Deciphering the Witches' Sabbath* by Carlo Ginzburg contains a passage that may be a historical reference to Aradia. On page 189 he speaks of a Pagan sect known as the *Calusari* who, during the Middle Ages (as late as the sixteenth and seventeenth centuries), worshipped a "Mythical Empress" whom they sometimes called "Arada" or "Irodeasa." The Calusari also used the term "mistress of the fairies" for her, just as the followers of Aradia called Diana the "Queen of the Fairies." There are certainly some very close similarities here, and we may be seeing a form of worship that evolved from the one Aradia founded over 100 years earlier.

According to the original legend of Aradia, she left Italy at some point in her quest and traveled out of the country. Serbia, the home of the Calusari, lies a short distance across the Adriatic from Central Italy, and travel by ship was not uncommon in that era. When Aradia left Italy she would not have traveled west to France because the Papacy was established there at the time, and Aradia was still being hunted by the Church. It would have been too dangerous to have gone to northern Europe because witches were being burned or hanged in that region (Italy did not begin the burning of witches until after the time of Aradia). So, in fact, an eastern exodus would have been the only logical action that Aradia could have taken. At the very least, there is a striking coincidence between Aradia's Witches and the Calusari of Arada.

---

1 Leland, p. 68.
2 T. C. Lethbridge, *Witches* (New York: The Citadel Press, 1962), pp. 13–14.

Appendix 3

MEDITERRANEAN/AEGEAN CONCEPTS IN MODERN WICCA

THE FOUR RITUAL TOOLS

The first appearance of the blade, cup, pentacle, and wand displayed together in a magical/ritual context is found in the symbolism of the early Italian Renaissance period. This image of the traditional tools of Western Occultism is captured in the fifteenth century Visconti Cary-Yale tarot deck, the oldest-known extant deck. The Visconti Magician card depicts a man standing before a table. In his left hand he holds a wand. On the table itself is set a large chalice, a sword, and a pentacle. Stuart Kaplan, acknowledged expert on the Tarot, says that all Tarot symbolism as we know it today evolved from the Italian Tarot.[1]

---

1   Stuart Kaplan, *The Encyclopedia of the Tarot* (Stamford: U.S. Games Inc., 1984).

THE BOOK OF SHADOWS

Italian Witches were hand copying from the Key of Solomon in the seventeenth century, and mixing it with spells and rituals from their private handwritten books.[2]

THE FOUR ELEMENTS

Empedocles (a student of the teachings of Pythagoras) was historically the first person known to have taught the concept of the Four Elements as a single cohesive doctrine. He lived around 475 B.C. in his native homeland of Sicily, where he presented the teachings concerning the four elements as the four-fold root of all things.[3]

THE ELEMENTALS

In book one, chapter 18, of the *Compendium Maleficarum* by Francesco Guazzo (1609), we read that Italian witches work with spirits of certain specific natures. Guazzo lists these as: fiery, aerial, terrestrial, and water. Here, of course, are the elemental creatures also related to modern Wiccan beliefs.

THE RITUAL CIRCLE

In *Compendium Maleficarum* (1609), there appears a woodcut by Guazzo depicting witches gathered for a ceremony in a circle drawn upon the ground.

DUOTHEISM

In classic Roman and Greek concepts we find the Divine Couple imagery in such matings as Jupiter and Juno, Zeus and Hera. At the second lectisternium in 217 B.C., for the first time in their history, the Romans selected a dozen deities and grouped them together into couples according to the Hellenic pattern. From this celebration arose the Roman version of the Twelve Principle Deities in Roman Mythology. In Leland's *Aradia; Gospel of the Witches* we read that Italian witches worshipped Diana and her consort, the Roman god Lucifer, the morning star.

THE WATCHERS

In the early Stellar Cults of Mesopotamia, there were four "royal" stars called the Watchers. Each one of these stars ruled over one of the four cardinal points common to astrology. This particular system dated from approximately 3000 B.C. The Star Aldebaran, when it marked the Vernal Equinox, held the position of Watcher of the East. Regulus, marking the Summer Solstice, was Watcher of the South. Antares, marking the

---

2 *Journal of Social History,* volume 28, 1995, article by Sally Scully, Department of History at San Francisco University.

3 Peter Kingsley, *Ancient Philosophy, Mystery, and Magic; Empedocles and the Pythagorean Tradition* (Oxford University Press 1995).

Autumn Equinox, was Watcher of the West. Fomalhaut, marking the Winter Solstice, was Watcher of the North. Towers were constructed as a form of worship, bearing the symbols of the Watchers, and their symbols were set upon the Towers for the purpose of evocation. These towers were called Ziggurats, or cosmic mountains.[4]

In Leland's *Aradia,* he recounts the tale of "The Children of Diana, or how the fairies were born," in which it is stated that Diana created "the great spirits of the stars." We also find a reference to an elder race:

> . . . Then Diana went to the Fathers of the Beginning, to the Mothers, the Spirits who were before the first spirit, and lamented unto them that she could not prevail with Dianus. And they praised her for her courage; they told her that to rise she must fall; to become the chief of goddesses she must become a mortal.

In archaic Roman religion, guardian spirits known as Lare were worshipped at the crossroads where small towers were erected. An altar was set in front of the towers, and offerings were given to the Lare. The Lare were originally Nature spirits of the fields, derived from the Etruscan Lasa spirit. Later they became spirits of demarcation associated with protection and with seasonal rites.[5]

THREE DEGREES OF INITIATION

The Italian Masonic group known as the Carbonari (circa 1820) had three degrees of initiation marked by colored cords or ribbons: blue, red, and black. A triangle marked first degree level. The Carbonari claimed to have been based upon the Mystery Cult of Mithra.[6]

STRUCTURE OF THE CIRCLE RITUAL

It is interesting to note that in the *Essay on the Mysteries of Eleusis,* by M. Ouvaroff, we find passages from the ancient philosopher Porphyry who reveals that the symbols of the Greek and Roman Eleusinian Mysteries included the circle, triangle, and cone which are all aspects of Wiccan rites.[7]

THE NORTHERN ORIENTATION OF RITUAL

The Etruscans who occupied central Italy (from whom the Romans borrowed heavily) placed their deities into quarter associations.

---

4 David Papon, *The Lure of the Heavens: A History of Astrology* (York Beach, ME: Weiser, 1972), and Richard Allen, *Star Names; Their Lore and Meaning* (Dover Publications 1963).

5 Georges Dumezil, *Archaic Roman Religion* (Baltimore and London: John Hopkins University Press, 1996), pp. 343–344.

6 Arkon Daraul, *A History of Secret Societies* (New York: Citadel Press, 1961).

7 As quoted in Manly Hall, *The Secret Teachings of All Ages* (Philosophical Research Society, 1962).

To the north was the chief god Tinia (and his consort Uni) who was king of the gods. The north was divided up into four sections that spanned from the north to the east quarter. In the east (the furthest extension of the northeast placement) dwelled the twelve major gods and goddesses of Etruscan religion. In the south were placed the lesser gods and nature spirits. In the west were placed the deities of Death and the Underworld. In this Etruscan view of the Cosmos, we have the earliest account of Italic beliefs associated with the four quarters.[8]

CONDUCT OF THE RITUAL BY A PRIEST, PRIESTESS, AND MAIDEN

A stucco relief from the Villa of the Mysteries in Pompeii, Italy depicts a woman leading a blindfolded initiate, assisted by a silenus priest and a female attendant (relief from the Farnesina 30–25 B.C., Rome, National Museum). The ancient cults of Rome typically involved both priests and priestesses with their attendant maidens. The Mystery Cult of Dionysus at Pompeii is a classic example depicted on murals.[9]

THE DESCENT OF THE GODDESS TO THE UNDERWORLD

The Eleusinian Mysteries, originating in Greece, involve themes of descent and ascent, loss and regain, light and darkness, and the cycles of life and death. In *The Secret Teachings of all Ages* by Manly Hall, the author tells us that the rites associated with these Mysteries were performed at midnight during the Spring and Autumn Equinoxes. Hall reports that the Eleusinian Mysteries spread to Rome and Britain where initiations into this cult were performed in both countries. The Eleusinian Cult contained the Greater Mysteries and the Lesser Mysteries. The Lesser dealt with the abduction of Persephone by the Underworld God, a classic descent myth. The Greater Mysteries dealt with the Quest for the return of the Goddess, and the rites were performed in honor of Ceres (an Agricultural Goddess who was Patron of the Mysteries).

In the general mythos, Persephone descends into the Underworld and encounters its Lord. The life of the world disappears with Her and the first autumn and winter befalls the earth. The Lord of the Underworld falls in love with the Goddess and wants to keep Her in His realm. Ceres intervenes on Her behalf and pleads with the Underworld Lord to release Persephone.

---

8   Yves Bonnefoy, *Roman and European Mythologies* (University of Chicago Press, 1992).

9   Joscelyn Godwin, *Mystery Religions in the Ancient World* (Harper & Row, 1981).

At first He refuses because Persephone has eaten the seeds of the pomegranate, an ancient symbol of the male seed (as we see in the Wiccan Descent Legend—they loved and were One). Eventually He agrees on the condition that She returns again to His realm for half of each year (cycle of the seasons).

LUNAR ORIENTATION AND FULL MOON MEETINGS

The writings of the ancient Roman poet Horace give us perhaps the earliest accounts of Italian Witches and their connection to a lunar cult. In the *Epodes of Horace,* written around 30 B.C., he tells the tale of an Italian Witch named Canidia. Horace says that Proserpine and Diana grant power to witches who worship them, and that witches gather in secret to perform the mysteries associated with their worship. He speaks of a Witches' book of Incantations (*Libros Carminum*) through which the Moon may be "called down" from the sky. Other ancient Roman writers such as Lucan and Ovid produced works which clearly support the same theme.

In Leland's *Aradia: Gospel of the Witches* (1890) we also find a reference to Italian Witches gathering for lunar rites:

> Whenever ye have need of anything, once in the month and when the moon is full, ye shall assemble in some secret place, or in a forest all together join to adore the potent spirit of your queen, my mother, great Diana. She who fain would learn all sorcery yet has not won its deepest secrets, them my mother will teach her, in truth all things as yet unknown. And ye shall be freed from slavery, and so ye shall be free in everything; and as a sign that ye are truly free, ye shall be naked in your rites, both men and women also. . . .

Appendix 4

THE WITCHES OF
NORTHERN EUROPE

Like many regions of Europe, the north is home to ancient Witch families who, despite the Inquisition, survived into modern times. In this chapter we will examine several of the mainstream personalities connected to northern European Witchcraft. Some of these individuals claimed to be hereditary Witches and others, while making no personal assertions to "Witch Blood" themselves, profess initiation into secret family traditions.

Several of the Witches presented in this chapter were proven to have mislead their initiates concerning their hereditary claims (primarily regarding the Book of Shadows everyone copied from.) In most cases the material claimed to be from family origin, if taken word for word, turned out to be essentially Gardnerian material written by Doreen Valiente, Gerald Gardner, or Aleister Crowley. Were these "hereditary" witches simply withholding traditional Witch Blood material and substituting Gardnerian material in its place, or were they making the whole thing up?

To say there is a bit of the Gypsy in the hereditary Witch would not be unfair. Rarely is Witch Blood material openly shared with nonfamily members, and when teaching unrelated initiates it is a common practice to use other available material as a foundation through which to introduce hereditary concepts. Yes, this is deception to a degree, but tricking someone into learning something is an ancient art, by whatever means.

There are several elements shared by those who claim hereditary affiliation. After reading about each individual presented in this chapter, these common elements should be very apparent. Are these signs of fraud, or are they indications of something quite different? Can it be that the desire to be a hereditary Witch may open one to possession by the earth-bound spirit of a Witch from olden times? Or is it just another con-game perpetrated for some odd sense of personal gain or self-satisfaction?

Clearly the people discussed in this chapter seemingly believed their own claims, or in time came to believe them, as did many people who worked with them. Rarely did such claims bring anything other than discord into their lives, and yet they maintained their claims to the very end. The zeal and steadfastness of these individuals was inspiring. Their devotion to the Old Religion is unquestionable, and without such individuals the growth of Wicca in the twentieth century may never have occurred.

Many questions are raised concerning the claims of the individuals discussed here. You will have to answer them yourself once you have finished this chapter. One possibility consistently overlooked is that some heredi-tary Witches, due to a longing for companionship and a sense of greater community, have reworked readily available material, and then presented it as older text in order to attract like-minded individuals. This allowed them to keep their personal sense of identity, while at the same time honoring their oaths of initiation. In this place, neither in shadow or sunlight, they shared their knowledge as best they could.

Whatever the case may be, or however you wish to view the matter, for me it is important only that these individuals opened the doors for so many sincere seekers, and for that I honor the memory of each one. So let us turn now and look at these curious figures who laid the foundation for much of the modern Craft as we know it today.

ROBERT COCHRANE

Cochrane was an English Witch claiming family ties to the Old Religion. Doreen Valiente first met him in 1964, eventually becoming a member of his coven—the Clan of Tubal-Cain. Cochrane made various inconsistent statements as to his Witch heritage, commenting that his great uncle on his mother's side was his teacher, and then at a later time that his mother taught him as she herself had been taught by her grandmother.

By all accounts, Cochrane was a very impressive and charismatic individual. His system of Witchcraft was largely based upon intuitive rituals and was more shamanic in nature than most Wiccan groups of this era. The ritual tools of his Craft consisted of a cauldron, knife, cord, cup, and a stone. Cochrane frequently expressed contempt for the Gardnerian Witches of his time, one of the factors contributing to Doreen Valiente's eventual exit from the coven.

Cochrane's coven disbanded due to several unfortunate events. He had become increasing more controlling of his group and, openly before his wife, began an affair with one of the coven's women. Cochrane's wife left him and the group became more and more disenchanted. The members of his coven felt he was too authoritarian in the final days, and his verbal attacks on Gardnerian Witches soon reached intolerable limits.

On a certain late afternoon in 1966, Cochrane spent some time with Evan Jones, a close friend and former coven member. Cochrane stated that his future was now in the lap of the Goddess. He returned home early that same evening and was found in his garden by a neighbor at four in the morning, unconscious due to the ingestion of belladonna leaves, also known as deadly night shade. He was taken to the hospital but died three days later. By some accounts Cochrane had become fascinated with psychedelic drugs derived from herbs, and there is some speculation that his death was an accident. However, those who were closest to him believed Cochrane had committed suicide.

GERALD GARDNER

Gardner is perhaps the best-known figure in modern Witchcraft. His books on modern Wicca became classics that inspired the growth and development of many Wiccan Traditions. Although never personally making any claims to being a hereditary Witch himself, Gardner did assert his initiation into an old surviving Tradition of the Old Religion in 1939. This coven was reportedly descended from one of the "Nine Covens" founded by George Pickingill some forty years earlier. Gardner maintained that this coven had hereditary roots, and according to Pickingill they stretched back eight centuries in an unbroken chain. The accounts vary concerning this coven; it was located either in Hampshire or Hertfordshire.

Around 1954 Gardner began to reveal aspects of the Tradition he practiced in his public writings. Not only was Gerald Gardner an author, he was a scholar in his own right, an anthropologist and archaeologist with findings published in the journal of the Malayan branch of the Royal Asiatic Society. He established several covens throughout England and eventually he opened a Witchcraft museum on the Isle of Man. Gardner worked closely with another famous Witch, Doreen Valiente, who helped him expand upon the material contained in his Book of Shadows.

Some people believe that Gerald Gardner and Aleister Crowley created the first

"Gardnerian Book of Shadows" between themselves. A rumor popular around that time alleged that Crowley was a former member of one of Pickingill's Nine Covens, and was later dismissed for reasons related to a lack of personal character and morals. Some people have noted that Gardner's Book of Shadows contained verses written earlier in Crowley's works. If Crowley had indeed been at one time an initiate of the Craft, it is possible that these verses were originally drawn from Craft sources by Crowley himself.

The Gardnerian Tradition, in time, took on elements of Italian Witchcraft as reflected in the earlier works of Charles Leland. One of the most famous of Gardnerian verses, the "Charge of the Goddess," is almost identical with the verses found in Leland's material over half a century earlier. Doreen Valiente, an admirer of Leland, later wrote the Gardnerian version of the Charge. Other elements drawn from Leland's works were full moon gatherings, worship of a goddess and god consort, cakes and wine ritual celebrations, and nude worship.

SYBIL LEEK

Sybil Leek claimed to be a hereditary Witch of Irish and Russian descent. Sybil traced her family tree back to A.D. 1134, and took special pride in being descended from Molly

Leigh, an Irish Witch who died in 1663. She even visited Molly's grave during one of her visits to Europe. Sybil was often accompanied by her pet Jackdaw, perched on her shoulder as she went about. Such was also the custom of old Molly before her.

Like the majority of hereditary Witches, Sybil was born with the birthmark sign of a Witch. She claimed to have met Aleister Crowley when she eight years old, and to have spent time climbing up the mountainsides with him near her home. Sybil wrote in her book *Diary of a Witch*[1] that Crowley had spoken to her about Witchcraft and also had instructed her on employing certain words for their vibratory qualities when working magick. It is interesting to note yet another indication of Crowley's involvement in Witchcraft.

Sybil lived in the New Forest region, one of the oldest forests in Britain. Her home was near Hampshire, the area that Sybil claimed was home to four covens that survived from the days of King William Rufus. New Forest is also the region where Gerald Gardner became associated with a coven claiming ancient lineage. Perhaps these groups were either related or were one and the same.

In her early twenties, Sybil lived with the Gypsies in New Forest for almost a year. From the Gypsies, Sybil learned a great deal concerning herbal potions and elixirs. The

---

1 Sybil Leek, *Diary of a Witch* (New York: Signet, 1969).

Gypsies taught Sybil their lore and their tricks. According to Sybil, the Gypsies knew she was a Witch and respected her, eventually accepting her into their camps like one of their own. When she finally left them, the Gypsies made her a "blood-sister" in the traditional method. This consisted of cutting her wrist and mixing her blood with the Gypsy leaders.

Sybil did a great deal to promote a positive image of the Old Religion, both as an author and as a lecturer. She toured and gave lectures throughout England and North America. During the later part of her life, Sybil worked as a professional astrologer, gaining much notoriety in the field. She was perhaps one of the most colorful Witches of the twentieth century.

Mrs. Paterson

Very little is known about this mysterious person. Occultist Austin Spare met her in London in the year 1902. Paterson claimed to belong to a hereditary Witch family, she herself having been initiated at an early age by her mother. Paterson worked as a fortune-teller, and according to Spare she had the ability to manifest her thoughts to visible appearance. Paterson would on occasion, during a psychic reading, mentally project visual images of the prophesied events she saw for her clients. Spare wrote in his journal that these visions would appear in the dark corner of the reading room, and always came true.

Spare wrote in his journal that Paterson was an elderly woman, yet could appear whenever desired as a beautiful, young, and sexually irresistible woman. Spare does not mention her age, but since he was only sixteen when they met, it is likely that she may not have really been "elderly" by social standards, but simply seen as such through the eyes of a teenager. Spare did several nude drawings of Paterson as both an old and young woman.

Paterson told Spare that she was a descendant of a Witch who lived in Salem, Massachusetts, circa 1692. She initiated Spare into her Tradition and taught him a secret technique for creating magickal sigils. He eventually expanded on this method and later called it the "alphabet of desire." Spare revealed the method for creating his magickal alphabet in several of his published writings.

Spare was never able to achieve the level of magick demonstrated by Paterson, although he did have fleeting moments in which he was able to manifest his visions through the use of sigils. Paterson reportedly could manifest spirits and thought-forms at will for any length of time she desired. As Spare became well known through his occult art, Paterson seems to have slipped off into obscurity. Other than what is noted here, little else was ever published concerning her.

GEORGE PICKINGILL

George Pickingill was born in 1816, and claimed to be descended from Julia Pickingill, "the Witch of Brandon," who died in England circa 1071. Pickingill had a sinister reputation in the village of Hockley where he was born. Many of the village folk were afraid of him and his magical abilities, a fact that he reportedly often used to his advantage whenever he was in need of something. If there is any truth to this story, it may lie in the simple ignorance and misunderstanding concerning Witchcraft in general. However, there is one curious allegation that may support the villagers' impression.

When Gerald Gardner began writing openly about Wicca, many elders within the Craft community became alarmed, fearing exposure and the resultant damage that could occur due to the distorted image of Witchcraft stamped upon the minds of the populace at large. Apparently the East Anglican Craft Elders of the period were concerned about associating George Pickingill and Aleister Crowley with Wicca. Pickingill openly advocated the demise of Christianity and tried to form an alliance with Satanic covens to expedite his vision. It has been alleged that the Elders of the Hereditary traditions in East Anglia set things in motion to discredit the claims of Gerald Gardner concerning the survival of Witch families in order to protect against discovery. This involved, in part, the eradication of as many traces of Pickingill and his Nine Covens as possible.

There is no doubt that Pickingill was a zealot. When he established a coven, its leader had to present evidence that she or he was of hereditary Witch blood. Pickingill's covens arose in Essex, Hampshire, Hertford, Norfolk, and Sussex. Each one had to meet his standards in order for Pickingill to pass his "power" on to the leaders. Although he taught his covens the basic structure of his tradition, Pickingill introduced many new concepts and embellished the ritual themes originally contained in his Book of Shadows.

ALEX SANDERS

Alex Sanders claimed to receive initiation from his grandmother at an early age. As the story goes he walked in on her unexpectedly, and found her performing some type of ritual. Alex was sworn to secrecy, and his grandmother broke his skin with a knife, saying "you're one of us now." This resulted in her taking Alex on as a student and bringing him into the Old Religion.

Sanders claimed to have copied from his grandmother's Book of Shadows, and later to have embellished it with material from the Key of Solomon, a Medieval text on ceremonial magick. Reportedly Sanders sought initiation in the Gardnerian covens but was unable to accomplish it. Eventually he founded his own coven. By 1965 Sanders claimed to have 1,623 Witches practicing what came to be called the Alexandrian Tradition. Janet and Stewart Farrar were both former members of this Tradition.

Sanders married a beautiful young woman named Maxine who served as his High Priestess for several years. According to Sanders he was given the title "King of the Witches" by the covens of the Alexandrian Tradition. This title, and his acceptance of it, caused many within the Craft community to view him with skepticism. Eventually, the material contained in the Book of Shadows (what Sanders presented as a copy of his grandmother's book) turned out to be largely Gardnerian writings, some of which was copied incorrectly.

Maxine and Alex soon went separate ways, and many of initiates left the Tradition. Sanders slipped off into obscurity and so ended the reign of the King of the Witches. Whatever the truth behind Sanders' claims, he made it possible for many people to enter into the Craft community and to learn ritual and magickal skills. Alex was reportedly a very skilled magician and ritualist. Even if the gift Alex presented to us was not "purchased" where he said it was, it was still a gift of great value.

LADY SHEBA

A true "pioneer" of modern Witchcraft, Lady Sheba was the first Witch to publish a complete Book of Shadows. She also registered "the Brotherhood of Wicca" as a religious organization in Michigan, one of the first people in the United States to officially establish the Craft as a legally recognized religion. Although she came under attack from within the Craft community for a variety of political reasons, Lady Sheba did much to open the doors for many who desired to follow the Path of the Old Religion.

In her book *The Grimoire of Lady Sheba,* she stated that she was a witch "by traditional heritage," and a "Gardnerian Witch by choice." Lady Sheba was of English descent on her paternal side; her maiden name was Jessie Wicker. Lady Sheba's maternal great-grandmother was a Cherokee Indian. Although raised in the United States, Lady Sheba spent some of her youth in England, and returned there for visits from time to time.

Lady Sheba reportedly died on the Cherokee Indian Reservation among family and friends. Those who knew her personally within the Craft community spoke of her as a powerful magickal person. Her name was tangled up in controversy following the publication of her grimoire in 1974, as it contained some Gardnerian material apparently written by Doreen Valiente. Fortunately the misunderstandings were all eventually resolved. We now remember Lady Sheba for her many contributions toward the furtherance of the Old Religion.

Austin Spare

Born in 1886, Austin Spare grew up to be an incredible artist and a practitioner of the occult arts. In 1902 Spare was initiated by a woman claiming to be a hereditary Witch. This was the beginning of what became a lifetime devotion to the ways of magick. Spare's art work soon caught the attention of Aleister Crowley, who commissioned Spare to create drawings for Crowley's magazine *The Equinox*. Eventually Spare was initiated into an occult organization created by Crowley, known as the Order of the Silver Star. In the 1950s Spare met Gerald Gardner, who employed him to create magickal talismans and other ritual aids.

Spare took the magickal Craft name of "Zos" after being initiated into Paterson's form of Witchcraft. Following his acquaintance with Gardner and his involvement with Crowley, Spare became obsessed with sex magick. He eventually emersed himself in the worship of Isis and other Egyptian deities, integrating this with his practice of Witchcraft. His art work then reflected this alliance of cultural themes.

Spare's obsession with sex magick turned him to many sexual practices that society would label as perversions. He believed that sexually repulsive acts caused certain chemical changes within the body transforming the magickal consciousness. Like Crowley, Spare was vilified by society and his name was treated with contempt by the press. He died in 1956 while working on a magickal grimoire that was to contain the accumulation of his magickal secrets.

Appendix 5

ITALIAN TEXT OF
RITUAL SPELLS

As promised in chapter 4, reproduced on the following pages are the Italian texts of many of the ritual spells described in that chapter. From page 50:

Non prendo questa chiave l'ho trovata
E lo porto con me, ma non porto
La chiave pero la fortuna
Che sia sempre appresso di me.

It's not a key that I have found
nor one that I shall bear around
but fortune that I trust will be
ever my friend and near to me.

From page 54:

Penne qui tanto nero quanto notte,
legame il briccone con magico stretto,
ed in azioni dell'oscurità reprime,
fino a tale tempo rilascio questo
incantesimo.

Feathers here as black as night,
bind the villain with magick tight,
and in darkness actions quell,
until such time I release this spell.

From page 55:

Una pietra bucata
l'ho trovato
Ne ringrazio il destino,
E lo spirito che su questa via
Mi ha portata,
Che possa essere il mio bene,
E la mia buona fortuna!

I have found a Holy Stone upon the
*   ground.*
O Destiny, I thank you for the joyful
*   find.*
And also the spirit who upon this road
has given it to me
May it prove to be for my true good
*   and fortune!*

From page 56:

Spirito del buono augurio!
Sei venuto in mio soccorso,
Credi ne avero gran bisogno,
Spirito del folletino rosso
Giacche sei venuto in mio soccorso,
Ti prego di non mi abbandonare!
Ti prego dentro questa palla d'intrare,
E nella mia tasca tu possa portare,
Cosi in qualunque mia bisogna,
In mio aiuto ti posso chiamare,
E di giorno e di notte,
Tu non mi possa abbandonare.

Good spirit of omens
who has come to my aid
believing I had need of you,
spirit of the red fairy
since you have come to aid me in my
*   need,*
I pray that you will not abandon me!
I beg you to enter now this sphere
that I carry in my pocket,
and when I have need of anything
that I can call upon you,
whatever need it may be,
and neither by night or day
will you ever abandon me.

From page 56:

Cornu, gran cornu, ritortu cornu;
Russa la pezza, tortu lu cornu,
Ti fazzu scornu:
Vaju e ritornu,
Cornu! cornu! cornu!

Horn, big horn, twisted horn;
Red the cloth,
crooked the horn,
I mock you:
I go and return,
Horn! horn! horn!

The next four spells appear in English on page 57:

O fuocco benedetto
chi brucia immensamente
e bruce tutte le gente
ti prego di brucciare
questo malocchio
e chi me l'ha dato!

O blessed fire,
you who burns so immensely
you who warms all mankind
I pray you to burn this evil spell
and the one who smote me with it!

Preparo questa corona
Per metterla sopra agli occhi
Di quella ammalata

(O ammalata, che sia)
Che possa ritornale la vista e che non
pouo suffire di nuovo.

I prepare this wreath
To place it on the eyes
Of that sufferer,
That her sight I may restore
And she may never suffer more!

Santa Lucia, Santa Lucia,
    Santa Lucia!
Del mal d'occhi fatemi guarire!

Saint Lucy, Saint Lucy, Saint Lucy!
Make me recover from the evil eye!

Cucio questo sacchetino
per la buona fortuna di me,
e della mia famiglia,
e che ci tenga sempre lontano
dalle disgrazie come pure
dalle malattie!

I sew this little bag
for my good fortune,
and also my family,
that misfortune be held far away.

From page 58:

Lucciola! Luciola!
Viene a gara!
Mette la briglia

a la cavalla,
mette la briglia
al figluolo del re,
che la fortuna
venga con me,
lucciola mia
viene da me!

Fire-fly! Fire-fly!
 come to the competition!
put the bridle
to the mare,
put the bridle
to the king's son,
so that fortune
comes with me,
my fire-fly
come from me!

From page 58:

Pena che colpi
con la furia di dragone sangue,
per l'amore di tutti spiriti
abbandona questo corpo,
rimuove la sua macchia.

Pain that hits
with the fury of dragon's blood,
for the love of all spirits
leave this body,
remove your stain.

From page 64:

Fuoco, fuoco benedetto!
Alla casa mia fortuna aspetto
e sempre a te vengo sperare
che l'augurio di buono,
fortuna tu mi voglio dare!

Fire, blessed fire!
My house waits for fortune,
and always comes to you in hope
that the wish of good fortune
you will devote yourself to!

GLOSSARY

Benandanti: An occult society of Renaissance Italy charged with Witchcraft by the Inquisition. It was their practice to "leave the body" and engage in ritual combat with the Malandanti during the Ember Days to ensure a bountiful harvest and the increase of herds.

Child of Promise: In pre-Christian European paganism, a mythical figure connected to the sun, the seasons, and to renewal of plant and animal life.

Compendium Maleficarum: A seventeenth-century Italian work on Witchcraft similar to the *Malleus Maleficarum* of northern Europe. It was commissioned by the Bishop of Milan, and was written by the Italian Ambrosian monk Francesco Guazzo while he was away in Germany.

Cult of the Dead: A Neolithic cult in which the dead were buried with personal items and supplies believed needed for the next life. This cult's practice was the origin of mythical fairy mounds.

Evocation: To magickally cause a spirit, deity, or some occult to appear in any given setting. To give outward form to a spirit or deity (see invocation).

Gnosticism: A mystical sect of philosophers that flourished in the first centuries of the Christian era. They were viewed as heretics by the Church. Their beliefs and practices were a blend of Eastern mysticism and Western Occultism.

Grigori: A race of spiritual beings who guard the portals to and from the physical dimension.

Hermetic: A doctrine of beliefs arising from the teachings of Hermes Trismegistus, an Egyptian mystic of Greek descent. The Hermetic teachings are a blend of Egyptian, Persian, Greek, and Roman paganism.

Invocation: To draw a spirit or deity into oneself, into one's own mind, body, or soul.

Key of Solomon: A Medieval treatise on occult magick rooted in Hebrew mysticism.

Malandanti: An occult society of Renaissance Italy charged with Witchcraft by the Inquisition. It was their practice to leave the body and engage in ritual combat with the Benandanti during the Ember Days to ensure the failure of the harvest and the decline of herds (mostly likely intended to harm the rich noble class).

Neoplatonism: A mystical philosophical system initiated by Plotinus of Alexandria in A.D. 233. It was based the teachings of Plato, but introduced Oriental concepts not professed by Plato.

Neopythagoreanism: A blend of the teachings of Pythagoras with foreign mystical concepts and Anglo-European traditions.

Of the Blood: A term used by hereditary Witches to denote lineage to Witch families.

Outdweller: A term used to denote people who do not practice the Old Religion. It means that they live outside of the Old Ways.

Strega: Literally, a female Witch.

Streghe: Plural for Witch.

Stregheria: The religion of Witches.

Stregone: Literally, a male Witch.

Stregoneria: Sorcery of a shamanic nature.

Treguenda: The Italian version of a Witches' Sabbat.

Selected Bibliography

Allen, Richard H. *Star Names: Their Lore and Meaning*. New York: Dover Publications, 1963.

Andrews, J. B. "Neapolitan Witchcraft." Volume three of *Folk-Lore; Transactions of the Folk-Lore Society* (March 1897).

Ankarloo, Bengt, ed. *Early Modern European Witchcraft*. Oxford: Clarendon Press, 1993.

Baroja, Julio Caro. *The World of Witches*. Chicago: The University of Chicago Press, 1964.

Barrett, Francis. *The Magus*. New Hyde Park: University Books, 1967.

Barstow, Anne L. *Witchcraze*. San Francisco: Pandora, 1994.

Bonnefoy, Yves, ed. *Roman and European Mythologies*. Chicago: The University of Chicago Press, 1991.

Bourne, Lois. *Witch Amongst Us*. London: Robert Hale, 1989.

Briggs, Robin. *Witches & Neighbors*. New York: Viking, 1996.

Cardini, Franco. *Il giorno del sacro, il Libra delle feste*. Milano: Rusconi Libri, 1989.

Catabiani, Alfredo. *Calendario; Le feste i mitti le leggende e i ritti dell'anno*. Milano: Rusconi Libri, 1988.

Cumont, Franz. *After Life in Roman Paganism*. New York: Dover Publications, 1959.

____. *Oriental Religions in Roman Paganism*. New Haven: Yale University Press, 1920.

De Martino, Ernesto. *Primitive Magic*. Bridgeport: Prism Press, 1972.

Dundes, Alan, ed. *The Evil Eye; A Folklore Casebook*. New York: Garland, 1981.

Elsworth, Fredrick T. *The Evil Eye*. London: John Murray, 1895.

Falassi, Alessandro. *Folklore by the Fireside: Text and Context of the Tuscan Veglia*. Austin: University of Texas Press, 1980.

Field, Carol. *Celebrating Italy*. New York: William Morrow & Co, 1990.

Frazer, Sir James George. *The Golden Bough*. New York: Macmillan Company, 1922.

Gardner, Gerald B. *Witchcraft Today*. Secaucus: The Citadel Press, 1973.

Gardner, Gerald B. *The Meaning of Witchcraft*. New York: Samuel Weiser, 1959.

Gimbutas, Marija. *The Goddesses and Gods of Old Europe*. Berkeley: University of California Press, 1982.

Ginzburg, Carlo. *The Night Battles; Witchcraft & Agrarian Cults in the Sixteenth & Seventeenth Centuries*. London: Routledge & Kegan Paul, 1966.

Ginzburg, Carlo. *Ecstasies: Deciphering the Witches' Sabbath*. New York: Pantheon Books, 1991.

Godwin, Joscelyn. *Mystery Religions in the Ancient World*. New York: Harper & Row, 1981.

Grimassi, Raven. *Ways of the Strega*. St. Paul: Llewellyn Publications, 1995.

Guazzo, Francesco. *Compendium Maleficarum*. New York: Dover Books, 1988 (originally published 1609).

Kaplan, Stuart. *The Encyclopedia of the Tarot* (three volumes). Stamford: U.S. Games Systems Inc., 1994.

Kingsley, Peter. *Ancient Philosophy, Mystery, and Magic*. Oxford: Clarendon Press, 1995.

Leek, Sybil. *The Complete Art of Witchcraft*. New York: Signet Book, 1971.

____. *Diary of a Witch*. New York: Signet Book, 1968.

Leland, Charles. *Etruscan Magic & Occult Remedies*. New York: University Books, 1963.

____. *Gypsy Sorcery and Fortune Telling*. New York: Dover Publications, 1971.

____. *Legends of Florence*. New York:

MacMillan and Co., 1895.

Lethbridge, T. C. *Witches.* New York: The Citadel Press, 1962.

Luck, Georg. *Arcana Mundi: Magic and the Occult in the Greek and Roman Worlds.* Baltimore: Johns Hopkins University Press, 1985.

Malpezzi, Frances. *Italian American Folklore.* Little Rock: August House Publishers, 1992.

Nuttall, P. A. *The Works of Horace.* Philadelphia: David McKay, 1884.

Ryall, Rhiannon. *West Country Wicca.* Custer: Phoenix Publishing, 1989.

Scully, Sally. *Journal of Social History* (volume 28, 1995).

Vecoli, Rudolph J. "Cult and Occult in Italian-American Culture; The Persistence of a Religious Heritage." In *Immigrants and Religion in Urban America,* edited by Randall M. Miller and Thomas D. Marzik. Philadelphia: Temple University Press, 1977.

READING LIST

Italian Paganism

Roman and European Mythologies, compiled by Yves Bonnefoy (University of Chicago Press, 1992).

Cults of the Roman Empire by Robert Turcan (Blackwell, 1996).

The Golden Bough by James Frazer (Macmillan, 1972).

Ancient Philosophy, Mystery, and Magic by Peter Kingsley (Clarendon Press, 1995).

Etruscan Magic & Occult Remedies by Charles Leland (University Books, 1963).

The Ancient Mysteries edited by Marvin Meyer (Harper San Franciso, 1987).

Italian Witchcraft

Ways of the Strega by Raven Grimassi (Llewellyn Publications, 1995)

The Wiccan Mysteries by Raven Grimassi (Llewellyn Publication, 1997).

Witchcraft; The Old Religion by Leo Martello (Citadel Press).

Early Modern European Witchcraft edited by Ankarloo & Henningsen (Clarendon Press, 1993).

Topics Related to Witchcraft in General

The Evil Eye by Fredrick Elsworthy (Julian Press, 1985).

Animal-Speak by Ted Andrews (Llewellyn Publications, 1993).

The Once Unknown Familiar by Timothy Roderick (Llewellyn Publications, 1994).

The World of the Witches by Julio Baroja (University of Chicago Press, 1975).

Hereditary Traditions

Witchcraft; A Tradition Renewed by Doreen Valiente and Evan Jones (Phoenix Publishing, 1990).

Diary of a Witch by Sybil Leek (Signet Books, 1968).

The Complete Art of Witchcraft by Sybil Leek (Signet Books, 1971).

Witch Amongst Us by Lois Bourne (Robert Hale, 1985).

West Country Wicca by Rhiannon Ryall (Phoenix Publishing, 1989).

Witchcraft the Sixth Sense by Justine Glass (Wilshire Books, 1965).

Ways of the Strega by Raven Grimassi (Llewellyn Publications, 1995).

Index

THE WICCAN MYSTERIES
Ancient Origins & Teachings

Raven Grimassi

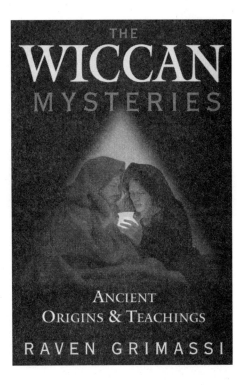

What you will encounter in *The Wiccan Mysteries* is material that was once taught only in the initiate levels of the old Wiccan Mystery Traditions, and to which many solitary practitioners have never had access. Learn the inner meanings of Wiccan rites, beliefs and practices, and discover the time-proven concepts that created, maintained and carried Wiccan beliefs up into this modern era. In reflecting back upon the wisdom of our ancestors, neo-Wiccans can draw even greater sustenance from the spiritual stores of Wicca—the Old Religion.

The Wiccan Mysteries will challenge you to expand your understanding and even re-examine your own perceptions. Wicca is essentially a Celtic-oriented religion, but its Mystery Tradition is derived from several outside cultures as well. You will come away with a sense of the rich heritage that was passed from one human community to another, and that now resides within this system for spiritual development.

312 pp., 6 x 9, softcover
1–56718–254–2   **$14.95**

ITALIAN WITCHCRAFT:
Its Lore, Magick & Spells
(formerly titled: *Ways of the Strega*)

Raven Grimassi

Discover, for the first time in one complete work, the rich legacy of magick and ritual handed down by Italian witches through the generations. *Italian Witchcraft* reclaims the beliefs and practices of southern European Pagan spirituality, giving you the best of the Old Ways and the New Age. Previously published as *Ways of the Strega*, this revised edition contains additional material.

Trace the roots of Italian Pagan tradition as it survives the times, confronted by Christianity, revived in the fourteenth century by the Holy Strega, and passed on as the Legend of Aradia to the present day. Learn the secrets of Janarra (lunar) witches, Tanarra (star) witches, and Fanarra (ley lines) witches. Their ancient wisdoms come together in the modern Aradian tradition, presented here for both theoretical understanding and everyday practice.

Italian Witchcraft gives detailed instruction on the practical how-to of modern Strega traditions, including making tools, casting and breaking spells, seasonal and community rites, honoring the Watchers, creating a Spirit Flame, and so much more. This bountiful volume throws open the door to the living tradition of Italian Witchcraft. (Available February 2000.)

**336 pp., 7 x 10, illus., softcover
1–56178–253–4**   **$14.95**

WICCA
A Guide for the Solitary Practitioner

Scott Cunningham

Wicca is a book of life, and how to live magically, spiritually, and wholly attuned with Nature. It is a book of sense and common sense, not only about Magick, but about religion and one of the most critical issues of today: how to achieve the much needed and wholesome relationship with our Earth. Cunningham presents Wicca as it is today: a gentle, Earth-oriented religion dedicated to the Goddess and God. This book fulfills a need for a practical guide to solitary Wicca—a need which no previous book has fulfilled.

Here is a positive, practical introduction to the religion of Wicca, designed so that any interested person can learn to practice the religion alone, anywhere in the world. It presents Wicca honestly and clearly, without the pseudo-history that permeates other books. It shows that Wicca is a vital, satisfying part of twentieth century life.

Here in this book are the theory and practice of Wicca from an individual's perspective. The Standing Stones Book of Shadows contains solitary rituals for the Esbats and Sabbats. This book, based on the author's nearly two decades of Wiccan practice, presents an eclectic picture of various aspects of this religion. Exercises designed to develop magical proficiency, a self-dedication ritual, herb, crystal and rune magic, as well as recipes for Sabbat feasts, are included in this excellent book.

240 pp., 6 x 9, illus., softcover
0–87542–118–0   **$9.95**

MODERN SEX MAGICK
Lessons in Liberation

**Donald Michael Kraig
with contributions by
Linda Falorio, Nema, and Tara**

Deep within you is a center of power so potent and strong it defies imagination. Now you can learn to control and direct it when it's at its most intense and explosive—during sexual arousal. *Modern Sex Magick* provides easy and precise exercises that prepare you to use the magical energy raised during sexual activity, and then it shows you how to work with that energy to create positive changes in your life.

This is the first book to clearly reveal the secrets of Western sex magick without relying on Tantric theory. It explores the latest scientific discoveries in the field of human sexuality. This unique mixture of science and magick produces a simple fact: practicing these techniques will help you increase and extend your sexual pleasure! You will uncover depths of ecstasy experienced by only a few, and the results can enhance and deepen your relationships. Three powerful women sex magicians also contribute articles to this book.

**384 pp., 6 x 9, illus., softcover
1–56718–394–8**   **$17.95**

TO LIGHT A SACRED FLAME
Practical WitchCraft for the Millennium

Silver RavenWolf

Silver RavenWolf continues to unveil the mysteries of the Craft with *To Light a Sacred Flame,* which follows her best-selling *To Ride a Silver Broomstick* and *To Stir a Magick Cauldron* as the third in the "New Generation WitchCraft" series, guides to magickal practices based on the personal experiences and successes of a third-degree working Witch.

Written for today's seeker, this book contains techniques that unite divinity with magick, knowledge, and humor. Not structured for any particular tradition, the lessons present unique and insightful material for the solitary as well as the group. Explore the fascinating realms of your inner power, sacred shrines, magickal formularies, spiritual housecleaning, and the intricacies of ritual. This book reveals new information that includes a complete discussion on the laws of the Craft, glamouries, and shamanic Craft rituals, including a handfasting and wiccaning (saining).

320 pp., 7 x 10
1–56718–721–8   **$14.95**

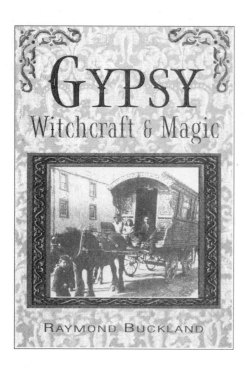

GYPSY WITCHCRAFT & MAGIC

Raymond Buckland

The Romany—or Gypsy—lifestyle has been a colorful one: living in brightly painted *vardos* and benders, cooking over campfires, moving about the countryside while scraping out an existence by one's wits. But the Gypsies, as an ethnic people, are disappearing. As a *poshrat* himself (a half-blood Romany), Raymond Buckland seeks to recapture the romance and charm of this culture's mystical past and present in *Gypsy Witchcraft & Magic*.

Learn of their origins and migration throughout the world, the truth about their religious beliefs, their daily life, and their magical practices. Try your hand at practicing authentic Gypsy magic, with spells and charms for love, healing, wealth, power, protection, and more. Learn to tell fortunes with beans, cards, coins, by scrying, and by reading the omens in nature.

192 pp., 7 x 10, illus., photos, softcover
1–56718–097–3   **$17.95**

ANCIENT WAYS
Reclaiming the Pagan Tradition

Pauline Campanelli, illus. by Dan Campanelli

Ancient Ways is filled with magick and ritual that you can perform every day to capture the spirit of the seasons. It focuses on the celebration of the Sabbats of the Old Religion by giving you practical things to do while anticipating the sabbat rites, and helping you harness the magical energy for weeks afterward. The wealth of seasonal rituals and charms are drawn from ancient sources but are easily performed with materials readily available.

Learn how to look into your previous lives at Yule . . . at Beltane, discover the places where you are most likely to see faeries . . . make special jewelry to wear for your Lammas Celebrations . . . for the special animals in your life, paint a charm of protection at Midsummer.

Most Pagans and Wiccans feel that the Sabbat rituals are all too brief and wish for the magick to linger on. *Ancient Ways* can help you reclaim your own traditions and heighten the feeling of magick.

256 pp., 7 x 10, illus., softcover
0–87542–090–7   **$14.95**

ANIMAL-SPEAK
The Spiritual & Magical Powers of Creatures Great & Small

Ted Andrews

The animal world has much to teach us. Some are experts at survival and adaptation, some never get cancer, some embody strength and courage while others exude playfulness. Animals remind us of the potential we can unfold, but before we can learn from them, we must first be able to speak with them.

In this book, myth and fact are combined in a manner that will teach you how to speak and understand the language of the animals in your life. *Animal-Speak* helps you meet and work with animals as totems and spirits—by learning the language of their behaviors within the physical world. It provides techniques for reading signs and omens in nature so you can open to higher perceptions and even prophecy. It reveals the hidden, mythical and realistic roles of 45 animals, 60 birds, 8 insects, and 6 reptiles.

Animals will become a part of you, revealing to you the majesty and divine in all life. They will restore your childlike wonder of the world and strengthen your belief in magic, dreams and possibilities.

400 pp., 7 x 10, illus., photos, softcover
0–87542–028–1   **$17.95**

EARTH POWER
Techniques of Natural Magic

Scott Cunningham

Magick is the art of working with the forces of Nature to bring about necessary and desired-changes. The forces of Nature—expressed through Earth, Air, Fire and Water—are our "spiritual ancestors" who paved the way for our emergence from the prehistoric seas of creation. Attuning to and working with these energies in magick not only lends you the power to affect changes in your life, it also allows you to sense your own place in the larger scheme of Nature. Using the "Old Ways" enables you to live a better life and to deepen your understanding of the world. The tools and powers of magick are around you, waiting to be grasped and utilized. This book gives you the means to put Magick into your life, shows you how to make and use the tools, and gives you spells for every purpose.

176 pp., 5¼ x 8, illus., softcover
0–87542–121–0 $9.95

MODERN MAGICK

MODERN MAGICK
Eleven Lessons in the High Magickal Arts

Donald Michael Kraig

Modern Magick is the most comprehensive step-by-step introduction to the art of ceremonial magic ever offered. The eleven lessons in this book will guide you from the easiest of rituals and the construction of your magickal tools through the highest forms of magick: designing your own rituals and doing pathworking. Along the way you will learn the secrets of the Kabbalah in a clear and easy-to-understand manner. You will discover the true secrets of invocation (channeling) and evocation, and the missing information that will finally make the ancient grimoires, such as the "Keys of Solomon," not only comprehensible, but usable. This book also contains one of the most in-depth chapters on sex magick ever written. *Modern Magick* is designed so anyone can use it, and it is the perfect guidebook for students and classes. It will also help to round out the knowledge of long-time practitioners of the magickal arts.

592 pgs., 6 x 9, illus., index, softcover
0–87542–324–8 $17.95

USING MODERN MAGICK
Donald Michael Kraig

Learn the secrets behind words of power on this 47-minute audio cassette. Hear how to say magickal words in their ancient Hebrew, Enochian, Greek or Latin languages.

0–87542–363–9, 47 min. audiotape $9.95

To Order, Call 1–800–THE MOON

Prices subject to change without notice

THE MAGICAL HOUSEHOLD
Empower Your Home with Love, Protection, Health and Happiness

Scott Cunningham and David Harrington

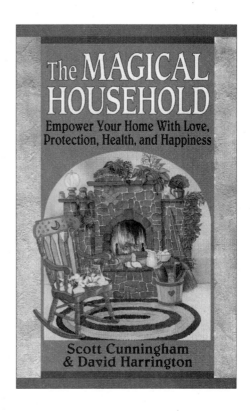

Whether your home is a small apartment or a palatial mansion, you want it to be something special. Now it can be with *The Magical Household*. Learn how to make your home more than just a place to live. Turn it into a place of security, life, fun and magic. Here you will not find the complex magic of the ceremonial magician. Rather, you will learn simple, quick and effective magical spells that use nothing more than common items in your house: furniture, windows, doors, carpet, pets, etc. You will learn to take advantage of the intrinsic power and energy that is already in your home, waiting to be tapped. You will learn to make magic a part of your life. The result is a home that is safeguarded from harm and a place which will bring you happiness, health and more.

208 pp., 5¼ x 8, illus., softcover
0–87542–124–5   **$9.95**